General

D0632781

ALCOHOLISM
Causes, Effects, and Treatment

JOSEPH F. PEREZ, Ph.D.
Westfield State College

ACCELERATED DEVELOPMENT INC.
PUBLISHERS
3400 KILGORE AVENUE
MUNCIE, INDIANA 47304

ALCOHOLISM
CAUSES, EFFECTS, AND TREATMENT

Copyright 1992 by Accelerated Development Inc.

10 9 8 7 6 5 4 3 2 1

Printed in the United States of America

All rights reserved. No part of this book may be reproduced or transmitted in any form or means, electronic or mechanical, including photocopying, recording, or by an informational storage and retrieval system, without permission in writing from Accelerated Development Inc.

Technical Development: Tanya Benn
                          Virginia Cooper
                          Sandra Gilmore
                          Delores Kellogg
                          Cynthia Long
                          Marguerite Mader
                          Sheila Sheward

Library of Congress Cataloging-in-Publication Data

Perez, Joseph F. (Joseph Francis)
    Alcoholism : causes, effects, and treatment / Joseph F. Perez.
        p.   cm.
    Includes bibliographical references and index.
    ISBN 1-55959-039-4
    1. Alcoholism.   2. Alcoholics--Rehabilitation.   I. Title.
    HV5035.P435   1992
    362.29'2--dc20
                                 92-53191
                                  CIP

LCN: 92-53191

ISBN: 1-55959-039-4

Order additional copies from:

ACCELERATED DEVELOPMENT INC.
PUBLISHERS
3400 Kilgore Avenue
Muncie, Indiana 47304-4896
Toll Free Order Number 1-800-222-1166

OTHER BOOKS
BY JOSEPH F. PEREZ

Counseling: Theory and Practice

The Initial Counseling Contact

General Psychology, Selected Readings

Mom and Dad Are Me

Family Roots of Adolescent Delinquency

Family Counseling: Theory & Practice

Family Counseling

A Father's Love (A Novel)

Counseling the Alcoholic

Counseling the Alcoholic Group

Coping in the Alcoholic Family

Relationships: Adult Children of Alcoholics

Tales of an Italian American Family (Short Stories)

DEDICATION

To Gerri

Wife, mother, grandmother,
nurse, scrabble player par excellence

PREFACE

This book is a substantial revision of an earlier book, *Counseling the Alcoholic*. The structure of this work follows the title. Part I treats **Causes** of alcoholism. Both the genetic and the dynamic aspects are considered. Part II addresses the **Effects** of alcoholism through cases of recovering alcoholics. In vivid fashion, these cases illustrate what happens to alcoholics and those close to them when one drinks alcoholically. Part III deals with both the theoretical and practical therapeutic aspects of **Treatment.** These are considered both in individual and group therapy.

Goals

The basic goals in writing this book were

1. to make it academically and professionally respectable (well over 150 citations), and

2. to make it readable and authentic.

Why this second goal for a textbook? Most therapists who deal with alcoholics are themselves recovering alcoholics. The experience of their disease has made them cynical and not a little suspect about any heavy intellectualized tone about an illness they know so well. What they demand are reliability and honesty. The autobiographical sketches in Part II **Effects** provide a riveting read precisely because of their authenticity.

Market

This is a basic text for alcoholism therapists. Practicing alcoholism therapists new to the field will learn much from it. It was conceived and designed for the individual planning to enter the field of alcoholism rehabilitation.

Veteran practitioners also can profit from reading the book as it provides much new information on genetic predisposition and innovative thoughts of the dynamics involved in learning to be addicted. The section on treatment, especially the chapter on group counseling, includes ideas and aspects which are unique to this book.

ACKNOWLEDGEMENTS

A book like this could not have been written without the help of others. I feel especially indebted to Mike McCartney, Rosemary Coombs, and Stacy Page for their candid and moving autobiographical sketches.

My acknowledgement, too, to Alice Welch, librarian in the Central Library of the Department of Public Health in Boston, for the invaluable assistance she provided searching the literature for studies to fit my hypotheses and the topic areas of this book. She responded always with alacrity, cheerfulness, and competence. Alice Welch is a veritable treasure in the Commonwealth's Department of Public Health.

My son, Christopher, who is an alcoholism counselor, gave me the idea to include material about alcoholism in the gay community. He also spent more than a few hours helping me to decide which studies from a vast array I should include in the final manuscript. Chris is my personal treasure.

After me, the person who spent the most clock hours in this effort is Doris Fecteau. She not only typed the manuscript but she edited it and rearranged whole sections. As ever and as Doris she did all that gracefully, coolly, and exceedingly well.

CONTENTS

THREE: ALCOHOLIC FAMILY 37

PART II EFFECTS 61

FOUR: THE COURSE OF ALCOHOLISM 63

LIST OF FIGURES

PART I
CAUSES

CHAPTER ONE

THE GENETIC VIEW

Whether or not people become alcoholic because of genetic endowment or because of learning is of interest and concern to the afflicted, their relatives and to the research scientist. In the latter part of the last century and for the first couple of decades of this one, the conviction of those who treated alcoholics, mostly physicians, was that alcoholism was an inherited disease.

ALCOHOLISM INHERITED OR LEARNED?

With the advent and popularization of personality theories, that conviction changed. For the past fifty years and more social psychologists, behaviorists, and humanists presented the view that we learn to be what we are. Adherents of such a view both within and without psychology became legion. Ergo, the new modern and conventional wisdom—alcoholism is learned.

Studies to determine whether alcoholism is a learned phenomenon or an inherited disease have been done (Goodwin, Schulsinger, Hermonsen, Guze, & Winokur, 1973). These researchers examined the records of men in their 30's who from the age of six months had been reared in nonalcoholic homes. What they found was that those men whose fathers were alcoholic were three times more likely to become so than those whose fathers were nonalcoholic. They found also that the sons of alcoholics were more likely to become addicted at an earlier age.

Another conclusion drawn from this study was that there were no significant differences in these boys with respect to personality dysfunctions or dispositions. The boys displayed comparable levels of anxiety, depression and psychopathic tendencies. In short, these boys functioned in pretty much the same manner on all measures of mental health.

In a follow-up study (Goodwin & Moller, 1974) the researchers compared sons of alcoholics who had been reared in homes of their alcoholic fathers with brothers who had been adopted and reared in homes that were not alcoholic. Based upon their statistics, the conclusion was that boys reared in the nonalcoholic homes were just as likely to become alcoholic as those reared by alcoholic fathers.

What Goodwin's studies have shown is that genetic endowment contributes far more than environment in the development of alcoholism.

The study which clearly validates the idea that alcoholism is a function of genetic predisposition was done by Vaillant at Harvard (1983).

This was a longitudinal study that spanned forty years, 1940-1980. The sample was composed of 660 males drawn from a variety of American socioeconomic strata: 240 were Harvard undergraduates and 456 were junior high school boys from various Boston schools. The object of the study was to determine if males carry personality traits or dispositions that one can use as criteria to predict, with a modicum of certainty, whether or not a person is or is not disclosed to alcoholism.

Vaillant concluded that no significant differences exist in traits or disposition between those who became alcoholic and those who did not. The men who became alcoholic and those who did not were comparably stable in their youth.

A criterion for prediction of alcoholism did emerge out of the study, however. Vaillant found that those boys who had a parent who was alcoholic were more likely to become alcoholic than those who did not. That likelihood, he found was astoundingly high, five times higher!

Today, considerable evidence has been collected on which to conclude that alcoholism is a genetically transmitted disease. Berk, Montgomery, Hazlett, and Abel (1989) have concluded that alcoholic fathers can genetically transmit physiological defects in the form of increased susceptibility to infection to both their sons and daughters.

The studies done with sons of alcoholics to determine if they acquire the disease from their fathers abound. Thus in one study (Newlin & Pretonious, 1990) the finding was that "the sons of alcoholics are dependence prone." In another study (Newlin & Thomson, 1990) the conclusion was that sons of alcoholics find alcohol more rewarding than sons of nonalcoholics precisely because certain blood factors work to give them more pleasure. Kubicka, Kozeny, and Roth (1990) investigated the effect of drinking at an early age on susceptibility to alcoholism in the sons of individuals diagnosed alcoholic. What the researchers found was that "early start of drinking led very frequently to early registered abuse in sons of alcoholics."

Pinl, Peterson, and Finn (1990) in a far ranging study found that sons of male alcoholics are at a markedly heightened genetic risk for the development of alcohol abuse: Athenelli and Shuckit (1991) apparently found that this genetic transmission can be accomplished with women as well as men. They discovered that the daughters of alcoholics have a much higher tolerance to alcohol than do daughters of nonalcoholics. A higher tolerance for alcohol ingestion usually means a potentially higher probability to become addicted because higher tolerance correlates strongly with production of an excessive number of enzymes that disease both the liver and the brain.

Electroencephalographic studies have been done to determine both the effect of alcohol on the brain and the genetic predisposition because of wave dysfunction. Researchers have concluded that indeed a predisposition to alcoholism may be as shown by abnormalities in brain waves (Little & McAvoy, 1945). The conclusion of the two men was substantiated in the work done by Begleiter, Porjesz, Binari, and Kissin (1984) with 25 sons of alcoholics. The boys selected for this study had not ingested any alcohol during their lives. These boys had a brain wave dysfunction identical to the one displayed by alcoholics in a state of recovery. The waves of these boys were markedly different from the normal waves of 25 boys who like them had never ingested alcohol but who had fathers who were not alcoholics. Begleiter, Porjesz, Rawlings, and Eckardt (1987) replicated these results.

Some early work in the biochemistry of alcoholism was done by MacLeod (1950). He was the first to surmise that alcohol interacts with acetylcholine in alcoholics in a far different way than it does in nonalcoholics.

MacLeod's early ideas were confirmed in a study by Schuckit (1985) done more than thirty years later. Schuckit examined the reactions to alcohol of 20 men who had a first degree relative (father or brother) who was alcoholic (termed Group A) and compared them to 20 men with no alcoholic first degree related (termed Group B). Each of the men in both groups was given three drinks of alcohol. Group A members quickly generated far higher levels of acetaldehyde than did the Group B members. Group B members displayed more signs of intoxication and they did not build up the quantities of acetaldehyde than did those in Group A. This finding was consistent with others' studies on genetic predisposition where when an increase was found in the acetaldehyde level of an individual a corresponding increase occurred in the individual's tolerance for alcohol.

Since acetaldehyde is produced by the liver, an abnormal increase in its levels means that if the liver is not dysfunctional, at least something is different about it. *And* if the liver is producing disproportional amounts of acetaldehyde (essentially a poison), a pertinent question raised might be "how is this affecting the brain?" (Metabolic substances are passed from the liver into the bloodstream and ultimately to the brain.)

The brain is composed of billions of cells that function through a marvelous system of neurotransmitters. These neurotransmitters signal the messages that precipitate *all* body functions from respiration to every iota of fibre involved in complex decision making.

The brain cells exist in a delicate equilibrium and are able to function only if they are permitted to maintain that proper equilibrium. A second and more specific question then might be "how does the acetaldehyde affect the equilibrium of these cells and their concomitant system of neurotransmitters?" The answer to both questions can be found in the work of the following researchers.

Gredd and Greengard (1990) in their work with post-mortem brain tissue of alcoholics and Harada (1989) in his research with the effects of aldehyde on alcoholics found that excessive ingestion of alcohol debilitates the brain by upsetting cell equilibrium. Worse, alcoholic drinking compounds the whole chemical system of neurotransmission between and among the cells. Please note that this is the system responsible for all human functioning. What can be concluded based on this research is that certain people become alcoholic because their body chemistry functions abnormally in response to the ingestion of alcohol. Ingestion of alcohol by the alcoholic follows a predictably destructive course—adaptation, acceleration, addiction. For people with such body chemistry, poison and alcohol are synonymous.

ADAPTATION

When alcohol is ingested into the body a byproduct derived from the metabolic process is the substance mentioned above, acetaldehyde, produced by the liver as it acts to process and expel the alcohol.

The body changes the acetaldehyde into an acetate which is in turn converted into carbon dioxide and water and eliminated through sweat, urine, and simple breathing. The effects of acetaldehyde include profuse sweating, vomiting, disorientation, rapid pulse, headaches, and the classic "hangover."

The liver of the average person can efficiently metabolize a little over one-half ounce of alcohol per hour. The serious consequences of acetaldehyde occur when one ingests alcohol at a faster rate than the liver is able to metabolize it. The excess of acetaldehyde enters the blood and ultimately the brain. Researchers now believe that it is precisely acetaldehyde excess which debilitates, ultimately atrophies the synapses which chemically transmit messages between and among brain cells.

The liver contains several enzymes which metabolize alcohol. One is called **alcohol dehydrogenase (ADH)**. This is the enzyme that converts alcohol into acetaldehyde. The other is called **acetaldehyde dehydrogenase (ALDH)**.

The National Institute on Alcoholic Abuse in 1980 discovered what many students of alcoholism had suspected for a long time: namely that the liver of alcoholics differs significantly from the liver of nonalcoholics. Like the nonalcoholic, the alcoholic liver contains both ADH and ALDH but when the liver of the alcoholic metabolizes alcohol it also produces two **metabolites** unique to them. They have been termed **2, 3, butanediol** and **1, 2, propanediol.** Researchers at the National Institute discovered that these two metabolites were present in the blood of the intoxicated alcoholic but *not* in the blood of the intoxicated but nonalcoholic.

These two metabolites increase enzyme production in the liver and precipitate an additional secondary metabolic process. This additional process helps the alcoholic metabolize *more* alcohol. The secondary process has been given a name, **Microsomal Ethanol Oxidating System (MEOS).**

The creation of this system contributes much to the making of an alcoholic. Why? Because MEOS speeds up and increases the alcoholic's ability to tolerate alcohol levels higher than normal. This toleration is what alcoholics find psychologically rewarding. It is why the alcoholic can maintain a "buzz" and a "high" for so much longer than a normal person.

The ability to tolerate alcohol for longer periods ultimately proves to be the prime cause for many physical dysfunctions. These dysfunctions come to plague the alcoholic because while MEOS helps the alcoholic liver to metabolize more alcohol into acetaldehyde it does *not* increase the liver's capacity to expel the acetaldehyde. If anything, it slows it down. The result is that the amount of the acetaldehyde poison increases in both the blood and the brain of the alcoholic.

ACCLIMATION

The blood contaminated with acetaldehyde enters the brain. The synapses, the message carriers which chemically transmit messages between the brain cells, are immediately affected. The acetaldehyde adheres and blends with these neurons; particularly with **norepinephrine** and **dopamine,** two chemicals found in the brain. The blending produces a substance called **TIQ.**

Alcoholics, probably because they manufacture more acetaldehyde for all the reasons indicated, also manufacture a disproportionate amount of TIQ. TIQ is an analgesic of remarkable potency. A veritable two edged sword, TIQ, precipitates feelings of relaxation and comfort. When it enters the brain, anxiety, regardless of the source, diminishes. The other side of the sword is that TIQ is as addictive as morphine. The conviction today among most biochemists involved in alcoholism research is that no one substance contributes to the making of an alcoholic more then TIQ. It's most salient, destructive effect is that it seems to cripple the person's willpower.

Virginia Davis (Davis & Walsh, 1970) discovered the relationship between alcohol addiction and TIQ. Prior to her discovery, it was thought to be manufactured as a function of addiction to heroine. Her work showed it can also be a derivative of the alcoholic process.

ADDICTION

Addiction occurs when the individual's body physically craves a substance, when the body has to have the substance to function, even shakily, when the substance becomes virtually a food-like sustenance. And that is precisely how the person addicted to alcohol perceives alcohol—as a food. All intelligence and every aspect of personality are put in the service of the craving. All the élan needed is mustered; whatever ploy or deceit that needs be employed is employed to obtain the food alcohol.

The biochemical irony is that the brain of the alcoholic does indeed come to *need* the alcohol to function if not optimally, then at best adequately.

The road to alcoholic addiction, while it varies in distance from person to person, ends inevitably the same way for all addicts. It is always destructive—especially to the brain.

The flow of nutrients in and out of a brain cell is controlled by the thickness of the membrane of the cell. **The stability of that thickness is the critical determinant for effective cerebral functioning.** The regular, protracted and heavy introduction of the acetaldehyde into the brain inevitably makes the delicate membranous tissue much thicker, confounding the crucial stability and inevitably the ebb and flow of nutrients. The neurotransmission of messages is of course disrupted. This thickening process, although unnatural, is a protective response by the cell to maintain a balanced equilibrium and to protect the integrity of the inner cellular layers from the killing alcohol.

Another reason the thickening occurs is that a third cell blends with the invading acetaldehyde. This is **gamma-amino-butyric acid (GABA).** When this blending occurs, a dramatic increase of chloride flows into the inner cell. The immediate effect of this melding is very comparable to the one affected by TIQ—a kind of perceptual nirvana where anxiety is nonexistent. That is the immediate effect of GABA but it is of course of short duration. The later effect is not so pleasant and over time cripples the brain. Why? Because to maintain the stability of thickness, unnatural because of excessive amounts of acetaldehyde, the cells cry out for alcohol, now perceived as a food by the cells. As the thickness of the brain cells increases, neurotransmission of chemical in pulses becomes harder and harder both to send and to receive messages between and among cells. Inevitably the addict becomes crippled cerebrally.

SUMMARY AND CONCLUSIONS

Based on research results with alcoholic parents and their children, genetic endowment contributes more than environment in the development of alcoholism. Based on results from electroencephlagraphic studies and biochemical research, support is lent to the point of view that a genetic predisposition exists to alcoholism. Results from the biochemical studies especially validate the genetic position.

Alcoholism is a disease that follows a predictably destructive course—adaptation, acclimation, addiction. In the adaptive phase the liver metabolizes and converts it into acetaldehyde. The liver of the alcoholic is different from the liver of the nonalcoholic. It produces unique metabolites that increase enzyme production in the liver and ultimately a secondary system to metabolize more alcohol. In the acclimation stage the acetaldehyde blends with neurons to produce TIQ a substance as addictive as morphine and one which contributes much to the making of an alcoholic. In the addictive phase, GABA blends with the acetaldehyde. Concomitant with this blending is a thickening of the brain cell membrane walls. The effect of this thickening is a progressive decline in the ability of the brain cells to function effectively. With continued ingestion of alcohol the progressive decline continues until the addict becomes a cerebral cripple.

QUESTIONS AND ANSWERS
FOR DISCUSSION AND REFLECTION

The following are answers to a list of questions most often asked of the author at workshops and conferences regarding the genetic predisposition to alcoholism.

1. ***How can I tell if I have a predisposition to alcoholism?***

At present, no definitive tests are available to predict that. There may well be in the future. At the present time a criterion with merit is that if you have a first degree relative—father, mother, sibling—who is alcoholic *and* you yourself are preoccupied with alcohol (you want to ingest some every day) you may indeed have a predisposition for becoming addicted to alcohol. Even if you do not, you are still displaying all the signs of a budding alcoholic.

2. ***If I have a genetic predisposition to alcoholism, am I doomed to be alcoholic?***

You are so doomed only if you drink. You are not so much doomed as you are **vulnerable.** Your liver is likely to produce excessive amounts of acetaldehyde. The melding of that acetaldehyde with cerebral neurons produces chemicals that can indeed lead to a life of doom. The simple truth is that alcohol will not enhance your body even though upon ingestion it might give *you* an especially nice feeling.

3. ***Both my parents are alcoholic. All this talk about genetic predisposition scares me. I drink in moderation now. Can I continue to? Should I? I have strong will power.***

Quite apparently you can continue to drink if you want to. Whether you should or not, I'll answer it like this. TIQ, the chemical produced in abundance by the individual predisposed genetically, is a powerful analgesic that in time can effectively debilitate even the most powerful will power.

4. ***Does a genetic predisposition make an alcoholic personality or does a person's personality make him/her alcoholic?***

The answer is not a simple either-or but can work both ways. Genetic predisposition can make an alcoholic personality but we know genetic predisposition is not the only reason people get drunk. It is not the only reason people engage in alcoholic behavior. While genetic predisposition may be a principle cause for the existence of an alcoholic personality, it is not the only reason. A person may develop an alcoholic personality who was not genetically predisposed to do so. The regular ingestion of alcohol is the only requirement to display behavior and characteristics associated with an alcoholic personality. People can drink to excess for any number of reasons: loss because of death or love affair broken off, humiliation, scandal, etc. They can drink to excess for a long enough time to bring on physiological addiction; i.e., their brain cells begin to crave the alcohol much as a hungry normal person's stomach craves food. Simply put, alcoholic drinking makes alcoholic personalities.

CHAPTER TWO

THE DYNAMIC VIEW

As many different personalities exist among alcoholics as there are alcoholics. At the same time, certain unfortunate commonalities seem to plague the personality dynamics of those individuals suffering from alcoholism. An examination of these commonalities provides another approach to understanding the alcoholic.

The elements of personality dynamics are

perception,

conscience, and

defenses.

PERCEPTION

Perception is a cornerstone of human personality. How we perceive others will determine how we interact with them. If others generally are perceived as accepting when they are so, our interpersonal relations and our emotional health will be enhanced. Conversely, if we generally perceive others as threatening when they are not, our health will be demeaned. In short, how accurately we perceive the world will determine how effectively we deal with it. Those judgments upon which the healthy adult acts are premised upon a mature and healthy perception of the world.

The alcoholic, by definition, is not healthy. Too often he/she unrealistically perceives a world filled with threat or, at best, indifference. Such a perception leaves the alcoholic unattuned to others and his/her sense of being devalued. Not uncommonly, judgmental responses by the alcoholic are overresponses manifested by impulsivity, escape into fantasy, and excessive personal gratification.

CONSCIENCE

The person without a conscience is one who engages in antisocial behavior and feels no guilt. This person is usually unable to trust or even to love. Such a person has been termed a psychopath. Most alcoholics, in their sober moments anyway, are not psychopaths. At the same time many alcoholics, drunk or sober, suffer from a conscience that fluctuates from too scrupulous to nonexistent. Thus, when in the overly scrupulous phase the alcoholic conscience will take over the ego's judgmental functions and will make decisions out of guilt. Invariably these are self-defeating, foolish, and socially inappropriate. In the latter phase, the alcoholic may behave as if he/she was an actual psychopath, demeaning, abusing, and beating on those whom they ordinarily love.

The alcoholic learns early that escape into booze can effectively drown his/her conscience, at least for a little while. Unfortunately when sober, the alcoholic's conscience returns in an even more awesome size. To escape this awesomeness is precisely why so many alcoholics keep returning to their booze, and also why so many choose to live in their nebulous, alcoholic haze.

DEFENSES

Defenses are an innate and necessary aspect of the human personality. They feed the ego and protect it from perceived threat.

Through defenses healthy people are able to perceive selectively. Defenses help human beings to perceive what they want to perceive and to ignore what they want to ignore. They help to create situations, events, and interactions that are satisfying, rewarding, and at times enhancing.

With alcoholics, this whole and very human process of defense becomes diseased. Their perceptions become not so much selective as distorted. So situations, events, and interactions tend to be unsatisfying, often even demeaning.

Alcoholics, especially in the initial stages of recovery, have fragile defenses. In counseling, this is usually reflected in their unsureness and conflicting statements. A major task of the counselor is to help these individuals rebuild and reinforce a defense structure that helps them to perceive more realistically. Then they can deal more effectively with the major problems with which they are beset. Principal among these are guilt, remorse, failure, and loss. Thus, the same defenses which were once self-defeating and kept the alcoholics in the throes of despair, now have to be redirected, and restructured to help them sustain their sobriety.

Explanation and illustrations on how to redirect and restructure alcoholic defenses are provided in Part III of this book.

Only those defenses most commonly used by the alcoholic will be considered. These are the following:

> denial,
>
> displacement,
>
> fantasy,
>
> projection,
>
> rationalization,
>
> reaction formation,
>
> regression, and
>
> repression.

Denial

A definition for denial is the emotional refusal to acknowledge a person, situation, condition, or event the way it is. The alcoholic who consumes a fifth of scotch per day, every day, for a time may honestly not recognize any addiction to alcohol. Denial prevents any recognition of the fact.

Displacement

The ventilation of hostility on a person or object neither of which engendered it in the first place is displacement. To illustrate, the person under the influence, or even sober, who beats a spouse because the person was hounded all day by a supervisor.

Fantasy

Daydreaming, a constant recourse for the alcoholic, is fantasy. It is a solace especially when the alcohol is first taking effect. It is the time when the alcoholic becomes expansive, talks too loudly, boasts, etc. Fantasy may take another form for the solitary drinker. It may be the nirvana to which the alcoholic retreats to escape boredom, frustration, and anxiety. In the world of fantasy, the alcoholic fulfills wishes, realizes expectations, and achieves power. For many addicts, alcohol becomes the catalyst which precipitates and facilitates the creation of a synthetic reality—one far more rewarding than the real world and one to which the alcoholic feels compelled to return repeatedly.

Projection

Motives which one harbors in oneself and attributes to another person or persons are referred to as projection. It invariably develops when a person becomes distanced from others. Estrangement and lack of communication, both plagues of the alcoholic, breed and feed this defense. Suspicion and an unhealthy-like sensitivity to others, manifested by a too quick to take offense attitude, are common manifestations of projection. To illustrate, while sipping a fourth drink the alcoholic becomes abusive toward a couple of strangers whom the alcoholic believes are talking about him/her.

Rationalization

This may be defined as making up excuses for actual or felt inadequacies or behaviors. This defense often is used to support denial—for example, the alcoholic who denies addiction and explains the routine need for three martinis before dinner as a way of relaxing.

Reaction Formation

This will be treated under Rorschach Test findings.

Regression

Use the term regression when referring to immature behavior— to behavior that is more appropriate to an earlier chronological age. Often the behavior is intended to manipulate and/or control. Temper tantrums, sulking, and pouting are common forms of regression in the alcoholic.

Repression

The term repression refers to the ego function of letting the memory of a person, situation, or event become unconscious because of fear and threat imposed by remembering it. Many individuals become repressed through the process of socialization. Some repression probably occurs whenever an individual is intimidated into doing and behaving in ways that are threatening or intimidating. Tahka (1968) found that alcoholics are more heavily repressed than people drawn from the normative population. Heavily repressed people are generally more unsure of themselves than lowly repressed. As developing children and adolescents, they saw threat and conflict everywhere. They learned to move in it without remembering any of it. If a teacher was especially scary, they repressed him/her as quickly as they could after leaving him/her. The effect of all this attitude, of course, is to diminish one's life experience and to reduce one's sense of sureness and one's level of maturity.

RESEARCH FINDINGS

Considerable testing has been done to assess the quality and strength of the alcoholic personality. Based on the results obtained, one must conclude that the alcoholic functions with a weak personality. One indication of this weakness is reflected in his/her impulsivity, and another in his/her low tolerance for frustration. Indications are clear that heavy drinkers are far more likely to show impulsivity than are alcohol abstainers (Cisin & Cahalan, 1968). Another study came up with comparable findings. It seems that alcoholics generally have a greater tendency to act on momentary impulse than non-drinkers (Harburg Gleiberman, Russell, & Cooper, 1991), and their tolerance for frustration is significantly lower than people drawn from the normal population (Lewis & Bucholz, 1991).

The abilities to perceive time accurately and patiently and to respond appropriately also are important personality functions. Much evidence is available on which to conclude that alcoholics are quite unable to perceive and appreciate the nature of time. Two separate studies (Roos & Albers, 1965; Sattler & Pflugrath, 1970) found that the alcoholic's perception of time is quite unlike that of the normal person. Briefly, these two studies showed that the alcoholic's needs are focused upon short-term gratification. Put simply, alcoholics want what they want when they want it—now. Three other studies confirmed these findings (Imber, Miller, Faillace, & Liberman, 1971; Smart, 1968; Roy, DeJong, Lamparski, et al., 1991). All of this research on the alcoholic's reaction to time discovered that generally they are quite unable emotionally to appreciate the effects of now behavior in their futures.

A healthy person is one who builds and maintains rewarding relationships. The alcoholic does not (Walter, Nagoshi, Muntaner, & Haerzen, 1990). Too often friends of the alcoholic are "drinking Buddies or Betties"—superficial acquaintances. Relationships are founded and maintained upon ingesting alcohol with these people. This seems to be true for both men and women.

Alcoholics get divorced at a rate higher than the national average. A probable reason for this might be the fact that alcoholics have difficulty identifying with their own sexuality.

They are not emotionally convinced or happy with the sex they are. Machover, Puzzo, Machover, and Plumeau (1959) using their own *Figure-drawing Test* compared a group of remitted and unremitted alcoholics with a group of homosexuals and controls. The alcoholics indicated more confusion about their sexuality than did the control group. These findings were corroborated in a study by Milliger & Young (1990).

Findings by Machover et al. (1959) seemed to be corroborated on a *Photo-preference Test* that was done by two researchers who found male alcoholics tended to favor the pictures of older people, especially those of women. This finding was interpreted as an indication of the alcoholic's discomfort with being a man and as a response to his dependency need.

One of the most revealing studies in this area of sexual identity of the alcoholic was done by Parker (1959). He used the *Termon-Miles Masculinity-femininity Scale* and compared two groups, one confirmed alcoholics and the other, moderate drinkers. What he found was that alcoholics by and large ranked significantly lower in masculine disposition than did the moderate drinkers. The alcoholics also displayed a strong maternal dependence and had been divorced. Interestingly too, these alcoholics had come from broken homes.

In a subsequent study, Parker tested a group of prealcoholics. His hypotheses were that these individuals would display a strong macho veneer and would be binding much unconscious anxiety about their sexuality. His hypotheses were confirmed (Parker, 1969). These last findings by Parker were proven in a subsequent study in which a group of alcoholics was tested on a difference scale of conscious masculinity (Zucker, 1968). In a more recent work, Roy et al. (1991) confirmed the findings of these last two studies. In addition, these researchers found that if individuals become alcoholic before age twenty they are even more likely to develop emotional problems of all sorts and to develop an intense anti-social disposition.

How a person projects self to others is a product of self-understanding. The indications are clear that alcoholics on the whole have low self-concepts and are hypercritical of themselves. The statistical evidence is strong that alcoholics don't like themselves (Connor, 1962; Craddick & Leipold, 1968).

Finally, on the same topic of self-concept, a group of 140 men was tested with the *Tennessee Self-concept Scale* and compared to a sample drawn from the normal population. On all ten aspects of the scale researchers found that the alcoholics scored lower than men in general (Gross & Alder, 1970).

WHAT PERSONALITY TESTS SHOW

Ongoing research with personality tests indicates that the alcoholic harbors a constellation of personality factors that set him/her apart from the nonalcoholic.

Objective Personality Tests

Minnesota Multiphasic Personality Inventory (MMPI). One of the most widely used tests to assess personality continues to be the *Minnesota Multiphasic Personality Inventory (MMPI)*. This test has nine different scales. The scale which has consistently reported significant difference between the alcoholic and the normal is lettered Pd and is concerned with measuring factors dealing with psychopathy (Cooney, Kadden, & Litt, 1990; Fuller, Lunney, & Naylor, 1966; Goss & Morosko, 1969; Kristianson, 1970; Spiegel, Hadley, & Hadley, 1970; Mungas, 1988). The prime ingredient of psychopathy has to do primarily with a conscience which functions poorly, erratically, or not at all. In the alcoholic sometimes it takes over the personality. The alcoholic often seeks relations with other people, behaves expansively, generously, and lovingly. Sometimes conscience seems to be totally absent. The alcoholic, however, may become a loner, embittered, and convinced that no one cares a whit about him/her, because everyone is really out for self. These last feelings are related to the second prime aspect of psychopathy, namely, an excessive concern for one's own self. (Smith & Newman, 1990). The alcoholic, when in the phase of conscience diminution, tends to view the world as a hostile, threatening place where people are unnurturant, uncaring, or even out to do him/her in. When in this phase, the alcoholic is beset by constant depression frequently associated with hostility.

The MMPI test confirms this depression (Hoffman, 1970a; Kristianson, 1970; Spiegel et al., 1970) as do a separate series of paper and pencil personality test by Hobson (1989). Alcoholics generally are more depressed than most normals. What this means is that alcoholics tend to resist developing goals and to resist solution of problems in their personal lives. They resist help and may vent their anger on those closest to them. This depression in alcoholics is understandable. They are tired. They are tired of the constant emotional conflict between an overpowering and virtually nonexistent conscience. They are especially tired of the excessive load of guilt that they must bear when the same conscience is functioning too strongly.

The Cattell Test-Sixteen Personality. Cattell (Cattell, Eber, & Tatsuoka, 1970) has developed a scale *(Sixteen Factor Personality Questionnaire)* which throws even more light on the alcoholic personality. Using this test, two researchers found a strong element of immaturity in the chronic drinker's personality (DePalma & Clayton, 1958). Alcoholics, especially during adolescent and college years, appear to be constantly looking for fun and especially are not inhibited by the possible consequences of their acts. Indeed they don't even think about consequences. Their focus is upon gratification—now. These last findings were proven in a more recent work by Mukasa, Nakamuna, Yamada, Inove, and Nakazawa (1991) and again by Windle (1990).

Jackson Personality Research Form (PRF). Hoffman (1970b) using the *Jackson Personality Research Form* found that alcoholics score higher than normals in their need for affiliation, nurturance, succorance, and abasement. What this finding indicates is that alcoholics need people but are uncertain about how to get close to them. Alcoholics don't feel that they are worthy enough to deal effectively with other people or to receive or accept the affection of others. Alcoholics in his study also scored low on aggression, autonomy, and dominance. These findings can be interpreted to mean that alcoholics also are likely to incorporate a strong element of passive dependency in their personality. This interpretation seems to be supported by low scores on achievement, play, endurance, and their high score on harm avoidance. Simply, alcoholics do not appear to be ambitious, particularly active, or interested in new experiences. Their general penchant seems to be toward a safe, warm, womb-like environment.

Projective Tests

Rorschach Test. This author scored and interpreted Rorschach protocols of 44 alcoholics ranging in age from 24 to 46 years. Thirty were men and fourteen were women. All were middle class, employed, and paying clients in this counselor's private practice. The sample, even though select, revealed certain common denominators in personality. Thus all exhibited

> a very rich fantasy life,
>
> a moderate to strong need to achieve and to be respected,
>
> an introverted orientation,
>
> a moderate to high expectation of rejection,
>
> a prima defense of reaction formation, and
>
> a weak self-esteem.

What the author concluded is that alcoholics live a disproportionate part of their lives in a fantasy world. They are daydreamers who commonly are beset with superstitions. Their need to succeed is strong as is their need for adulation. At the same time, they are bedeviled by a latent but constant feeling that they are doomed losers. They are obsessed about this feeling. Even when they are able to put this kind of "stinkin' thinkin'" out of their cognitive minds, it remains a core part of their emotional self-understanding. It is a major reason for their fixated preoccupation with self.

Among the debilitating aspects of alcoholics' characteristics is their fearful and constant expectation of rejection. Indeed, what this counselor has learned in dealing with alcoholics is that the latter always seem to be surprised when people are accepting and a little shocked when they do for them. This perception of a rejecting world leads to problems. Frequently they take offense too quickly and worse, do it secretly, obsess about it, and may show displeasure much later to the bewilderment of the supposed offender, thereby weakening or even destroying another relationship.

Such erratic behavior may puzzle those who interact with alcoholics, but it is perfectly understandable to the therapist. This behavior is a product of the psychological defense called **reaction formation.** When they use this defense, alcoholics are trying to protect themselves from perceived threat by behaving in a way which is diametrically opposed to how they really feel. Too often this is a major defense in the alcoholics' repertoire of protection. This author is convinced that reaction formation is a major debilitator of alcoholic personalities. Why? Because it alienates alcoholics from their individual selves. When they respond by reaction formation, alcoholics do not know how they truly feel. They can't because reaction formation like all psychological defenses, is unconscious.

An insidious function of reaction formation is that it effects and maintains a low self-esteem. The importance of self-esteem cannot be overstated. It is at the very heart of all human functioning. An individual's life performance is basically a function of self-esteem. If one thinks one is good, one performs well. If one thinks one is unworthy, then one performs unworthily—or one doesn't perform at all.

During the counseling process the counselor learns quickly that the alcoholic's self-esteem is low. The counselor who remains constantly aware of the alcoholic's low self-esteem can better appreciate the client's periodic embitterment, excessive concern for self, and pessimistic perception of the world to which he/she jealously adheres. The counselor can better understand also that his/her client's focus on gratification is nothing more than a puerile-like attempt to feed a badly impoverished self-esteem. Hoffman's (1970b) findings with *Jackson Personality Research Form*, explained previously, also can be understood in this light.

Thematic Apperception Test (T.A.T.). The author compared the T.A.T.'s of 21 male alcoholics, who were residents in a rehabilitation center, with a group of nonalcoholic men who were hospitalized for physical disabilities. The alcoholics' tests were strikingly different from those of nonalcoholics. Thus, the latter told mostly stories with optimistic outcomes and focused on themes of success and effective coping strategies. The alcoholic stories, however, were characterized by themes of (1) impotence, (2) inebriation, (3) dominance, and (4) hostility. Also the author was struck by the paucity of heroes in the alcoholics' tests when compared to those of the nonalcoholics.

A recurring theme among 14 of the alcoholic protocols was impotence. Apparently alcoholic men feel that they do not have the emotional means to cope with the stresses of lives. They feel pains of stress acutely and exquisitely. Even worse, they fully expect many painful outcomes and are pretty much resigned to victimization. In short, they feel hapless, helpless, and hopeless.

Surprisingly, many stories related by alcoholics dealt with drunkenness. Central in these stories was a sense of loss: loss of relationships, job prestige, and status. Quite apparently, the alcoholic is fully cognizant of the potentially destructive effects of drinking.

Probably this cognizance together with the concept of victimization can explain the alcoholic's insatiable need to dominate and control the environment. It also explains the research findings of McClelland, Wanner, and Vanneman (1972) that the male alcoholic drinks to escape into a fantasy world where he can indulge his illusions about being a powerful man.

Even in his fantasy world and too often when he's out of it, the alcoholic is laden with deep, deep feelings of hostility. What was especially interesting to this researcher was that most vitriolic stories were told by the alcoholics who related in a warm, healthy way. A comparable finding was discovered by Gynther, Presher, and McDonald (1959). Another finding, which corroborated Gynther et al. and the author's work, was the relative lack of hero types to be found among the alcoholic stories. This finding is not surprising. This lack of hero worship by the alcoholic can be attributed to lack of ability to put trust in others, i.e., in the conviction that everyone has clay feet. Even more, the alcoholic's inability to identify with heroes reflects his/her abiding sense of hopelessness about others projected from his/her sense of inadequacy.

Figure 2.1 contains an illustrative self-esteem cycle of the alcoholic. The poor self-esteem contributes to the drinking which causes more depression and so forth.

Self-esteem Cycle of the Alcoholic

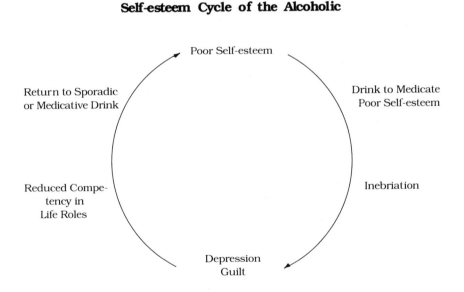

Figure 2.1. Schematic illustration of the self-esteem cycle of the alcoholic.

SELF-ESTEEM RESEARCH

The problem of low self-esteem has been the object of much research. Evidence is clear that a major motive for excessive drinking is a low self-esteem (Segal, Huba, & Singer, 1980). Many alcoholics drink because their self-image is so radically different from the idealized image they have of themselves (Eastman & Norris, 1982). Phrased another way, alcoholics don't like what they are and what they seem to be to themselves. They don't accept themselves. For whatever reasons, they desperately seek to be more than they feel they can ever be in their real lives. So, they seek it in the private world of fantasy. In this fantasized world, alcohol helps them to embellish the constant nagging version of themselves with which they are plagued.

In this fantasized world, the male alcoholic especially is able to fantasize about power—that which he lost or that which he seeks to gain. Research by McClelland and Davis (1972) and McClelland, Wanner, and Vanneman (1972) has focused on this need for power in the male alcoholic. Alcoholics, these researchers have discovered, drink to accentuate their need to dominate others and because drink makes them feel powerful.

Resorting to drink because of acutely low self-esteem is not a male province alone. Women drink because of self-esteem problems too. Indeed, one researcher (Beckman, 1978) found that the woman alcoholic suffers even more than the man in this regard.

Within the family, low self-esteem can be insidiously infectious. It was found in at least one study that a woman who comes from a family with a history of alcoholism is likely to develop important self-esteem problems and is probably a candidate for alcoholism (Beckman, Day, Bardsley, & Seeman, 1980; Winokur & Corgell 1991). The irony of drinking is, of course, that while the alcoholic drinks to raise self-esteem, the effect is precisely the opposite (Konovsky & Wilsnack, 1982).

ALCOHOLIC PERCEPTION

Alcoholics do not perceive the world or their internal selves in the same way that nonalcoholics do. Normal people are able to differentiate between people and their settings. Alcoholics are not. For alcoholics, people and settings blend emotionally. For example, the difference for them between hospital and doctor, doctor and nurse, nurse and hospital is small, if any. Each and all are the institution. This inability to differentiate between figure and ground has been explained as a major reason for the alcoholic's constant dependence. Their inability to articulate perceptually has led them to surrender to their environment. Witkin, Dyk, Faterson, Goodenough, and Karp (1962), in their research, substantiated these views. The conclusion based on research is that the perception of alcoholics is far more distorted than that of nonalcoholics. Indeed, the alcoholic dependency as a function of distorted perception is even more acute than that of nonalcoholic psychiatric patients. These studies by Witkin et al. (1962) have been corroborated by a number of researchers (Chess, Neuringer, & Goldstein, 1971; Goldstein & Chotlos, 1965; Karp, Poster, & Goodman, 1963; Moss, 1989).

The alcoholics' view of the world seems very much in tandem with their view of themselves. Wisotsky (1958) and then again Laird (1962) found that alcoholic men when asked to *Draw-A-Person* were not as likely to draw a man first as are nonalcoholics. Wisotsky (1958) found that almost 95% of normals drew themselves while only 70% of alcoholics did so. Laird's (1962) findings were not too dissimilar. Eighty-one percent of the alcoholics drew themselves first compared to 95% of the normals. One conclusion is that the alcoholic man does not view his body as favorably as he does the woman's. Another is that he is threatened by women.

The last thought seems to find support in another study which found that male alcoholics, when asked to *Draw-A-Person*, consistently drew the female figure taller than the male figure (Craddick & Leipold, 1968). Quite apparently alcoholic men have problems with how they perceive and accept their bodies.

PAIN TOLERANCE

Some evidence is that the alcoholic's threshold for pain is lower than the normal person and that his/her perception of pain is more acute than that of the normal person. Petrie (1967) in some sophisticated research found that the alcoholic who touched the same shock stimulus as the nonalcoholic tended to overestimate the subsequent stimulus shock. The implications of this initial research (1960s) made for interesting speculation. Could it be that some people innately feel pain—physical and psychological, more intensely than others? Could this fact be a reason that some people drink to excess? Subsequent research indicated that the answers to both questions are "yes." This study confirmed that alcoholics are more exquisitely sensitive to pain and that alcohol has a considerable reducing effect in this sensitivity. The researchers in this study hypothesized that alcoholics may be alcoholics precisely because alcohol for the heavy drinker is simply a way of effecting a physiological sensory equilibrium (Buchsbaum & Ludwig, 1981). Their hypothesis is supported in subsequent studies where it was found that alcohol effectively reduced pain more in alcoholics than it does in normals (Barnes, 1980; Brown & Cutter, 1977; Cutter, Maloof, Kurtz,, & Jones, 1976).

A related characteristic to a low threshold for pain is hypochondriasis. Alcoholics consistently score higher in this characteristic than do normals. What the research shows is that alcoholics complain more about their bodies and their emotional problems than do people drawn from the normative population (Goss & Morosko, 1969; Hagnell & Tunving, 1972; Sargent, 1966).

PREALCOHOLIC PERSONALITY

As of 1992, whether or not a prealcoholic personality actual exists, is uncertain. The reason for this uncertainty is that no research has assessed potential alcoholics and reassessed them after they have become alcoholic.

However, considerable research has been done with results that have been the bases for suggesting that alcoholics in their prealcoholic phase may differ from normals in selected personality traits. One study compared selected personality characteristics of individuals who had become alcoholic after college with nonalcoholics. Both groups had taken tests while college freshmen. What the researchers found was that the alcoholics, while freshmen, were more lackadaisical and unfocused. They also were inclined to manipulate and "cut corners" without too much worry. In addition, researchers found that alcoholics tended toward a high level of unproductive activity (Loper, Kammeier, & Hoffman, 1973). These findings gibe in part with an earlier study which found that men tended to be rebellious, impulsive, and nonconforming. A third study on this topic compared the test profiles of alcoholics who had been patients in a mental health clinic. They compared these files with those of a control group and found the incidence of hostility and nonconforming behavior much higher among the alcoholic group (Robins, Bates, & O'Neal, 1982). What these three studies indicate in a clear fashion is that individuals who later become alcoholics have at least one common denominator: an inability to exercise controls effectively over hostile impulses.

Research has been done to determine if factors were in the alcoholic's home environment that were conducive to the development of alcoholism. What was found was that alcoholics develop poor self-esteems as children. Those alcoholics in this sample were seldom reared by affectionate mothers, were exposed to much parental ambivalence, and had encountered ambiguous communication. As a child, the alcoholic rarely had a clear understanding of what was expected of him/ her by adults in control of the environment. The budding self-esteem became stunted. The coordinator of this work speculated that the later addiction to alcohol was a function of this stunted self-esteem (McCord, 1972).

A study with undergraduates found the college problem drinker already has a poor self-concept and it is comparable to that of the older alcoholic. The problem drinker in this study displayed a high incidence of self-depreciation, a low self-acceptance, and a remarkable distancing between real-self and ideal-self (Williams, 1965). The question to ask is, "are these self-views a function of already heavy drinking or are they innate predispositions?" The answer is still unclear. More longitudinal research needs to be done to confirm or deny the existence of a prealcoholic personality.

ALCOHOLISM IN THE GAY COMMUNITY

Yori (1989) in a study with homosexual men in California found that gays feel alienated in our society. Their perception of themselves and of other gays is of people who do not belong. Their perception of the general society is that it is a dangerous place in which to live, work, and play. Their constant mood sense is one of vulnerability and of acute discomfort with themselves and with being gay. Alcohol, they find, helps considerably to palliate the stresses and discomfort encountered in being gay.

These findings are substantiated by the work of McKirnan and Peterson (1989). In a study with 3,400 homosexuals, these researchers found that the perception and expectancies of gays were structured and molded by the cultural values and norms of the general society.

Gays are at a greater risk to abuse alcohol because of how they perceive themselves in relation to heterosexuals and in relation to alcohol. Critical in their socialization is the "bar scene." The bar, usually segregated from the heterosexual community, is of prime importance for socialization. Socialization for the gay person is virtually always in an alcoholic context. While socialization frequently involves drinking in the general heterosexual community, in the homosexual community socialization without drinking is a rare phenomenon. For most gays drink has become the catalyst which precipitates relationships and which maintains them. While the bar may be viewed as a place to meet and socialize by many heterosexuals, by most gays the view is that it is the only place. With such a view, alcohol takes on exaggerated importance. With such a view the inducement to drink is stronger. With such a view learning to become alcoholic is easier. These thoughts would seem to be substantiated in a subsequent study by McKirnan and Peterson (1989). They found that a substantially higher proportion of the homosexual than the heterosexual sample abused alcohol and that "homosexual men and women"—are at a—"high risk for alcohol abuse due to psychosocial variables such as the importance of bar settings."

SUMMARY

Perception is a cornerstone of human personality. How we perceive others will determine how we interact with them. Too often the alcoholic perceives a world filled with threat, or at best, indifference. This is manifested by impulsivity, escape into fantasy, and excessive personal gratification.

The alcoholic conscience is characterized by fluctuation between over-scrupulousness and nonexistence. In the former phase, the alcoholic's behavior is a function of guilt. In the latter, the behavior brutalizes those near him/her.

Alcoholics' psychological defenses do not work. Often this is because they are used immoderately and because an undue quantity and intensity of threat is perceived.

Alcoholics experience difficulty in building and maintaining relationships. A probable reason for this variable is that they have trouble identifying with their own sexuality. This difficulty with self-identification is reflected in a low self-esteem and, paradoxically, in an excessive concern for one's own self. This constant conflict results in depression, and when depressed, the alcoholic withdraws into the safe, warm womb-like environment of addiction.

In the author's research with the Rorschach, he discovered that the alcoholic has a rich fantasy life, a moderate to strong need to achieve and to be respected, an introverted orientation, a moderate to high expectation of rejection, and a weak self-esteem. Reaction-formation is a prime defense.

The author's research with the T.A.T. indicated that the alcoholic is characterized by feelings of impotence, is obsessed with the need to drink, feels victimized, harbors deep hostility, and has trouble identifying with hero types.

The alcoholic's perception is that of one who has surrendered to his/her environment. The alcoholic man tends to view the woman's body as threatening and more prestigious than his own. Alcoholics perceive and anticipate pain more sensitively than do normals. Alcohol seems to have a more soothing effect upon them than upon normals. This perception and anticipation helps to explain why the alcoholic has a stronger penchant for hypochondriasis than does the normal person.

At this time, whether a prealcoholic personality actually exists or not is unknown. However, some evidence is available that individuals who lack controls may have a higher predisposition toward alcoholism than do those with normal controls. Also, an emotionally depriving home environment may be conducive toward the development of a prealcoholic personality. However, the view by most professionals is that more longitudinal research needs to be done to confirm the existence of an alcoholic personality.

Gays in our society feel alienated. Their perception of themselves and of other gays is of people who do not belong. This perception is precisely what exacerbates their abuse of alcohol. Critical in their socialization is the "bar scene." Indeed, in gay life, socialization is virtually always in an alcoholic context.

TOPICS FOR DISCUSSION AND REFLECTION

1. How do alcoholics perceive themselves? How do they perceive others?

2. When the alcoholic is in an overly scrupulous phase of conscience, he/she tends to make decisions out of guilt. Why is this undesirable?

3. How do defenses help the alcoholic to persevere in his/her alcoholism?

4. Of the defenses described which one(s) do you consider to be the most and least difficult to break down? Why?

5. Most alcoholic men have a lower self-esteem than nonalcoholic men. What are the implications of this for them? For others?

6. The Cattell Test—Sixteen Personality shows that many alcoholics are not inhibited by the possible consequences of their acts. What does this mean about such alcoholics?

7. What do you believe to be the most important findings in the author's research with Projective Tests? Why?

8. On the T.A.T. test, alcoholics were found to have a paucity of heroes in their stories. What significance do you attach to this?

9. On the evidence presented, do you think further research will confirm the existence of an alcoholic personality? Why? Why not?

10. On the basis of the research presented, do you think the gay alcoholic has a better or worse chance to attain a state of sobriety? Why?

CHAPTER THREE

ALCOHOLIC FAMILY

A number of studies show that if the alcoholic lives with family, then the addiction is a familial problem not just a personal one (Cook & Goethe, 1990; Gross & McCaul, 1990; Penick, Nickel, Powell, Bingham, & Liskow, 1990; Tweed & Ryff, 1991). When an individual begins to drink to excess, effects are felt by all members of the family. Alcoholism sickens not only the addict but also the entire family. As has been indicated, the emotional deprivation suffered as a child within the family is an important factor in the development of one's alcoholism. This seems to be truer for women than for men (Beckman, Day, Bardsley, & Seeman, 1980). One study found that when both parents are alcoholic, their children are more likely to be the same than when only one of the parents is alcoholic. The same study found that the probability is higher for an individual to become alcoholic if one parent was alcoholic than if neither were (McKenna & Pickens, 1983). Quite apparently, children can identify with the worst as well as the best of the parental personality.

Families have emotional equilibriums just as individuals do. Such an equilibrium has been termed a "homeostatic balance" (Jackson, 1957). This balance is achieved by how the family members perceive one another, by what they expect from one another, and by how they interact with one another. Each member has a role, and each plays a part in maintaining the equilibrium of the family. Examples include the wife who always drives home from a party because of her husband's inebriation, the adolescent who has learned to do the family's food shopping because mother isn't feeling well—again, and the husband who serves as a scapegoat for his alcoholic wife's verbal abuse. Each member consciously or unconsciously has an emotional stake in maintaining familial equilibrium. What the author has learned is that when a member no longer wants to play the role, a change is effected within the family. The adolescent may rebel and refuse to do the family shopping, may refuse to accept mother's protestations about not feeling well, and may finally confront mother and father too, about mother's addiction. The crisis may effect a change to which members must adapt or the family separates. The author remembers just such a case.

The client, a successful architect, married for twenty-one years, was convinced by the head of his firm to join Alcoholics Anonymous. He stopped drinking and referred himself to the author for counseling. The presenting problem was not his long-term drinking but a bad marriage. The wife was asked to join the counseling session but steadfastly refused. The client was in counseling for thirteen months and concurrently attended AA faithfully. What came out in the counseling was that the client, who had always had a penchant for passivity and dependence, had married a controlling, protective mother figure. She had reinforced his dependency by tolerating his drinking but had kept the knowledge secret from their children and their friends. She even bought his booze. In a real sense, she had fed his alcoholism. When his drinking stopped, his need for a protective mother figure also stopped and the family equilibrium changed. She could not adapt. Simply, she functioned better with an alcoholic husband than with a sober husband. She filed for divorce.

Research data are available for the conclusion that the self-esteem of married couples drops as their consumption of alcohol increases. Without doubt, an alcoholic man can wreak emotional havoc in the family setting. The research evidence is even stronger that the effects of a woman's alcoholism are even worse. Curlee (1970) compared male and female patients in an alcoholic treatment center and found that once a woman took to drink, her problems became more acute more rapidly than they did for a man. Curlee's findings are supported by Nespor (1990).

Apparently effects of female alcoholism on family members can be severe. Indeed, two researchers found that student's reasons for drinking were positively related to the frequency of maternal intoxication (Harford & Spiegler, 1983). A male or female student's risk of becoming a problem drinker increased if he/she had been exposed to what the authors of the study called "maternal deviant drinking." A subsequent study by the same principal author indicated that genetic factor may be the predisposing reason for this. Whatever the reason(s), the negative impact of an alcoholic mother is greater than that of an alcoholic father. This is probably because maternal alcoholism is less socially acceptable than is paternal alcoholism.

THE ENABLER

More than just one star is in the tragic drama played on the stage of the alcoholic family. Costarring with the alcoholic is the **enabler.** Usually a spouse, the enabler also can be anyone living with the alcoholic—parent, child, uncle, aunt, or simply a live-in friend. The enabler is any person who unwittingly abets and promotes the alcoholic's addiction.

Just as no two alcoholics are alike, neither are two enablers alike. At the same time, certain denominators are in the personalities of enablers which facilitate the alcoholic process in family member(s). Enablers are disposed to be

1. overprotective,

2. compulsive, and

3. worriers.

OVERPROTECTIVE ENABLERS

Overprotective enablers, like overprotective parents, are not loving but rejecting. The overprotective parent does not view the child as a separate and independent human being. The overprotective parent does not understand that the child's emotional health, growth, and maturity lie in making his/

her own choices and decisions and in being responsible for his/her own behavior. In short, the overprotective parent perceives the child (regardless of age) as basically helpless and inept which is more often than not the parent's unconscious self-view (projection defense). Both perception and defense are used by this type of enabler toward the alcoholic. The overprotective enabler serves as a buffer between the alcoholic and the rest of the world. The rest of the world may even include the rest of the family. Thus the enabler may lie, explain, and/or defend that alcoholic to children, parents, and outsiders. Most enablers, in their zeal to protect, defend, and explain the alcoholic's behavior, do not see that they are actually feeding and nurturing irresponsibility and immaturity. Indeed, their overprotectiveness creates a womb-like world for the alcoholic's mundane physical needs and insulates him/her from the normal, usual demands and anxieties of daily living. The alcoholic is excused from family chores, from most social obligations, sometimes even from holding a job. Such an alcoholic seems excused from life. A cocoon-like existence maintains the alcoholism and thereby accelerates the physical, intellectual, and emotional deterioration.

Overprotective enablers are people who need to control and manipulate. In the domineering type enabler, this need is easy to see in the arbitrariness, in the fits, and so forth. In the submissive or more deferential type of enabler, this need is more covert but is just as, if not more, demeaning. In these latter types, it usually can be seen in the intense inordinate interest which they take in their alcoholics' lives, in what they eat, whom they see, where they go, and where they are at any moment. Through this interest, complemented usually with the disposition to do, do, do for the alcoholic, the enabler is able to control the alcoholic's meals, social life, and virtually all the alcoholic's movements. Overprotective enablers who find reward in achieving such control of another's life seem to fill an acute need for personal security.

This need for personal security is a prime motivator for overprotective enablers. Simply, they can best be understood as being concerned primarily with their own selves. Why? Because their intent, conscious or unconscious, is to turn the alcoholic into an overdevoted and obligated companion.

This is especially true of those who persevere in their enabling even after they become aware of it. These enablers seem to exist with a latent but constant anxiety that in the end they will be left alone. The irony is that often their enabling accomplishes just that, since enabling does nothing to engender loyalty.

COMPULSIVE ENABLERS

Enablers tend to be **compulsive.** Their constant and most important mission, among many, is to solve any and all family problems. They set up and implement schedules, not only their own but those of the rest of the family members, alcoholic or not. They tend to the myriad of family chores that need tending. If they cannot, for whatever reason, deal with a minor task themselves, they will bully or manipulate another family member into doing it. Then they will supervise to see that whatever was to be done was done to their satisfaction— meaning in letter perfect fashion.

This concern with letter perfection distinguishes the compulsive enabler from the normally efficient person. Some enablers acquire it late; in others it seems to be positively congenital. Regardless at what point they incorporate this trait into their personalities, it is the one which is most apparent and the one which precipitates arguments, fights, and stresses of all kinds in the family. This trait alienates children especially. Usually, because of this trait, children come to sympathize with the alcoholic, turn to him/her for closeness. Indeed, *the enabler's compulsive ways may well be a prime reason that so many children of alcoholics become themselves alcoholic.* Many come to conclude that it's better to be a relaxed drunk than a frantic, compulsive enabler.

Why are most enablers compulsive? The answer seems to lie in the alcoholic's withdrawal from the family. The enabler's compulsiveness in most cases can be understood as the response to that withdrawal. They feel that their compulsive ways bring order and sanity to the chaos and indifference which alcoholism brings into the family.

Compulsiveness in the enabler is a response to something else too. Please note that compulsive people are usually people in constant motion—physically, intellectually, and/or emotionally. They're always doing something. Now, such activity has an important benefit to alcoholic enablers as it distracts them from seeing the alcoholic's drinking. Such activity has another important benefit for enablers in that it prevents them from focusing on their inner selves and on how they continue to contribute to the family's alcoholic dynamics. In short, compulsiveness helps enablers to deny the reality of their own and the family's situation.

ENABLERS AS WORRIERS

Enablers are worriers who are unwilling or unable to see alcoholism or the insidious effects of it in the family. Like the alcoholic they tend to see the drinking problem as being outside themselves. They see little or no connection between themselves and the problem. Despite this myopic view of their situation, or perhaps because of it, they worry a lot.

The worry of many enablers comes in waves. Sometimes they feel inundated by it, at other times, free of it. When worried, they have to go into action—"do something" for the alcoholic or for another member of the family to assuage the constant sense of guilt with which they live. The guilt can be derived from the abuse they inflict on others in the family or for the abuse others inflict upon them. Both worry and guilt seem to keep them on an emotional roller coaster.

The dependent enablers are sometimes physically abused. When that is the case, they usually develop an alcoholic-like view of being victimized by life and circumstances. Too often they develop a masochistic outlook and learn to suffer in silence. Occasionally these enablers develop a martyr complex much as if they are ennobling their suffering by doing so. They conclude that happiness of any kind, even a modicum of it, is not for this life but in the next only.

What people think is of critical importance to enablers. Indeed, it determines and explains much about their behavior. Typical enabler thinking goes like this:

"What will people think if they find out my wife is alcoholic?"

"If I leave him?"

"If they were to stop in when she's roaring drunk?"

"If he/she lets the lawn go too long?"

"If he/she gets into an auto accident when he/she is drunk?"

This obsessive concern for appearances and propriety is a major reason enablers persevere in their enabling, a major reason they have so many worries.

ALCOHOLIC ADOLESCENTS

Drinking among adolescents today is rampant (Alexander, 1991). The National Institute on Alcohol Abuse estimates that 30% of all adolescents who drink have little or no control over it. This inability to control drinking is the reason that more than ten thousand adolescents are traffic fatalities every year (Hawthorne & Menzel, 1983).

One estimate places the number of alcoholic adolescents at 10% of the adolescent population (comparable with the adult drinking population). If these estimates are accurate, this would mean that today approximately 600,000 adolescents have a serious drinking problem (Keller, 1980).

Even more alarming than these statistics is a report that a "very substantial evidence of alcohol use exists throughout the drug treatment population" (Hubbard, Cavanaugh, Rachal, Schlenger, & Ginzburg, 1983) and that the programs designed to treat adolescent alcoholism have not had the positive effect expected. Thus, over one-third of the adolescents treated in programs funded by the National Institute on Alcohol Use continue to use alcohol in excessive amounts (Hubbard et al., 1983).

The evidence is that adolescents (both boys and girls) take their first drink during age 13. This fact has been true for over 20 years. What has not been true for over 20 years, however, is that adolescent boys report their first experience of being drunk as occurring at age 13 (Fromme & Samson, 1983). In short, the intensity of the addiction, as well as the generality, among adolescents, seems to have become more acute.

For a long time adolescents have viewed drinking as an important complimentary rite to facilitate passage into adulthood. Drinking in their view was and is the *"cool thing"* to do (Rachal, Guess, Hubbard, Maisto, Cavanaugh, Waddell, & Benrud, 1983). *"Has to be,"* they reason, *"all the adults do it."* Thus, as a child, the adolescent observed that men drink. Women drink. Dad drinks. Mom drinks. *"So why shouldn't I drink?"* becomes the logical next question. And each does.

We shouldn't be surprised nor especially alarmed at that fact. What is alarming is that a disproportionate number of adolescents are growing up without experiencing the adolescent years. They relate to parents, teachers, and peers through an alcoholic haze. So they are unable to acquire the social and interpersonal skills historically acquired during adolescence. The alcoholic "buzz" does not permit them. By this buzz, they are able to escape any and all potential anxiety, pain, frustration, and ambiguity (Milman, Bennett, & Hanson, 1983).

In short, they emerge from the teen years with the social sophistication and emotional wherewithal of children, and they know it. Probably for this reason the male adolescent problem drinker continues to be a problem drinker in his twenties. The negative effects of alcoholic addiction during the adolescent years are not all emotional or social. Supplemental evidence causes one to conclude that other negative factors exist. For example, Hannon, Day, Butler, Larson, and Casey (1983) found that a decline in intellectual competence occurs with constant alcoholic addiction.

Many people who study the alcoholic adolescent point to the peer group as the critical cause for the adolescent's addiction. Thus, they will cite studies which show that a given adolescent's drinking increases as peers increase their drinking (Harford & Speigler, 1982). They report that excessive drinking during the early college years is a function of peer pressure (Shore, Rivers, & Berman, 1983).

Without doubt, peer groups are an important factor in the development of adolescent alcoholism (Barnes & Welte, 1990). This author, however, believes that the family can obviate destructive peer group influence. A peer group assumes major importance in an adolescent's life, especially when the family is not meeting his/her basic needs of security, love, and self-esteem (Hays & Revetto, 1990). Generally speaking, *when a family has been successful in meeting those needs during the childhood years, drinking during adolescence is not a problem.* The notable exception to this generalization, of course, is when one or both of the parents are alcoholics (McKenna & Pickens, 1981).

What most adults forget, too easily, is that adolescents are still in the formative learning years and at some level still want guidance. If home was always the place that the adolescent received solid, valid information, then he/she will continue to seek modeling there first. This is particularly true about drinking. Much research evidence has been collected, and researchers have concluded that an adolescent's drinking behavior is very much a function of parental approval and disapproval. Adolescents reported that they drank little if their parents disapproved and much if their parents approved (Rachal et al., 1983).

ADULT CHILDREN OF ALCOHOLICS (ACOA)

Children, who grow up in alcoholic families, grow up emotionally deprived. Sometimes they are reared in situations where the climate is explosive. Temper tantrums, sudden and unpredictable, happen, seemingly for no reason. Here people scream, cower, and cry. Sometimes the climate is just the opposite. It is so undisturbed that the children learn to live in an environment which could be described as tomb-like; one where no talk or communication occurs and where members function in isolation and keep secrets from one another. Sometimes the climate is between these extremes. Even so, in these "middle climates" the children are often abused verbally and/or physically. If they are not abused themselves, they see other members so abused they come to understand that hypercriticism and nagging are viable and legitimate ways of interacting. They learn that promises are not necessarily binding as they may or may not be kept.

Climates such as these promote insecurity. Climates such as these promote a sense of isolation and of never having been loved. Climates such as these promote a poor sense of self worth. ***Children of alcoholics come to negate the worth of their own love and feel unworthy of anyone else's.*** For many, the giving and taking of love becomes a mystery. The feelings of insecurity, the ineptness with love, and the low self-esteem are the major reasons that these children as adults exhibit a veritable host of debilitating personality traits. Chief among these are

1. a constant need for approval;

2. a low ability to persevere;

3. an inability to trust;

4. unreliability;

5. a tendency to lie a lot and often for no reason;

6. an attraction to pain;

7. vacillation;

8. an inability to get close to others;

9. a tendency to become involved in relationships which are based upon pity, not love;

10. a terror of being evaluated; and

11. a frantic way of life.

Before proceeding, please note. The intention here is not to imply that the children of alcoholics are all alike. Quite the contrary. Like their parent alcoholics and enablers they are seen here as all different from one another. The previously listed traits and descriptions which follow can best be understood as characteristics in their unique personalities. In some children of alcoholics, some of these characteristics are dominant, in other children barely discernible, and in still others some of these characteristics do not exist at all.

Constant Need for Approval

Adult children of alcoholics tend to have an acute and constant need for approval. More often than not this stems from the emotional paradox in which many were steeped in childhood. They grew up in sharply contrasting emotional extremes. One parent (usually the alcoholic) was indifferent or rejecting. While the other one, out of misguided good intention to balance the emotional equation, was studiously over solicitous, if not overprotective. A worse situation (more common too) for such a person was to live a childhood where the same alcoholic parent(s) vacillate(s) between superabundant love, attention, and caring and icy indifference and/or hostile rejection. Behavior at both extremes of the emotional continuum is, of course, common among alcoholics as it is a function of the guilty conscience and inebriation.

The constant need for approval can be and often is channelized in doing for others. The gratitude and recognition they receive fuels them to continue to do for and to serve others through their lives. This is especially true among those who themselves never become alcoholic. They seldom, if ever, examine the why of their constant need to do and serve others. Their frenetic activity is the alternative they choose to self-examination. It has a fringe benefit too. It salves their conscience, albeit never fully. Their conscience, in most cases, is oversized and is the reason they make so may decisions out of guilt and not out of choice. Of course, this person is the ideal candidate for the role of enabler. As a result many do become so. They do because like most people they gravitate consciously or unconsciously toward those whose ways are familiar and which they feel they understand. If nothing else, potential enablers do indeed understand the ways of the budding alcoholic. Therefore, they often marry one.

An unfortunate effect among those with an oversized conscience is that they feel guilty all the time. Their guilt may be such that they seldom take a stand on anything, even if their integrity is involved. What they believe depends upon to whom they are talking. This is true especially with strangers. Such a submissive approach results inevitably in a loss of self-respect and the respect of others. The anger engendered in the child of the alcoholic by such submissiveness by those outside the family (and there is usually a lot) is often displaced upon family members. It is a reason why so much nagging, hypercriticism, and physical abuse occur in the alcoholic family.

Low Ability to Persevere

Children of alcoholics have a low ability to persevere in most activities, even those which they enjoy. In those activities which are unappealing or which are threatening, their ability seems virtually non-existent. As college students, their class attendance is at best spotty, and frequently downright poor. If they have chores at home, their style is to do them sporadically, not at all, or frantically. Most projects, even minor tasks, seem to be finished with little enthusiasm— often grudgingly. They change their jobs often and are the ones who suffer "burn out" most. In short, achievement and striving for success are not prime motivating factors in their lives. This is because many children of alcoholics are plagued by the latent but constant fear that they are going to fail whatever the endeavor, project, or work. This is especially true when they are confronted by new tasks and fulfilling obligations. Their response invariably is to procrastinate. Their emotional rationale seems to be, *"If I don't try, I can't fail."* Their inability to persevere and their penchant for procrastination can best be understood as a defense against lowering further their already pitifully low self-esteem.

Inability to Trust

Children of alcoholics are unable to trust. Trust is learned in a stable home, one where the child can predict with a high degree of accuracy what's going to happen. The alcoholic home, filled as it is with acute emotional vacillations and broken promises, quite apparently militates against such learning. The children of alcoholic families emerge from childhood distrustful and suspicious people. Their distrust costs them much. Because of it, they are unable to get emotionally close to others. As children, they are unable to identify with adults and peers and thereby enrich their personalities.

This inability to identify with others is the reason that during childhood these children appear so bland and apathetic in both appearance and disposition. The blandness and apathy seem to evaporate during adolescence and adulthood, but in truth, are merely veneered beneath the social sophistication which comes with an increase in age. The core suspicions and distrust learned in childhood are very much present. These suspicions and distrust are the prime reasons for the poor quality of their interpersonal relations. The simple truth is that people can't get close to others if they can't trust. Children of alcoholics can't trust.

Unreliable

The children of alcoholics tend to be unreliable. This unreliability is a function of their low self-esteem. Self-esteem influences performance mightily, i.e., if we think we're good, we perform adequately. A disproportionate number of children of alcoholics believe that they are inadequate. Because of this self-view, they resort to the emotional rationale previously noted, *"If I don't try, I can't fail."* The result of these unfortunate cause and effect dynamics is that they present themselves as unreliable. Doing so is not of special significance to them because they grew up with unreliability. In most instances being surrounded by one or more unreliable persons was an integral part of their childhood milieu. As adolescents and adults, they do like most people do. They mirror behavior with which they are familiar and which they understand. Also like most people, **they are far more concerned with maintaining some semblance of respectability in their self-esteem than they are in projecting an image of reliability.** In their view, they have to do that if they are to function at all.

Lie Frequently

Children of alcoholics tend to lie a lot—often for no reason. Several reasons exist for this. As children they spent much of their lives in fantasy to escape the chaotic, harsh reality of their real world. Many learn to find so much reward in their world of imagination that their fantasy lives become as important to them as the real world. For some, it becomes more important. For all of them *fantasy has become an integral defense for the harsh reality which they continue to perceive in adolescence and adulthood.* To mitigate that harshness, they invariably blend their fantasies with reality. The effect of all this fantasizing is to develop a distorted perception of self, of reality, and, simply, of what's true. More often than not, they come to believe the reality which they perceive even though it is a blend of their own imagination.

For these reasons, children of alcoholics view all their lies as "white" lies. If something is not exactly as they said it was, they feel justified in feeling and believing that it should be! Most of them are quite oblivious of the fact that when they blend fantasy with reality they are really telling themselves and others that reality and truth are really not important.

Attraction to Pain

Many children of alcoholics seem beset with an attraction to pain. The reason for this is not difficult to fathom, if one keeps in mind the fact that conscience is a very real and major factor in the alcoholic family. It is usually evident, if not dominant, in all intra-familial interactions. More often than not, conscience is the critical determinant for both major and minor decisions made. In families such as these, conscience literally inundates the children with guilt—guilt which precipitates the need they have to punish themselves. They punish themselves with worry, useless anxiety, imaginary ailments, accidents, a constant scene of unworthiness, and so forth. Bizarre, but true, in the view of some of those reared and steeped in the crazy dynamics of alcoholism, such punishment is a kind of penance to atone for the original sin of being born into an alcoholic family. Thus, *children of alcoholics gravitate toward pain because they find that feelings of hurt salve their feelings of guilt.*

The most salient manifestations of their need to punish themselves are probably reflected in the harshness with which they judge themselves in all that they do and especially in the constant denigration of their physical looks. They are never pleased with how they look. If nothing else, this constant displeasure reflects the basic sense of self-loathing with which they live.

Vacillation

Children of alcoholics tend toward vacillation. This is not surprising because most were reared by role models who were indecisive, indifferent, and of low self-esteem. Most of these children became what they were exposed to.

Decision making for them is a painful experience, filled with much doubt and even more dread. They feel that making decisions reinforces their basic self-understanding that their judgment is terribly poor. If they do not make decisions, such reinforcement can not occur. So they vacillate.

What is ironic about vacillation is that it is both a product and a precipitator of anxiety. Thus, the vacillators who are too anxious about making a decision only increase their anxiety by not doing so when finally caught between the proverbial "rock and hard place." At that point, their anxiety is such that their judgment may indeed be poor and their decision faulty. In this way, they realize their basic self-understanding about their ineptness to make decisions. What also should be noted is that through this self-fulfilling prophecy they structure the anxiety for the next decision they have to make.

Emotionally Distant from Others

The children of alcoholics find it difficult to get emotionally close to others. This is not surprising because the ability to get close and to love is founded on learning feelings of trust. Such feelings are learned best and most easily during the childhood years.

Now, if we are not exposed to closeness as children but to rejection and indifference, like children are in the alcoholic family, our sense of trust is developed poorly if at all. Why? Because when we let ourselves get close to others, when we love, we open ourselves up to potential hurt. We trust that our love will not be rebuffed but returned.

If the love we give as children is returned in kind or even more bountifully, we learn to trust. We learn to love. We learn to get close. Children of alcoholics learn early in life that they cannot trust because they never saw much love between their parents. More often than not, they themselves were the object of a love which was at best sporadic and unpredictable. In short, **what they learned in childhood was that the chance of being hurt was very strong if they got emotionally close.** Unfortunate but true, throughout their lives most of them are not willing to risk that chance.

Relationships Resulting from Pity

Many children of alcoholics, though unable to get close, still develop relationships with others. However, these **relationships are not based upon love but upon pity.** These relationships then are not relationships of give and take and are not peer-like, but are characterized by emotionally sophisticated condescension.

To be in a relationship where one is the pitier is not threatening. One can feel kind and noble about oneself in such a situation and any demands made upon the pitier can or cannot be met without guilt. Love—especially peer love—is something else. Peer love necessarily involves not only the sense of trust, already noted, but also a healthy self-esteem, a feeling that one has something of emotional worth to offer the other person. Quite apparently, peer-love means being loved and accepting the love of another. Such acceptance involves obligation; i.e., one has to pay love back. This is a critical rub for the children of alcoholics. They are acutely threatened by obligations of any kind. Paying back love is threatening indeed. To obviate such an occurrence and **to still feel that they are giving of themselves, they seek out, find, and relate to people whom they can pity.**

In this way they are able to deny their inabilities to love in a peer and meaningful way.

Terror of Being Evaluated

The children of alcoholics live constantly with a terror of being evaluated. To most of them, being evaluated means to be demeaned, because they believe they will be found wanting. They go to extreme, sometimes self-defeating lengths, not to be evaluated. If college students, they are emotionally paralyzed by every test they have to take. They procrastinate about submitting papers on time and, thereby often have grades lowered. As workers, they tend to gravitate toward lower paying, fringe-benefited, bureaucratic-like jobs which are not truly evaluated. They prefer such jobs to those where the compensation is higher but where productivity and competence are truly evaluated.

Although children of alcoholics seldom get into positions of prime leadership, responsibility, and accountability, they do sometimes rise into minor or middle managerial type jobs. In such positions **they live with the constant dread that they will be found unsuitable if not inept.** To protect themselves from any such eventuality, they become clerks par excellence. They keep minutes of all meetings and then distribute the minutes immediately afterward if the agenda was not personally threatening. They distribute the minutes much later when memories have become fuzzy or blended if even the slightest threat to them was present. In these ways they are able to color what transpired and put themselves in a more favorable light. Of course, such behavior is not peculiar to the children of alcoholics but is indeed common in any hierarchical structure, be it industrial or governmental. Nevertheless, **the need to protect one's derriere is an acute and compelling one for children of alcoholics.** However, doing so is not their only method of dealing with the constant threat with which they live on the job. **The other way is namely, not to take a definitive stand, or any stand, where one might become the focal point of attention and possibly be wrong.** To be wrong to the child of an alcoholic raises the specter of being demeaned, disciplined, or dismissed. This is not so likely to happen if they never take a stand.

So they don't. This elusive response to threat is learned from an alcoholic parent or enabler. A manifest purpose of elusiveness is to present a low self-esteem from being lowered further. Ironically it does just the opposite. More often than not, elusive people come to think less and less of themselves precisely because they don't know what they believe.

Frantic Way of Life

Children of alcoholics lead a frantic way of life. The reason for this is a function of their oversized conscience and the super-abundant guilt which it precipitates. As we have noted in various contexts, love is a rare commodity in the alcoholic family. One of the unfortunate effects of that rarity is that children learn that if they are to obtain any at all, they must do, act, work, and contribute.

A grateful glance from a harried enabler mother or a bleary-eyed alcoholic father is usually enough to cause an emotionally deprived six-year-old to continue doing the dishes every night throughout his/her child life and to assume other duties far beyond their child-like competence. What these children learn is that if they want even the tiniest crumb of emotional acceptance, they have to earn it. They have to do so with an undue expenditure of effort, too. Very often their efforts go unrewarded. Even the crumbs are withheld. Still they persevere, because they see no alternative. With the advent of adolescence, the indifference and the sporadic crumbs of the alcoholic and/or enabler take their toll. Their perseverance to contribute, indeed their perseverance for whatever, ends. Their constant frenetic activity does not. Productivity is not the issue for them anymore, just activity. In this way they are able to justify their existence to themselves.

Case of Linda R

This case exemplifies the insidious, destructive hold that alcoholic parents can have upon their children. The author dealt with Linda while a consultant in a school department. The reports which follow are the actual ones. Minor editing and name changes were done to protect identity of the subject.

Linda was referred by her guidance counselor. She was reported as being out of contact in her classes. "Unreachable" was the word used most often to describe her class behavior. Linda was failing in all of her classes. She was suspected of drinking. A teacher had caught her in the girls' room nipping from a bottle of wine. Twice liquor had been smelled on her breath.

Psychodiagnostic Report

Name: Linda R

Testing Date: 13 Jan. 1984

Date of Birth: 17 Sept. 1970

Test Administered: Wechsler Intelligence Scale for Children (WISC),

Bender Gestalt Test,

Thematic Apperception Test (TAT),

and

Rorschach

Behavioral Observation. Linda is a short, slender, pale faced girl who wears glasses. She showed up for testing in a skirt and blouse which were clean but wrinkled and ill-fitting. Her shoes were well-worn and of a vintage passé. Linda covered her mouth when she spoke or smiled to hide a missing tooth and a few badly crooked ones. Initially she was detached and shy but warmed up as the testing proceeded. Quite apparently, she enjoyed the attention she received from the testing session.

Test Results. Linda is currently functioning with a verbal IQ of 115, a performance IQ of 115, and a full scale IQ of 116. Scores such as these indicate that Linda functions in the bright-normal range of intelligence. Approximately 75% of the people in her age score *below* her on this test. Linda has the ability to obtain A's and B's.

In the verbal sphere of competency, Linda functions best in general fund of information, vocabulary, and reasoning. In all of these areas, she functions like a person two years her senior. Her memory and ability to reason arithmetically are consistent with her general level of competency. She functions in the low normal ranges in social comprehension.

In the nonverbal spheres her ability is in the superior to very superior ranges in spatial relations but below average in both perception and social awareness.

The WISC findings seem to be substantiated by Rorschach findings. What we have here is a confused little girl who is growing up with glaring deficiencies in the social and interpersonal spheres. Linda is bewildered, shy, confused, and socially scared. She perceives a world filled with hostile or, at best, indifferent strangers. Such a perception has led to a general mistrust of acquaintances and teachers. (She reports she has no friends.)

Quite apparently this is a girl who has been emotionally shortchanged during most of her life. She is in desperate need for attention of any sort. Her failing record can be understood as a function of her self-perception. Simply stated, Linda sees herself as a failure.

Recommendations: Home visits to assess conditions. Counseling at earliest possible time.

Joseph F. Perez, Ph.D.
Consulting Psychologist

Report of Social Worker. Linda lives on the one street of this town which could be accurately described as "slummy." An only child, she lives with her parents in a duplex house which sorely needs a coat of paint and the two front steps repaired.

I visited the home without benefit of an appointment because there is no phone and Linda was always vague and unwilling about helping to arrange the visit. I learned why when I got there. Both parents were home. I never got to see the father but I heard him only too well. He snored loudly in the bedroom off the kitchen throughout the interview. Mrs. R told me that he was sleeping off a half gallon of wine.

Mrs. R seemed oblivious to the untidy, even dirty, kitchen. The small living room was only a little better. Mrs. R told me she was 38 years old. She appears to be ten or fifteen years older. Her bleary look and confused speech convinced me that she too had had her share of the half gallon of wine.

The interview was a very short one because Mrs. R was uninterested and not a little embarrassed by my presence. I did learn that Mr. R is an unemployed welder who suffers from a "bad back." The family is on the city welfare rolls and has been for almost a decade.

What I saw in her house convinces me that Linda's problems are considerable. Both parents are alcoholics and oblivious to any problems Linda might have.

I concur with Dr. Perez. Linda should be in counseling. After seeing her mother and her home, I am not optimistic.

M. Corcoran
School Social Worker

Comments. After reading this report, the author arranged to see Linda on Monday mornings and Thursday afternoons. Our sessions lasted forty-five minutes each. Linda was so starved for attention that despite her suspiciousness and shyness, and perhaps because of our prior testing session, rapport was almost immediate.

Toward the end of the first session and continuing for many weeks she spent the entire forty-five minutes describing the utter deprivation in which she had been reared. The author still remembers some of her lines. "I was always alone. I don't even remember ever being held even . . . I saw the boy next door being spanked once for playing on the street. I remember going on the street to play. I guess I wanted to be spanked. My mother and father didn't even notice. They were both too drunk." Once after a particularly tearful session she confided her abiding fear that she would end up like her parents. Despite the defeatist attitude which threaded through her talk, Linda had an engaging way about her. The utter simplicity and candor with which she related the rejection and loneliness of her life was touching. So much so that the author stepped out of his counseling role and began to try to manipulate her life outside of counseling. He arranged through a dentist friend to have dental work done, her tooth replaced, and the others straightened.

He continued seeing Linda for the balance of that academic year and for all the next. Throughout he knew she had a crush on him. He used it and began to communicate his expectations about her school work. By the end of the first year of counseling, Linda was making first honor roll, had a part-time job, and new clothes. She began dating.

The following September Linda turned sixteen and never came back to school. She had obtained a full-time job at a local factory. She called the author at Christmas time of her sixteenth year to say that she was happily married and pregnant. The guidance counselor subsequently informed the author that Linda had never married.

Personal Note. Once while driving, I saw Linda coming out of her parents' house with a baby in tow. I stopped to talk. She never met my gaze but kept glancing away with a vague, defeated look. I had seen that look before, but never in anyone so young. It was the look of the alcoholic who has surrendered to life.

SUMMARY

If an alcoholic lives with a family, then the addiction is a familial problem not just a personal one. Indeed some studies show that if one parent is alcoholic the risk for a child becoming alcoholic increases.

Equilibrium within a family is crucial and each member consciously or unconsciously has an emotional stake in maintaining it. Familial self-esteem is tied to consumption of alcohol. Such self-esteem drops as alcoholic consumption increases.

Costarring with the alcoholic in the tragic drama of familial alcoholism is the enabler. Three types of enablers were considered: (1) the overprotective, (2) the compulsive, and (3) the worrier. Overprotective enablers are basically rejecting because they view the alcoholic as basically helpless and inept. The compulsive enabler is characterized by an intense need to solve any and all family problems. The worrier enabler is one who tends to develop a masochistic outlook and suffers in silence.

The high incidence of alcoholism among adolescents is a legitimate cause for alarm because a high percentage of them emerge from the teen years with the social and interpersonal skills of children. The peer group contributes toward the destructive—like drinking—but the author holds that the family can be a critically important factor for obviating or aggravating the process.

Feelings of insecurity, ineptness with love, and a low self-esteem are the major reasons adult children of alcoholics exhibit a host of debilitating personality traits. Eleven were described.

TOPICS FOR DISCUSSION AND REFLECTION

1. If the alcoholic lives with the family, the addiction is a familial problem, not just a personal one. Explain this.

2. Why do you think that the effects of woman's alcoholism are worse for a family than a man's.

3. Explain how an overprotective enabler is not loving but rejecting.

4. Discuss how the enabler's need to control is a response to a need for security.

5. How can an enabler's disposition toward compulsiveness engender stress in a family?

6. Discuss how the enabler's concern for propriety exacerbates the alcoholic's problems.

7. As noted, a disproportionate number of adolescents grow up without experiencing the adolescent years. What are the implications of this?

8. Of the personality traits noted among adult children of alcoholics, which do you believe to be the most dysfunctional? Why?

9. Vacillation in adult children of alcoholics is both a product and a precipitator of anxiety. Explain this.

10. Adult children of alcoholics are attracted to pain. How and what does this bode for relationships?

PART II
EFFECTS

CHAPTER **FOUR**

THE COURSE
OF ALCOHOLISM

Alcoholism is a progression. Figure 4.1 contains illustrated acts which occur during alcohol addiction and recovery.

In 1951, E.M. Jellinek delivered a series of lectures entitled, "The Phases of Alcohol Addiction in Males." This series was later expanded by Glatt (1959). The description of the four progression stages toward and recovering from alcoholism is derived from their work.

The following description is intended only as a general guide. Few alcoholics actually progress step-by-step through the four stages as described. Indeed, some alcoholics may become addicted with their first drink and touch on steps of the fourth stage in a matter of months or even weeks. Others might take decades to do so.

ALCOHOLISM—THE PROGRESSION
(See Figure 4.1, Left One-half)

Stage One

1. Regular social drinking. The individual is uncomfortable when there is no booze at a party or social event.

(Continued on page 66)

Social drinking

S   Alcohol tolerance increases
t
  a
    g   Regular drinking after work
      e

        O   Drinking faster and more than others
          n
            e

              ——
              S   Occasional drinking at odd times
                t   Sneaking of drinks
                  a   Guilt feelings about drinking
                    g   Memory blackouts begin
                      e   Projections of blame for drinking onto others
                          Guilt increases

                  T
                    w
                      o
                      ——
                      S   Addiction
                        t   Auto accidents, major and minor
                          a   All attempts to stop drinking fail
                            g   Resentments and anger become acute
                              e   Social and vocational problems increase

                          T
                            h
                              r
                                e   Meals taken sporadically
                                  e   Blackouts increase

                                ——
                                S   Job loss
                                  t   Family breakup
                                    a   Alcohol tolerance decreases
                                      g   Malnutrition
                                        e   Indifference to physical appearance

                                    F
                                      o   Acute medical problems
                                        u
                                          r   Death by accident
                                          ————————————

Alcoholism—The Progression

The descriptive behaviors in this figure are derived in part from a chart first composed by M. Glatt. Glatt, M.M. (1959). A chart of alcohol addiction and recovery. *British Journal of Addictions, 54*(2)

Figure 4.1. Schematic for alcoholism—progression and recovery process.

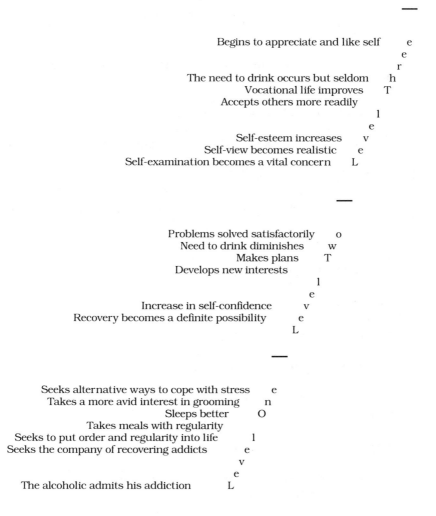

Productive Life

Begins to appreciate and like self

The need to drink occurs but seldom
Vocational life improves
Accepts others more readily

Self-esteem increases
Self-view becomes realistic
Self-examination becomes a vital concern

Problems solved satisfactorily
Need to drink diminishes
Makes plans
Develops new interests

Increase in self-confidence
Recovery becomes a definite possibility

Seeks alternative ways to cope with stress
Takes a more avid interest in grooming
Sleeps better
Takes meals with regularity
Seeks to put order and regularity into life
Seeks the company of recovering addicts

The alcoholic admits his addiction

Alcoholism—The Recovery Process

Figure 4.1. Continued.

2. Seldom leaves a party not high.

3. A gradual almost imperceptible increase in tolerance for alcohol.

4. The two "quick ones" after work and/or before dinner become a regularity.

5. Occasionally resorts to alcohol under pressure.

6. Drinks more quickly and uncommonly more than others.

Stage Two

1. Begins occasional drinking at odd times during the day.

2. Drinking under pressure increases.

3. Sneaking of drinks begins.

4. Delays eating to continue drinking.

5. Guilt feelings about drinking.

6. The onset of memory blackouts.

7. Begins to project blame for drinking onto persons, situations, or events.

8. Begins to find fantasy rewards in drinking.

9. Friends and family begin to notice. Reproofs and chastisement begin to occur.

10. Guilt increase. Attempts made to stop.

Stage Three

1. Psychological addiction has occurred. Control over drinking at a very low ebb.

2. Speeding tickets and auto accidents, minor and major.

3. All attempts at stopping drinking fail.

4. Resentments, anger toward friends and family become acute.

5. Social and vocational problems increase.

6. Keeps problem hidden.

7. Meals are taken sporadically.

8. Seeks out drinking "Buddies and Betties."

9. Solitary drinking increases.

10. Blackouts increase.

Stage Four

1. Beset by a constant stage of anger and/or depression.

2. Job loss may occur.

3. Drinking becomes the lone interest.

4. Family break-up may occur.

5. Lives in an alcoholic daze or constant binge, drinking for days at a time.

6. Alcohol tolerance may decrease.

7. Malnutrition may set in.

8. Overnight stays at a hospital.

9. Lack of concern in grooming and physical appearance.

10. Acute medical problems appear, i.e., liver cirrhosis.

11. Death by accident.

ALCOHOLISM—THE RECOVERY PROCESS
(See Figure 4.1, Right one-half)

The first step in the recovery process levels (admission of alcoholism) is a very personal and private matter. Why it does or does not occur remains a mystery. For some individuals, it occurs in Stage One of the Progression outlined previously, for others not until Stage Four, and for some, never.

The following three levels for the process of recovery, like that of the four stages for progression into alcoholism, is intended only as a general description. This process is not an easy, neat, and simple step-by-step movement, level to level to level. Indeed, the return back to a meaningful life is fraught with peril, anguish, temptations by the score and occasionally, despair. In short, few alcoholics make this return with ease, but some do make it. The autobiographical sketches in the next chapter show that.

Level One

1. The alcoholic admits alcoholism.

2. Honestly asks for help.

3. Learns about addiction, is willing to see it as an illness.

4. Seeks the company of recovering addicts.

5. Begins to find reward in a chosen form of therapy, individual, group or recreational.

6. Seeks to put order and regularity into life.

7. Takes meals with regularity.

8. Sleeps better.

9. Takes a more avid interest in grooming.

10. Seeks to find ways to cope with normal stresses of living.

Level Two

1. Recovery becomes a definite possibility.

2. Increase in self-confidence.

3. Takes a more active interest in others.

4. Develops new interests.

5. Makes plans.

6. Gets verbal rewards and encouragement from family and friends.

7. The need to drink diminishes.

8. Problem solving, obligations are dealt with, if not always perfectly at least satisfactorily.

Level Three

1. Self-examination becomes a vital concern.

2. Self-view becomes realistic.

3. Self-esteem increases.

4. Guilt is put into proper perspective.

5. The need to drink occurs but seldom.

6. Sees recovery as a life process toward a sense of fulfillment.

7. Accepts people.

8. Vocational life improves dramatically.

9. Begins to appreciate self and own productivity.

10. A life-long process of coping with guilt and confidence.

ALCOHOLISM—THE RELAPSE

Frequently, alcoholics who are in counseling and who have seemingly made an emotional commitment to stop drinking, return to the bottle. For some it is because their commitment is something less than genuine. For others, it is because of the fear engendered by what they see in the self-examination process of counseling. For still others, it is because of the threat imposed by the realization that continued sobriety requires a radical change in self-perception, perception of others, and life-style in general.

The counselor should know that clients lapse back into drink also because of another reason. ***They are testing the hypothesis upon which the whole process is premised; namely, that they are alcoholic.*** Thus, they reason if they are drinking they aren't really alcoholic, and so don't really have to self-examine. In short, they don't really have to change. In their fuzzy way of thinking, their ability to drink is proof of their normalcy and of their health.

The relapse can be short term, protracted, or the pathway to death. In every case, the relapse is a classic illustration of denial defense.

Symptoms of the relapse frequently can be found in sudden and new client behaviors. These fall into four general categories:

1. behavioral,

2. verbal,

3. emotional, and

4. body language.

Behavioral

The most obvious evidence of relapse is the ***odor of alcohol.*** Too many counselors (especially new ones) deny that they smell or think they smell liquor on their client's breath. They like to perceive the new gum chewing or peppermint sucking habit displayed by a client as a healthy alternative to booze.

If counselors think they smell booze, they should verbalize it to their clients, especially if the client is one who never chewed anything before. The counsel's verbalization may be a blunt question or an observation toned facetiously. The style should gibe with the counselor's manner and personality. In any case, once the counselor makes the remark he/she should observe the response carefully and proceed from there.

Another possible evidence of relapse is **the client who comes in one day heavily perfumed or cologned.** The author's experience is that the client is trying to mask the odor of alcohol or is trying to redirect the counselor's perception. A remark by the counselor, pointed or subtle, is not inappropriate.

Being unusually early or late for an appointment is often a sign of a relapsed client. In the former situation the client may be showing an inappropriate zeal for counseling (he/she protesteth too much). At the same time the client who suddenly starts showing up unusually early may be crying out that he/she is indeed on the brink of relapse.

Clients who suddenly start coming late for their appointment communicate that their motivation for counseling is on the wane. Often, such behavior reflects a client in or tending toward relapse.

Continued missed appointments because of "sickness" may well be a sign of relapse. Clients should always be asked about the absences. Again, their responses should be carefully observed.

Sudden weight gain is frequently a symptom of relapse. If the counselor one day observes that the client seems heavier, the counselor should inquire about it. In any social context and in other counseling contexts, this would be considered inappropriate. In alcoholism counseling, it is appropriate and very worthy topic for discussion. Why? Because the simple truth is that when a client stops drinking, he/she ordinarily loses weight, or at worst, maintains it even if he/she increases his/her nutritional or junk food intake.

In sum, behavior by clients, which seems out of the ordinary, should be confronted by the counselor. The counselor's obligation is to let clients know that the counselor is sensitive to any and all changes which might be symptomatic of a relapse.

Verbal

The verbal manner of the client in relapse is different. The difference can be subtle, blatant, or somewhere in between.

Clients in relapse frequently *fudge their replies.* They suddenly seem unable to make a statement without couching it in qualifications, i.e., "Yeah, I'm going to try to do that. That just might be a good idea you got there, doc, and if I get a chance and if things are right, I might just do it."

Clients in relapse frequently *change the subject* especially if it even remotely borders on the possibility of their being in a relapse. Such clients seem to verbally flee from questions posed by the counselor and from subjects which smack of the client's attempted con of the counselor.

Clients who suddenly develop a new verbal style—launching into *long, rambling monologues*—are legitimate suspects of relapse. This is a ploy used by the client who needs to control the counseling hour because of the fear of being found out.

Discussions about former drinking associates delivered in almost nostalgic tones should be viewed suspiciously by the counselor. At its most innocent level, such talk should tell the counselor that the client has not yet learned to fill the time or social void provided by the client's prior drinking bouts.

A common verbal manifestation of relapse is the client's sudden *request for additional appointments.* Often what this means is that the client is in conflict and is crying out for help. If at all possible, such a client should be given the additional appointments. At the same time the counselor should make it transparently clear that finally it is the client's decision to drink or abstain and that the client's ego, not the counselor's, is the locus of control.

Emotional

The client in relapse always seems more nervous. Frequently a dramatic increase in the amount of tears shed in a counseling session occurs. This is true for both males and females.

Client voices seem to be more strident and far less modulated. Unaccountably, client sentences seem to be punctuated inappropriately with nervous laughs, giggles, and guffaws.

Body Language

The client in relapse tells the counselor as much with his/her body. The sudden onset or uncommon increase in each of the following signs may be symptomatic of a relapse:

> averting of the eyes;
>
> fidgeting;
>
> nervous twitching, hand drumming;
>
> slight, almost indefinable eye glaze;
>
> facial puffiness;
>
> constant, latent, unaccountable glint of fear in the eyes, a vulnerable look, scared rabbit look; and/or
>
> client begins to sit at attention and seemingly listens too intently, or the vice-versa.

If any of the above signs were to be manifested with one or more of the others, the counselor should be especially concerned.

A point worthy of reiteration is that the **body language which communicates a relapse most clearly is that which the counselor finds "foreign" and new in the client's personality.**

SUMMARY

The Jellinek and Glatt curves served as the basis for the description of alcohol progression and recovery. Progression began at Stage One with social drinking and continued into the fourth stage with death as a possible outcome. The recovery process was explained as beginning with denial and continues lifelong.

Alcoholics go into relapse for a variety of reasons and manifest their relapse in a myriad of behaviors. These behaviors fall into four general categories: (1) behavioral, (2) verbal, (3) emotional, and (4) body language. The counselor should be suspicious of sudden, new, and inconsistent behavior by the client, as it may be a sign of relapse.

TOPICS FOR DISCUSSION
AND REFLECTION

1. At what point in Stage One of the Alcoholism Progression do you feel an individual should be concerned? Why?

2. Do you see any point at Stage Two of the Alcoholism Progression where an individual might be receptive to help? If so what might that be?

3. Can the alcoholic in the throes of Stage Four in Progression be helped? Why? Why not?

4. Why alcoholics admit to their addiction is a mystery. Do you believe some experiences could precipitate an admission? Why and what might they be?

5. Can you think of any life experiences which can facilitate and/or accelerate recovery for an alcoholic? If you can, describe them.

6. What elements make for a stronger commitment to stop drinking than others?

7. What fears specifically engendered by self-examination in counseling can precipitate a relapse?

8. Which of the specific signs of relapse listed under Behavioral do you believe to be a "sure" sign that the alcoholic is drinking? Which of them do you think at best only a weak one?

9. Which of the Verbal signs of relapse would you describe as subtle? As blatant? As somewhere in between?

10. Which combination of signs in body language would most likely communicate alcoholic relapse? Explain your feelings/reasons.

CHAPTER FIVE

CASES—WHAT IT MEANS TO BE ALCOHOLIC

SEVEN CASE STUDIES

The following seven stories explain as well as, perhaps better than, any research study or statistical chart what the cruel effects of being addicted to alcohol are.

Figure 5.1 illustrates the cycle of addiction. This cycle is found in each of the seven stories.

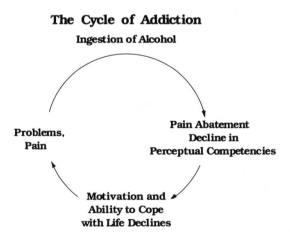

The Cycle of Addiction

Ingestion of Alcohol

Pain Abatement
Decline in
Perceptual Competencies

Problems,
Pain

Motivation and
Ability to Cope
with Life Declines

Figure 5.1. Schematic Illustration of the Cycle of Addiction.

CASE OF MIKE
Male, Divorced Father, a College Teacher

For 16 years I had lived as a hunted and haunted man, struggling each day to avoid detection and, when trapped, frantically trying to escape the truth and its consequences. On Saturday night, May 2, 1981, there was no safety left in the small apartment I shared with my girlfriend and I knew I had to flee. I was too drunk to get myself out of there, having polished off three quarts of gin in the preceding 24 hours. Still, I had to make a getaway because the hideous gnarled gnomes and glowing bugs and disconnected voices had slipped through the walls and windows and were amassing for a final assault on my alcohol-soaked body and brain. If they broke through the last thin membrane of my exhausted psychic defenses this night, I knew they might drag me forever into that living nightmare of stark-raving madness from which there seemed no escape.

*I asked my girlfriend to drive me to my sister's home some fifty miles away, and when she asked me **"why"** I had no answer. To this day I don't know why I chose that particular place as an attempted refuge, but I was insistent. Although she saw no point in it, the urgency of my pleading and the absence of any notion as to what else to do persuaded that confused and frightened woman to oblige my request.*

Once there, my sister, her fiance, and my girlfriend tried to fathom my condition and to make me comfortable, and then they went to bed. I wanted to sleep too. So often in the past few years all I longed for was the chance to fade into a state of numb nothingness, of painless unconsciousness and unfeeling oblivion, that would last forever.

But when I tried that night, sleep would not come. I was terrified to find that I had been followed by the phantoms I had sought to escape. When I closed my eyes my mind turned over and over like a whirling flywheel, flashing a kaleidoscope of images and thoughts and fears that had no relationship to each other, or for that matter to anything. I dug my fingers into my scalp to stop this insane parade inside my skull, but ugly little trolls just laughed at the vanity of my feeble effort to control something I could not touch or influence or understand. My arms and legs twitched and jumped involuntarily, as if those phantoms were jolting me sadistically with a cattle prod. I wrapped the pillow around my head, to no avail.

I got up and went to the living room and put on the light and spent the rest of the night pacing the carpet trying to walk around the ragged edges of panic. I knew the landscape of panic well, for I had lived with it or the threat of it every day since a March Sunday in 1965. I was at Mass that morning when it first began as a slight tremor in my hands, a pounding in my chest, clammy sweat on my forehead, and a vague sense of anxiety about nothing in particular. I was sick with a terrible hangover that day in church and I first attributed the symptoms to that. But then, like a tidal wave sweeping up and over me, a sense of abject terror and imminent doom produced a violent shaking, a profuse cold sweat that drenched me, a heart that seemed about to explode, a sense that my knees had vanished and left my lower legs disconnected from my thighs and a ringing alarm in my intestines. I had felt that I was literally coming apart at the seams of my skin and that my mind was escaping the confines of my body and slipping into a hellish twilight zone of horror never before visited by another human being.

That day I knew for the first time the incredible terror, the total unworldliness, the horrid fright of abject helplessness a person feels when the mind and soul somehow disconnect themselves from some delicate tether of flesh and blood that moors them to the mainstream of humanity, of acceptance, of rootedness, of belongingness. With alarms clanging in every fiber of my body and my mind eluding my grasp like wind-swept vapor I felt that all possibility of communication was lost. I felt I was on the verge of losing all control over my behavior. I saw myself being wrestled down, placed in a straight-jacket, and salted away in an asylum. To prevent that, I knew I had to get a grip on myself and pull myself back from the edge of madness, but I literally rattled with fear as I realized that I did not know how. I knew hell, that day.

I did not know that five years of heavy daily drinking had brought me to this mental cliff. All I knew was that I wanted to draw back from the edge and never get near it again. I bolted out of the church, ran home as if pursued by devils, and wrenched the cap off my gin bottle. With the neck clanking against the lip of the glass, I poured myself a tumbler full and drank it like water. Slowly, the alcohol eased me back into the tranquillity of a lazy Sunday morning. It seemed I had my answer, and from that day forward for 16 years I never allowed myself to be more than an arm's length from the toxic medicine, the deceitful distilled spirits that seemed to be the only friend I could rely on to ward off the evil spirits of insanity that lurked in wait for me everywhere.

Unwittingly, I had like Faust, sold my soul to the devil, in exchange for alcohol's promise to spare me from slipping away forever from the farthest reaches of any human contact or self control. To keep me from the desolate moonscape of total loneliness and depravity, I surrendered everything I ever owned of both a material and spiritual nature. I had planned to be with my father on a July night in 1972 when he called and asked me to come—I simply wanted a couple of martinis to make the trip more pleasant. I was still drinking alone, hours later, when he gave up the wait and died. The death certificate said it was a miocardial infarction, but only I could know he was killed by a broken heart. I was drunk at his wake and at his funeral.

I wanted to give my little son the only thing he asked, a few hours of my time. But I needed to drink, so I said "no" to the hope in his freckled face. When his eyes dimmed and his tiny red head hung, I did not relent, but stood there torn between love and addiction as he moped away, dejectedly kicking at the stones in his path to confusion, hurt, and loss. I wanted the love of my picture-perfect daughter, a kid so inside-out beautiful that she's a blessing to the human race, but I so much needed to put alcohol first that I was able to bear hearing her make but one request of me, her brown eyes blinking back the tears, "Daddy please! Just go away and don't come back!" I knew the colitis that ate my gorgeous wife's guts out was caused by my drinking and I saw the *scars of my disease mar her body and I knew she was right when she sobbed and stamped her foot and screamed, "You're murdering me!" I wanted it to be different, but what could I do? I had to drink or go crazy, and only I could know that, for only I had been to the brink. I would lose all before I lost my mind.*

Then that May in 1981, as the sun rose and still I paced, I knew I could no longer move fast enough or far enough to survive. I had tried everything. I had, a few weeks before, even gone with a gun and parked on a deserted dirt road in the woods. I had put a barrel in my mouth and tasted it, a cold, blue-black, acidic, iron assurance on a fuzzy, fermented tongue that a simple twitch of my finger would bring the eternal relief from remorse, despair, and self-contempt that plagued my every conscious hour. I was killing the living love of so many innocent people. Why should I not do something noble, and at the same time, achieve what I now believed to be the only final answer to my pain? I was a bum, now. My family had thrown me out. I was divorced from everything tangible and intangible that I had ever belonged to or that had ever belonged to me. My girlfriend said she could no longer tolerate my behavior, and I was only headed back to the cheap flops peopled by troubled transients from which she had given me refuge. I would be back on the streets that led nowhere, toting all I had left in the world in the half-filled sea bag. Soon, I would probably be totally unable to work and I would lose my job, and with it, the money I needed to pay the ransom to alcohol which held my mind hostage. Why not pull the trigger?

*The headlights of my car reflected on a white sign nailed to a tree on those woods. I read it. It said, **"No Hunting."** This was what I had come to. I was going to shoot myself on a dark and moonless night in a lonely place where sane people had decreed it illegal to shoot even the wild rodents that foraged in the night to feed off of each other. Wasn't there a sign somewhere that protected me? Or had I sunk too low? Or was this the sign?*

In a sense, it was. That had been the early part of my last drunk, a desperate, downward spiral that had led me to the home of my sister, who happened to work at a hospital that had an alcohol detoxification and rehabilitation program. **"Why,"** she asked that Sunday morning, **"don't you let us take you there? They can probably give you some tips on how to handle your drinking better."** She wasn't, she promised, saying that I was an alcoholic or that I should admit myself to the hospital. She was just saying I might get some good advice. I went, not to get good advice, but in the hope that I would get some tranquilizers, for hospitals and doctors had always come to my rescue with pills.

But this ward of this hospital was different. It was staffed by alcoholics and people especially trained in the symptoms and treatment of alcoholism. They said I should stay there for 21 days and I protested. What would my friends think? The answer was that any friends who did not know I belonged there were not the kinds of friends I needed. What about my job? The answer was that my job could and would wait. But what about my life? If I stay, I'll be admitting that I'm an alcoholic and won't that mess up my whole life? The answer was raucous laughter. My hands shook so badly I could not sign my name on the admitting forms and I could not hold the cup of water they gave me to wash down the librium. My fingers were swollen with fluid; my face was puffy and scaly red; my liver ached; my stomach was queasy; my esophagus burned, and I was 46 pounds overweight. Maybe I did have a problem. I just didn't know.

I agreed, at first, to stay in that hospital only four or five days. As sick as I was from alcohol, I could not, even then, allow myself to admit that alcohol itself was the primary source of all my problems. If I did that, I felt I would be confessing that all the harm my behavior had caused was my fault. My whole life had dissolved into a process of doing things I never intended to do and not doing things I had always resolved to do, and I desperately wanted to find some other plausible explanation for failure that absolved me of the guilt. But how many excuses did I have left? I had convinced myself that I was a creative genius, misunderstood by ordinary people, but I had never created anything but common chaos. I had convinced myself that I was a great intellectual and that I drank to relieve myself of the lonely pressures caused *by my gifted insights into difficulties that lesser mortals could not see. But, in fact, I had never had an original thought. I had happily agreed at one time to a psychiatrist's diagnosis that I was a manic-depressive, feeling that a certified psychosis was a more acceptable explanation of my destructiveness than was alcoholism. Almost wildly, at one time or another, I had blamed my mother, my father, the nuns, the priests, my wife, and later my girlfriend, my many jobs and bosses, my friends, my relatives, the Internal Revenue Service, the criminal justice system, and even the weather. Only alcohol had escaped my cynical judgment, for of all my desperate fears, the greatest was the idea of having to face a single day without that drug. I agreed to stay a few days only because I was so close to delirium tremens. I dared not chance another night alone. By the end of the week, when I knew I would feel better and safer, I intended to leave and start drinking all over again.*

But during that week I was immersed in the stories of people who were recovering from the disease which they admitted had afflicted them. Very slowly—against my will in fact— I began to realize that I had not been the first traveler to that horrid hell of panic and dread from which I had spent 16 years on the run. It became clear that they had been there too; for the experiences of that God-forsaken limbo of alcoholism are so bizarre that no human imagination could counterfeit them. It became clear also that they had found a safe way out and that they were fully confident of going back. It became clear, too, that each of them had triumphed only through total defeat and complete surrender to the truth of the disease and had risen like the Phoenix from their own ashes. Most surprising of all was the fact that they seemed content and looked happy, hopeful, and confident.

Most of that week I had spent crying, anchored in deep depression, and flogging myself with the whip of guilt and remorse, and truly wishing I was dead. Somehow I began to realize, at least in an embryonic and tentative way, how very sick I was. I knew I was a thoroughly beaten man and that there was no fight left in me and no place else to run. I wanted to feel like those recovering alcoholics looked.

Finally, with as much dignity as I could muster, trying to look like General Lee at Appomattox, I surrendered upon their terms. Still I choked on the words, my throat tightened around them, and my jaws pulsed to warn them back, but I forced them out, **"Hi, my name is Mike, and . . . and I'm . . . an . . . alcoholic."**

The answer was simple, **"Hi Mike! Welcome!"** That's all. No thunder, no lightning, no clucking of tongues or pursed lips or hands covering the mouth, or fingers pointing shame. Just, **"Hi Mike! Welcome!"**

By the end of the three weeks I had fully admitted to myself and to the others that I was an alcoholic, that my life had become unmanageable because of the disease, and that I was powerless to restore myself to sanity. Only by coming to the end of my rope did I come to the beginning of God. I had taken my first beer as college freshman in a desperate attempt to overcome the grief of homesickness and I found in that saloon the quicksand of false camaraderie and a warm sense of belonging. Among other alcoholics, I found that same lost feeling again—a sense of oneness, of rootedness, of understanding, and belongingness, this time based on genuine caring and sharing and compassionate love. I had cried when I entered the hospital, and three weeks later, I had to fight back tears at leaving.

Over the past ten years I have attended Alcoholics Anonymous meetings in dozens of cities and several states. The fright, the remorse, and the despair are gone, as is the desire to drink. At the age of 41, I am, for the first time, enjoying life and rising with the sun each morning, full of hope and full of wonder, for I am among the chosen who live now on borrowed time. I don't want to waste it. Each day has all the ups and downs of any normal life, and for the first time I am learning to handle it all like a normal person.

My prayer was answered when I realized that I'm Mike and I'm an alcoholic, and I now feel like other people look.

CASE OF MARIE
Female, Unmarried, College Undergraduate

I was brought up in an upper-middle class family. Both my parents are in helping professions. My father is alcoholic but now sober. I was third born in a series of four girls.

During my childhood my parents had many fights and separations mostly because of my father's drinking. I was basically a happy kid but very fearful of my father when he drank. At one point his drinking drove my mother to drugs and eventually an institution. Upon her return I became very fearful of her also, but in a different way. Dad was frightening because of his power. Mom was frightening because of her fragility. They were divorced when I was about ten. I had a very low opinion of myself by this time. I became a people pleaser to my friends. My grades were not too good in school. I cried a lot in classes and found I received attention for this and began to force myself to cry and talk to the guidance counselor.

After grammar school I began to get very interested in pot and alcohol when in the past I had thought of it with fear and disgust. My older sister noticed my interest and she and her boyfriend got me high. I loved it. I felt free. I laughed. I spoke nonsensically. I felt I could do anything.

Although my mother was not alcoholic she began to go to A.A. meetings and dating men she met there. Ron and his daughters soon became part of the family. Our get-togethers consisted of drinking and smoking pot. At first they were very discrete about smoking when I was around which made me feel left out. I was too young but my sisters weren't.

Junior high school wasn't a happy experience. I never felt as good as the others. I wasn't popular enough and I never got the boyfriends I wanted. My grades were still mediocre and I didn't participate in school sports anymore. I knew I wasn't the best athlete and refused to be second best so I didn't try at all.

Not many kids smoked pot yet so I felt mature and cool. Soon though I found other kids that smoked and began to hang around them. I finally started to feel better about myself. I had more friends and was more popular.

Ron and my mother got married and we moved away. At first I hung around kids I didn't like much because it was better than being alone. I eventually became apart of the clique I wanted to hang around with. I started to feel even better about myself. I was cool. Many of my friends were older than me so it was easy to get alcohol. I knew where to get drugs.

I skipped school a lot and when I was there I was high. I participated in no school activities. I began to do other drugs like acid and speed. By the time I was fifteen I had experienced blackouts, hangovers, convulsions, and was busted for possession of marijuana.

My family relations were almost nonexistent. My stepfather was drinking very heavily. He and my mother went on many vacations for at least a week at a time and we kids were left at home to take care of ourselves. I liked it when they were gone because I could come home at any time, have parties, and get as drunk and stoned as I wanted—not that how drunk I was mattered because I was never punished for being drunk.

I started to get paranoid and my thoughts of suicide had increased. Often I thought my mother was poisoning my food. I felt she and my stepfather were trying to get rid of me. I began to hate and resent my stepfather for taking my mother from me. They began to have marital problems and slept in separate bedrooms. Eventually my stepfather went into an institution. Group therapy was a joke. I wanted no part of it. I refused to say anything. I became very rebellious against my parents. I stole money from them and started to shoplift.

My father had quit drinking and remarried. We thought he could provide a better home for my sister and myself and so we decided to move in. I was scared to death because I knew my drinking and drug taking would have to slow down. It didn't. In fact I was high more of the time. Nothing was good. I was afraid of my father, and my stepmother was boring. I had a love-hate relationship with my sister. Sometimes I would be kind to her, other times I would beat her and threaten that if she told on me I would beat her harder.

Eventually my father started drinking again. My stepmother's bags were packed, and Kim and I decided to run away from home

Kim was forced to go back with my Mom and Ron where she was terribly emotionally abused for the next five months until Ron committed suicide through an overdose of seconal. I lived with another family in a city I had previously lived in. I got into a lot of trouble with them. I was not a good influence for their daughter and I got busted again, this time for shoplifting. They forbade me to hang around with the girls I stole with after that.

School was a joke. I was never there completely, always stoned.

After Ron died, I decided to go back to my mother. I didn't cry over his death. I was glad he was gone. I still am.

Living with my mother was crazy. I did anything I wanted. I abused her often. She bought me alcohol and pot. I was drunk all the time, stoned all the time, and didn't come home nights. I was sixteen years old. I slept with everyone and his brother as long as he was good looking. It hurt real bad.

My senior year of high school kind of blew by me. I wasn't there often but I seemed to attain good grades. Stoned all the time, I got into a relationship which lasted a year and a half. We were in love, I guess. My mother allowed us to sleep together in our house. My friends thought that was real cool. It was real sick. My responsibility where sex was concerned got me pregnant twice. After the second abortion in four months, I became very depressed and ended up quitting cosmetology school. I was drinking almost every night. No more pot or other drugs—they made me too paranoid. I had just turned eighteen.

I went back to live with my mother for almost a whole year except for a few months in which I lived in Florida with my boyfriend. My relationship with him became more childish. The only things we really shared together were pints of rum at the movies and sex. He called me a baby for wanting to go back to my mother to save money for college. I ignored him. I became bulimic.

I managed to save my social security checks to pay for school. Work money went to supporting my heavy habits. I tried to stop drinking and was successful for about a week with the help of pot. I went into withdrawal. I became paranoid. I thought people were after my life. I heard voices. My mom took me to a psychologist. He referred me to the drug abuse clinic. I didn't go. I started drinking again.

I really wanted to do well in college. I tried my best but I didn't realize that drugs and booze engulfed my life. It was my only love, yet it didn't do for me what it used to. I still got excited about drinking but it was more a need than a want. I would battle with myself during the day to keep from drinking until the night. I was doing a lot of acid, pot, and alcohol together—a great combination. I thought I was so worldly and experienced because I tripped.

I had a lot of friends. It seemed the closer one was to me the more I would hurt them. I had become violent in blackouts from time to time toward close friends. I tried to hide my blackouts from my friends but wasn't too successful. I had been blacking out for years but now they had become very frequent. I'd wake up in strange places. I'd wake up with bruises all over me. I'd wake up with last night's clothing on or no clothing. Sometimes I didn't wake up. I lost my car often, my keys, my license, my head.

My second year of college was worse. I had suicide on the brain constantly. Paranoid all the time. I was convinced the cashiers at the small food stores knew I was bulimic, and of course, they knew I was alcoholic, but that didn't bother me. My dad had told me I was alcoholic a year earlier but I didn't care anymore. It was too much when people knew I was a pig though. That was disgusting. Paranoid, I kept the curtains closed. I didn't answer the phone. Sometimes I'd go for days without brushing my teeth or showering. I'd cross the street when someone I knew I was coming my way. I'd spit at myself in the mirror, repeatedly knock my head against the wall and hit myself in the face. I was either crying or numb. I had fewer friends and no boyfriends. By the end of the year my roommate looked at me with hate and disgust. I felt awful, guilty, like a burden.

My mom considered my summer a calm one. I was down on myself. I couldn't get out of bed. I was convinced it was because of the light blue curtains that gave my room a gloomy look. I spent the summer mostly by myself, lying around the pool drinking, going to bars alone, and hiding in my closet.

My third year of school started like the others, a lot of motivation to do well, and less partying. As usual, the plan failed. Within a month I had spent an enormous amount of money on booze and drugs. I thought I had gone crazy. I had no idea my addiction had the power to drive me out of my mind. Finally, after a fairly light night of drinking and drugging, I drove home to my mother's and became hysterical. I wanted to be put away somewhere. I thought I needed a rest from reality for a while.

My father knew what my problem was being an alcoholic himself. I was sent into rehabilitation for four months. It was a horror show. My moods changed constantly. I was very depressed much of the time but soon I started to feel better for longer periods of time. I started to care about myself and other people. I was becoming able to listen to them. I started to accept my alcoholism.

I moved back in with my mother. I felt stronger but my feelings were very confused still. Somewhere in the back of my mind I knew I'd get drunk again and I still wanted to be crazy (it was the only cop-out left). I went to outpatient alcoholism counseling and as time went on I made it to fewer and fewer A.A. meetings. I started meeting my old friends in bars and soon I found myself alone with my disease. For the first time I experienced the power of my alcoholism and I got drunk again. The same old things happened, nothing had changed. I got paranoid, blackouts, violence, suicide attempt, jail.

I entered another alcoholism treatment program for four months. It was very painful and frightful but I experienced a lot of growth. I became much more open to try new things when in the past I thought life was in the bottle. I have fun without alcohol. I am a living miracle. I love. I respect. I care. I have the ability to be honest with myself and others and I have real sharing friendships with others. I don't need to or have to drink or drug with the help of people I have met in A.A. After fifteen months of sobriety I actually love myself, and life gets better with every day I stay straight.

CASE OF BARBARA
Female, Married, Mother, a Librarian

Discovering when I was an alcoholic is probably one of the most vivid moments in my life. It was Tuesday, October 11, 1978. I had slept late that morning which was my pattern then, and waited until everyone had left the house for work or school. My oldest daughter was a freshman in college in Rhode Island, and our youngest was a senior in high school. There I was 39 years old, no job, no college education, and not knowing who in the hell I was. Just like any other morning of the past three years, I proceeded downstairs to where I had hidden a bottle of sherry in the kitchen cabinet underneath the sink. Sherry was my morning drink primarily because it was cheap. I remember always pouring my drinks into a coffee mug, knowing that if anyone came home or dropped by for a visit, they would not see what I was drinking.

At this point in my drinking career I did not seem to worry too much if my husband came home unexpectedly for lunch, because by noon I was usually feeling no pain and things did not seem to be so bad. Occasionally he would come home but our relationship had deteriorated so badly that our conversation was very limited. Everything about him disgusted me. He was to blame for all my problems and was a major reason for my drinking, so my alcoholic thinking went. I felt smothered, gasping for freedom, but not knowing exactly what

I was looking for. I thought perhaps some other person could make things right, or perhaps a good job, or perhaps new clothes. Always searching for happiness and ending up drinking to relieve the pain. Towards the end of my drinking days all kinds of physical ailments appeared and I found myself drinking more to relieve them.

My afternoons were spent shopping. For some reason I found comfort in being with strangers in stores. I also think that I knew if I stayed home all day that by dinnertime I would not be able to function. On these afternoons I also bought my booze. In the last two years of drinking, I spent more time thinking about alcohol and plotting where I would buy it. I always selected liquor stores that were out of town and made mental notes not to frequent them more than once a month. I would always strike up a conversation with the clerk about a special dinner party I was planning and how I knew so little about what to serve. Vodka became my drink for several reasons: (1) it was odorless—a fallacy, it smells as bad and as much as any other alcoholic drink; (2) it looked like water—true, and I put it in my coffee mug, or in juices, or in tea or in diet soda; and (3) it had less calories so I thought. I gained fifteen pounds, but was never aware of the weight gain until I stopped drinking.

My whole life was based on lie upon lie. I remember a time when my oldest daughter was in high school and was home sick. I returned home that day and found her in her room crying. She was the first person to confront me about my drinking. The clothing bag in my closet was my ultimate hiding place for my bottles of vodka. I usually kept one at a time in there, but I was careless and had left several empty bottles as well as a full one in there. She had discovered them and asked me why they were there. I could not answer her and walked out of her room quite shaken by the idea that someone else knew my secret. Disposing of the bottles always posed a problem. We live in the country and do not have garbage pick up, so my husband made weekly trips to the local dump. What I usually did with the bottles was wrap them in a paper bag and place them in the bottom of another brown bag and add garbage during the day on top of the bottle. I thought this was very clever, and it was until a week before I hit bottom. For some reason I had put three or four quart bottles and two half gallon bottles in the garbage in one bag. My husband had seen them, and along came the second confrontation. I had been out shopping and when I entered the kitchen there were the bottles lined up on the kitchen counter. He asked me where they came from and I remember saying I don't know. I think he thought that perhaps our oldest daughter had put them there, but I know today that he probably accepted that explanation in order to deny the fact that his wife had a problem.

The feelings I had when I was drinking varied greatly. In the beginning, in my early twenties, alcohol made me feel great. Most of the drinking then was strictly social and occasional. As the years progressed it increased to drinking every weekend and I was consuming more alcohol to feel that certain high. I always felt attractive, loving, and at ease with other people while I was drinking. In the last two years of my drinking, I began to hate myself and my life. I remember getting up in the morning and looking in the mirror and asking myself what is the point of getting up. I felt so useless, ugly, and very depressed. Deep down in my heart I knew I was in trouble with alcohol, but kept right on denying it with something like, only bums in bowery are alcoholics, not me. Then I would think, what would my husband say, what would my children say, what would everyone else say? But I knew, and it even made me drink more to hide the pain of guilt and shame. I wondered often how to get off the merry-go-round my life was in but did not know how. I finally reached a point where I wanted help.

I recall one evening six months before the end of my drinking, my husband and I were eating dinner in a restaurant. Prior to going out to dinner or a party I always fortified myself with plenty of alcohol. At the restaurant I had several cocktails and by the time dinner arrived I could barely see the plate in front of me much less eat the food. I remember crying and saying to my husband, I need help over and over. Perhaps something was planted that night because I remember him saying there was help and it was called A.A. I wasn't quite ready for that at the time, but later A.A. would appear more desirable to me.

The emotions of guilt, shame, and total isolation from everyone began to build up and I began to notice that I needed more alcohol in order to cope and to function each day. A week before I reached bottom, I remember saying, God please help me. I had not been to church in more than fifteen years, somewhere deep inside of me I knew I needed help desperately. The help I needed had to come from a source other than myself. I knew I could not do it by myself, but who or what I was not sure.

On that Tuesday evening in October of 1978, I had been drinking more than usual and remembered my husband calling to say he would not be home for dinner that night. I was furious with him—how dare he not come home, after all I had done in preparing a lovely meal. Feeling angry and lonely, I was so overcome with emotions, I grabbed the dinner off the stove and dumped it all over the kitchen floor. The gates of emotion opened and I got down on my knees in the middle of the kitchen floor and kept saying over and over as the tears poured, God please help me. Almost like a light being turned on, I stood up and reached for the local telephone book and looked in the classified under alcoholism information. Standing there, trembling, I reached for the telephone and dialed the number. Someone answered and all I could say was when is the next meeting. I remember the man saying tonight at 8:30 and he gave me the location. I knew where it was. I proceeded to clean the kitchen floor and pour myself another drink. I needed the drink, I told myself, in order to go to the meeting.

Today as I reflect on that night, it was a miracle that I arrived there safely and returned home that night safely. To me A.A. gave me back my life which I had lost through excessive drinking and nondirected living. I remember someone in the program saying we are reborn. I believe that my life began that night. A.A. taught me a whole new way of living day by day with myself and others. For me it was a very spiritual experience. I firmly believe that a person can change with help and guidance. Why the program works has been the topic of discussion and research. My own thoughts are it works for those who want it to, but even more it works for those who believe in a power or God much stronger than the individual.

And now, five years later, I have a full-time position of responsibility, have completed a B.A. degree, and have the love and respect of my family and friends.

Many rewarding moments have arisen from my being sober. I hold fast to the principles of A.A. which guide me daily in all my affairs. I like myself and have begun to formulate some new goals for myself, one of which is to go on to graduate school.

When I first went to that A.A. meeting five years ago, I remember saying over and over to someone there, **"Why me?"** I do not question anymore. I know why now. Being a recovered alcoholic is a very vital part of my being and identity as a person.

The desire to drink left me a long time ago and I can go to parties and other social functions where alcohol is served and enjoy myself and the company of others and be totally at ease. I could not do that before.

CASE OF JULIA
Woman, Mother, Saleswoman

When I was asked to write this article I was nine years away from my last drink. The request produced a variety of emotions and I became very interested in exploring that part of my life.

A flash of a blond-haired blue-eyed six-year-old girl on a rainy Saturday morning came to mind. She is much like other six year old girls—bright, precocious. Unlike most six-year-olds on a Saturday, she is not watching cartoons. She has been in the kitchen making Kool-Aid. A great achievement most little people are proud of. She comes into the living room with her gourmet treat and makes a profound statement: "Drink this mommy, it won't make you sick like that scotch does!" It took six months and $6,000.00 in an alcoholic treatment center to make me realize that same simple truth—"Scotch makes me sick."

Truth is what I struggle greatly with these days, but in the days of my self-inflicted madness it was the thing I dreaded facing the most. Being confronted with the destructive effect that alcoholism had on my children is probably the most difficult truth I face today. The inescapable fact is that I did it to them. I reared them in an alcoholic setting.

At age eighteen I had completed my mandatory education and supposedly was an adult ready to face the world. I didn't know that one searches for an identity, because I was busy looking for a label: good, pretty, intelligent, loved, cared-for. At age twenty I had my first child followed by two other births of healthy babies. At age twenty-eight, I began full-fledged alcoholic drinking.

Having been abandoned by my own parents at age two, I had no genuine role model of what a mother should be. I had the fairy tales and poems on Mother's Day cards. These cards said mothers were kind, caring, giving, and wonderful creatures—almost saintly and madonna-like—certainly, not drunk.

What stands out most vividly about my drinking days is how frantic they were. I was always dashing here and there, like a Keystone Cop going off in three directions at once. I'd have a sudden craving—a pizza, a sundae, an Italian grinder. I decided I wanted it. Decided I needed it and I had to have it. I got it.

I remember arguments too—lots and lots of arguments with my children. I never could stand being contradicted and would never admit to being wrong especially with them. I learned in counseling that I did that because I had a "fractured self-esteem."

I remember being in bed "sick" a lot. I had migraines all the time. I realize now they were probably all part of my hangovers.

What my two younger children remember vividly is their older sister cooking meals and eating with them, taking them for walks and picnics in the backyard, and reading them bedtime stories in her bedroom. They remember Mommy "crying" and "hanging-on" to them a lot when she was drunk. I remember early in recovery being in a woman's therapy group where the topic was the inability of one particular woman to hug her child. With my ego and arrogance I stated, **"Oh I hug my children all the time."** The verb used by my children was "hanging-on." The reality is that in sobriety I had to learn to hug my children too. I still haven't digested the fact that I've never really been close to my kids. I'm still learning how. I'm still learning how to be a giver rather than a taker. Most women know motherhood is giving. In search for self with alcohol you become a taker of more than just a drink. Nothing is safe from your taking—friends, family, husband, or children.

If ever there was a model adolescent, my eldest was. She was my greatest enabler. She didn't date, party, or act irresponsibly during her high school years. She was a caretaker, dependable. Always prepared for any emergency. Life in a home with an alcoholic mother is not secure and one never knows what is going to happen. She learned to drive at age fourteen because one night when all the kids and mom went out to dinner mother got drunk, backed into four cars in the restaurant parking lot and was unable to drive. She could have called someone but she didn't want them to know about her mother, so she drove home.

I awoke the next morning in absolute panic from the blackout. How did we get home? Were the children O.K.? If they were, who had gotten them ready for bed? I struggled out of bed, inched down the hall, peeked into each bedroom. Thank God they were safe! Then down to the kitchen to get a drink to get rid of this awful feeling! One of many, many similar incidents. Yet, I remember telling my eldest daughter, **"I'm an alcoholic and I'm going to get help."** Her response was, **"Mom you're not that bad, don't do that."** I understand now her fear of loss of her role. Today at 25 she is in the Army, a very predictable orderly place to be. She has had several short-term relationships with very dependent men and is beginning to want answers for why this keeps happening. I'm hopeful, for she wants answers not labels, as I did.

Being married to an active alcoholic can be very lonely, confusing, and frustrating. To compensate for this, my husband took as his confidante and friend, our second child, our son. There was always a power struggle for this child's attention and affection between his father and me. It was a "no-win" situation for our son, so he chose to escape. He became involved in karate, little league baseball, basketball, and other sports. He made the All-Star team and won many trophies in karate. He developed a close circle of friends with whom he spent many hours. He did anything he could to spend time away from the rest of the family because it was such a painful place to be. At eighteen he left home to live on his own. He has not been back. He is successful in terms of school, career, responsibility. He is in a relationship with his high school sweetheart. From time to time in the last two years he pops in to see his mother. There is always a connection and always a distance. There is always a Christmas visit and gifts. Some years there is even a Mother's Day card, but it is not consistent. He will not accept a commitment, for it may not be safe. Recently he was hospitalized for ulcers. He was told not to drink and he is finding that difficult to do. I have shared with him the fact that the children of alcoholics are at high risk to develop the disease.

At sixteen my third child (a difficult position even in a normal family) became heavily involved with drugs and alcohol. She dropped out of school. I was angry as hell. Not at her. My feelings were, **"Come on God. We have had our share of alcoholism in this family!"** I refused to enable her. She had to move out. Her older sister, the great enabler, took her in. Two years later she hit bottom. Today she is home. Progress is slow. She lacks confidence and needs a lot of support. Sometimes I wonder if that is a true statement or my excuse to protect her because of guilt.

At fourteen the youngest child had a serious suicide attempt. As I sat by her bed in the intensive care unit and listened to a machine beep out her heartbeat, I kept asking, **"Why!"** **"Why!"** The guilt was tremendous. I had had several suicide attempts during my heavy drinking and her early childhood. Months later after much therapy, I asked her why she hadn't shared her feelings with me. Most were feelings adolescents experience during crucial times of growth. She answered with **"I was afraid you would drink."** At that time, I hadn't had a drink in six years!

After about three years of being sober, we were sitting at the dining room table and one of the kids said, **"Mom, remember the time you were drunk and we were watching Peter Pan and you thought you could fly!"** My heart sank, fear and guilt were my immediate reactions, but they continued the story. **"You jumped off the couch. Hit your head on the beamed ceiling and fell down. You leaped so high and hit so hard you got a concussion. Boy did you look funny flying through the air!"** They started to laugh. I started to laugh. We laughed and laughed until tears came. It was the beginning of WE.

So how do you deal with all this? First of all, **"I"** don't deal with it. **"They"** don't deal with it. **"WE"** deal with it!

Alcoholism happened to me! The effects happened to us all—to our whole family. You see, the nineteen year marriage ended in divorce after two years of being sober. Some damage can never be repaired.

CASE OF TERESA
Woman, Mother, Secretary

When I seriously think about me and my being an alcoholic I can't believe it happened to me. I never really liked the taste of any of it—I had to "acquire a taste for it." But oh boy! did I like what it did to me—how it made me feel and not feel.

I can't remember much about growing up, like little incidents in whole stages. I can only remember feeling afraid all the time but still having to cope, to perform, to do well. My mother had a vicious temper and no one knew when she would explode. No, she wasn't an alcoholic just angry all the time. My father was gentle and did little or nothing to protect me from my mother's wrath. So I lived in constant fear. I don't remember *seeing and feeling much love—not at home, not in school, not in church, nowhere.*

I remember feeling very secure and able to love when I was a junior in college. I felt very good about me. A lot of people admired me and praised me for my looks and brains. I began to believe in me. I met Marty and we got married. It was during the early fifties and we were busy having kids and acquiring a house, car, things. The thing for a woman to do then was to stay home. So I did and I let all of my secretarial skills evaporate. We had three kids in three years. So during the mid-seventies I had to go to work to help pay for college tuition. My husband kept badgering me to get a job and the anxiety increased. The fear, the one that I'd had all my life, that I would never, could ever really succeed at a job began to gnaw at me. Constantly feeling scared, I couldn't sleep. So I began to have a glass of muscatel before going to bed. Then I needed a bigger glass before I could feel relaxed so I switched to gin. God knows what happened after that. It's all a blur.

I remember being alone in the house and starting to shake. It was about 2:00 p.m. or so (or maybe it was 10:00 a.m.). Time was always a blur. The important thing I recall is walking into my bedroom at this inappropriate drinking time, dashing for the booze, gulping it down, and breathing a deep, relieving sigh when it hit me. I walked to the mirror, looked in it and said, **"Jesus Christ, you're an alcoholic! Now how in hell did you get into this mess. Oh my God, what am I going to do?"**

I remember trying to stop and instead increased the amount I drank. I hid bottles everywhere. I drank morning, noon, and night. My kids (all three) were in Junior High School and doing very well. I now had another baby and she was perfect. (I didn't have a drink, not one, during this pregnancy. All the public information regarding fetal alcohol syndrome was being ballooned on T.V., radio, etc.) After she was born I tried so hard to control the amount, the times, and the location of my drinking. Since I hadn't had a drink in nine months, I decided I wasn't an alcoholic. I drank again. I think in nine weeks' time I made up for nine months of sobriety. I helped to build a new house, moved into it, took care of 3 adolescents and a new baby and I was tipsy, drunk, or in a blackout all the time. My booze increased from a pint to a fifth to a quart bottle each and every day. Like a baby I took a bottle to bed every night.

I remember one day about 1:00 P.M. I called A.A. and a man answered. I told him, **"I'm an alcoholic."** I cried saying these words. They meant I had no willpower. They meant I would end up in the gutter. They meant I was less than human. I wept. The man asked me if I could come to the "center." I told him "no" because I had a baby napping. He then asked if he and another man could come to the house. I hung up. Two strange men coming to my house when I was alone confirmed my trip to the gutter. I definitely needed a drink to get through that one!! (Even as I write all this I feel there is pain, a heavy weight, a feeling deep inside me, a lump in my throat. All the pain resurfaces and again I cry.)

I knew the older kids knew. Sometimes I saw it in their questioning glances. At times I felt guilty, at other times hostile and flaming angry and at other times I just didn't care.

I went to soccer, basketball, tennis games, plays, and teacher conferences. I did it all and remember very little.

I had always been a very patient type of person. Suddenly I had patience with nothing and nobody. I couldn't, wouldn't put up with the least frustration. I refused to wait in lines or waiting rooms. I took to leaving my shopping cart piled high with food at the supermarket's checkout counter if I thought the line was too long. I walked out of the doctor's office if I had to wait more than a few minutes. Like it or not, sometimes I had to wait, for example at the bank to cash a check. Those times I would yell and make a scene. I remember ranting at bank tellers a lot and more than once at various bank officers.

Life was like that whenever I left the house, as if I had become injected by a mania serum. Suddenly I couldn't sit or stand still. I felt like I had to be in constant frenetic motion.

The crazy frenzy left me as soon as I came back home, back to my sedative.

What finally pushed me to go to the center was a confrontation I had with Marty. I was to stop drinking or leave because **"your drinking is ruining this family and I won't let that happen"** he said. I went to a motel that night. The next day I returned home to get clothes and to plead with him. I told him that I really tried to stop but couldn't. He told me he would do anything he could to help me. Right then I knew I had all the support I would ever need. I called the center.

The "center" was located in the worst section of town. I was definitely not from the worst section. I couldn't conceive walking on that street let alone into a building on that street. How strange my thinking was at that time. I didn't think anybody knew I was drunk and at the same time I knew they knew. When I walked into the center I wasn't saved. It took several months. Finally my non-drinking alcoholic counselor asked me to take Antabuse. I knew I couldn't get through one day without a drink so he asked me not to drink for at least eight hours. When I went that day I lied and said it had been eight hours since I drank. He warned me that if any physical symptoms occurred he would rush me to the hospital. The one and only hospital in our small town. I knew that if I swallowed that half pill that if I had to go to the emergency room everyone in town would know that I was drunk. I remember hesitating. Wanting to say **"Let me die."** **"Don't take me there."** Instead I popped the pill and swallowed it. Immediately I wished I hadn't. I was a coward. I was sick and tired of living but very scared of dying. I felt like such a nothing that I didn't want anyone to know me. I'd rather be dead than to be known as a drunk. I broke out in a rash. I itched. I sweated. I had trouble breathing. I paced. I got through day one. I almost didn't make it through the night. No big physical reaction, just an overwhelming feeling of anxiety and dread. The center opened at 9 a.m. I flew there at 9:01 a.m. I paced . . . paced . . . paced. Day two passed. Then days three and four.

What finally pushed me to stop drinking was a major confrontation with my counselor after one of my "slips." He said he knew I was still drinking and soon I would start drinking on the job. (I had gotten a job three months previously.) I liked my job and the people I met there. One evening I began shaking at work. I couldn't wait to get to my car to have a gulp of gin and I knew my counselor was right. I couldn't keep it at bay any longer. It was a lion devouring me. I had to stop or kill myself. Nobody likes a drunk but everybody feels sorry for a suicide victim. The problem was that I was too scared to die!!

The hardest things for me were to drive by a liquor store and to live through the nights. I knew where every liquor store was located. I clenched the car's steering wheel everytime I drove by one. About three weeks after practically living at the center I drove by a liquor store and I didn't realize it was looming in the corner of my eye. You know what I wanted to do? I wanted to stop the car in the middle of this busy street, jump out, and yell to the whole town, **"Free at last! Oh, my God, I'm free at last."**

About one year after I had stopped drinking I came home from work in a very silly mood. My elder 17 year old daughter very cautiously asked if I was drinking again. I was furious with her and it hurt inside me. This episode was another milestone. I realized I had hurt many other people and also that it would take a long time, maybe forever, for my family to forgive and to trust me. But it was my own doing that caused this suspicion. It may never happen. Nevertheless, it was worth trying to recapture their esteem and love.

Much of my life is forgotten. The early years were lost by fear, the middle years by booze. Perhaps the later years I'll remember because I'm loving again. I remember stating earlier that saying **"I am an alcoholic"** meant many negative things. Now I'm mostly glad that it happened. I'm a much better human being because of it. I'll tell you something, though. I wish I could have learned from a dream instead of from a nightmare. I have been eleven plus years without booze. It just dawned on me, learning by living is the best.

CASE OF HENRY
Man, Divorced Father, Computer Programmer

When Dr. Perez asked me to write this two months ago I said, "Sure! Why not? Glad to!" and I meant it. When he told me that I could take two months to do it if I needed that long, I told him I'd have it ready a lot sooner than that. The two months and then some have gone by and I'm just beginning it. It's been like that all my life. Time slips like water through my fingers. I wink my eyes and a month has passed. I'm forty-two years old now and time still is very much of a mystery to me. I wonder if it is to everybody else.

I taught French in high school for thirteen years. I didn't like teaching. I never did. I hated the kids. They shit all over me. Right from the first day I had a discipline problem. My first principal told me that my problem was that I was not strong enough. What he really meant was that I was a weak man. I hated him but I was scared of him. That's why I took the crap from him. I guess I was a very scared guy because I took that crap from everybody. My shrink said that it was all probably due to low self-esteem. If it was, then mine had to be below my toes. The reason I got tenured was that the principal never wrote me up, never told the School Board about me. He had a heart attack the week before the School Board passed on the tenure applications. A week later he died. I figure he must have found out that I got tenured.

You might wonder why I even wanted to teach if I hated it. Simple. I had a wife, a month old baby, a mortgage, and a cat. Besides all that, I didn't know what else I could do for a living. What do you do with a major in French? As a senior in college and before I met my wife, I took the Foreign Service exam and flunked. No surprise. I knew I would. Even though I learned to read and speak it, I can't understand it. Much of the exam had to do with comprehension. Anyway, I got the teaching job. Nobody else applied.

I started drinking like a drunk the afternoon after I put in my tenure application. I couldn't bear the anxiety of waiting to hear. After I got the "good news" I stayed drunk for three days. My wife Linda in those first months of our marriage and while she was still pregnant took care of me and protected me. She was my enabler par excellence. Anyway she called me in sick for those three days.

I developed a very careful schedule for buying my beer. I never hit the same package store twice in one month. I did all my drinking at home. I went right there after buying my booze. My drinking began at four o'clock and ran to about ten when I would stagger to bed. Weekends and holidays it began about 11:30 a.m. Once I started I just continued until I passed out, usually watching T.V.

Except for the three days lapse when I "celebrated" my being tenured, I never missed another day of school. I'm convinced today that that three day spree happened because I was scared and depressed. I saw being tenured as a sentence to a vocational hell.

I'm sure my alcoholism began to show. Until my tenure, I'd always weighed about 160. I ballooned out. Within a year of my "serious drinking" (that was my name for it) I weighed close to 190. I also ate like a pig. My newly developed beer belly helped me look like that pig. I must have really looked like hell on those days I forgot to shave. There were a lot of those.

At lunch one time in the school cafeteria I was on one side of a partition eating alone when I heard one secretary talking to another about me. I never forgot her comment, **"Everytime I see that man I want to put in a Maytag washing machine."** I remember finding some kind of perverted delight in her disgusted tone. I didn't increase my showers.

Looking back I find it amazing that no one at school ever commented to me about my appearance. My wife didn't either. She didn't seem to notice my drinking. For that matter she no longer noticed me at all. The baby was born. Right from the day she came home from the hospital, she was completely wrapped up with the baby.

See, Linda and I had to get married. I never loved her. I certainly never wanted to marry her. I had to. I was brought up in a strict Baptist home. There were a lot of rules in my house. All don'ts. Don't drink. Don't smoke. Don't swear. Especially don't screw. My father, mother too, were the types who punctuated every sentence with a hallelujah and finished every paragraph of their lives with a biblical quote. That's exaggerated but only a little bit. Anyways if I hadn't married Linda, I would have spent the rest of my life marinating in my guilt.

What was ironic about the whole pregnancy was that I was never much with girls. I never dated anyone in high school, in college either. Girls made me nervous. No brag, just fact. Linda chased me. She was on a church committee with my mother. I met her in my house. We went out a couple of times. She was the only girl I ever went out with. I went out with her because I figured I was supposed to. Boys went out with girls. She seemed very receptive to my fumbling sexual advances. In fact, I'd say she was more aggressive that way than I was. It's interesting after she got pregnant she seemed to lose all interest in sex. What I realize now is she wanted a baby, not me! I was used.

My life began to change a little over two years ago when Linda's parents were killed in an auto accident. A week later she walked out on me with our 14 year old and went to live in her parents' house. The divorce became final six months later. She had asked for nothing—not even child support. I wasn't hurt, only relieved.

The central theme of this story was supposed to be my experience as an alcoholic parent. I can't do that because the truth is that I don't have much experience as a parent. I'm a parent but only biologically. I never was a father to my daughter Brenda. I never fed her, diapered her, played with her. I never tucked her in or kissed her goodnight like you see on T.V. or in the movies. Like I said, I never did as a parent. Funny but I never felt I had to. Linda never asked me to and I never wanted to. It's an awful thing to say but it's true. I always saw my daughter as Linda's child, not mine. She reared her, not me.

I never developed any real affection for her because I never had any experiences with her. We lived in the same house but we didn't have much to do with each other. I came home from school, went into the den and watched T.V. She stayed near her mother. I guess I was kind of a phantom for her, there in spirit but not really there. My experience as a parent taught me that you really aren't, if you're an alcoholic. It may sound awful but it's true, I'm not especially sorry about what I missed because I just don't know what I missed. I know this all sounds a little insensitive, and it is. It is because that's what alcohol does. It desensitizes. That fact explains my alcoholism to me better than anything else. I wanted to be desensitized to being a husband and a parent. That's why I was drunk during my whole marriage and all of Brenda's life.

Anyway I stopped needing drink that day Linda and Brenda moved out. My need to be desensitized and insulated from them and my whole life just plain evaporated. Suddenly I didn't want to be drunk anymore. I went to see Perez. I learned a lot of things about myself. Basically what I learned was that I can be in control of my life if I want to be. I learned that I didn't have to be a teacher if I didn't want to be. I did it. I quit teaching. Today I'm working as a computer programmer. It suits me. I'm always in control. Unlike kids, computers never shit on you.

CASE OF JUDSON
Grateful Dad

As I walked along the street on a September evening with my son, recently turned 16 years old, I pointed out the beauty of the sky.

"But it's the August sky you like the best at night, isn't it?" *he asked.*

He was right. Years ago, in the summer before the divorce, I used to love the August nights on Nantucket when the moon was full and low and shooting-stars criss-crossed the sky. But I was surprised that he would know this and I said so.

"Don't you remember," he said, **"how you used to come in and wake us up when we were kids and make us go out and look at the sky in August?"**

I said that I remembered but, in truth, I did not.

"You kids must've thought I was crazy," I said.

He looked at me and smiled the kind of smile that conveys understanding and a bit of forgiveness. He was now almost my height and he was a polite and modestly self-assured star athlete and an "A" student, well adjusted and at home both among kids his own age and among adults.

"No," he said, **"we didn't think you were crazy."**

I was grateful for that kindness and I dropped the subject. It had been nearly five years since I had taken a drink of alcohol and often during that time of sobriety I had wondered just what my children really did think of me. But despite my occasional resolve to find out, the question always seemed inappropriate when I was with them. What does one ask, **"So, anyways, how'd it feel to have a father who was a drunk?"**

My relationship with my son and daughter was like my relationship with everybody I knew. It was distant. Never had I been able to talk with either about feelings and emotions and this inability has always loomed large as a void in my life. Their mother could do so. I recall the persistent sense of loss I would feel each night when they would go to her and hug and kiss her, then turn to me and from a respectable distance bid me a goodnight. It was as though I was somehow crippled or handicapped—wanting very badly to express my affection both verbally and physically while at the same time being incapable of even the simplest gesture. How could they be expected to understand the true depth of my feelings for them when even I could not understand my failure to show them? It seems that I tried to pressure my sanity by denying my own feelings, and the ultimate tragedy was that I failed both at admitting my feelings and at denying them. That doesn't leave you much.

What it leaves you is . . . well . . . wondering. That's what I've been doing during the years since the divorce. I wonder. I wonder why I've not been able to emit or relate to others and to my children especially. Sometimes I think it's due to the curse of us alcoholics, a sense of inferiority that permeates our very soul. The shrinks call it low self-esteem. We alcoholics live with the notion that we are different, that we are a lower form of people. To too many of us our disease is a sign of our unworthiness. That we don't feel worthy enough to share our love is the best sign of the sense of that unworth. Besides what normal person can really understand how and what we feel? Why would they ever want to? What do we really have to offer anybody? Even our children? These awful thoughts, this awful wondering still plagues me.

I don't remember what fantasy of fatherhood I was entertaining when, after a couple of years of marriage, I forced the idea of having our first child on my reluctant wife. However, I do recall that idea was entirely my own and only months of demanding and arguing caused her to relent. She cried upon learning that she was pregnant and they were clearly not tears of joy.

Years later, at the time of the divorce, I would learn from her the source of her reluctance. **"I knew it was a mistake to marry you even before the wedding,"** she would confess, **"but things had gone so far it was just too embarrassing to back out."**

What she knew even then was that there was only one constant in my life, constant drinking. Beyond that reliable trait I was given to all manner of impulses, unpredictable behaviors and moods. I had begun a year after the marriage and a year before the arrival of our daughter to medicate my anxiety, my depression, and my fears with gin and to fuel my drives and fantasies with it as well. She was a remarkably stable person, very steady and reliable, and her senses warned her, darkly, of the potential disaster of sharing parenthood with me.

From the very beginning, alcohol would insinuate itself between me and my children. This first happened on the very day that I was to bring my first-born, my daughter, home from the maternity ward. The hospital had scheduled the discharge for anytime after 10:00 a.m., and I had arrived at about that time. As I entered the hospital lobby I could feel the ghostly fear, the anxiety that plagues the alcoholic began to stir within me. I boarded the elevator and as I rose to the maternity floor the fear erupted into panic, as I knew it would, as it had for the past year. I was trembling for want of a drink and I was certain that I might go insane if I tried to function without one.

Without getting off when the elevator arrived at the maternity floor I pushed the button to return to the lobby. Once there I hurried back to the parking lot and drove to a package store where I purchased a half pint of vodka, still believing it was odorless. I drove around for nearly an hour, drinking the alcohol and allowing this "medicine" to relax me and control my mood. All the while, as I drove and drank, my wife and infant daughter waited, fully clothed, to be taken home.

Finally satisfied that I was in control of myself, which is to say finally half drunk, I returned to the hospital and went directly to the maternity floor. But even then I had miscalculated the amount of gin necessary to deal with fatherhood. I still trembled as the nurse tried to hand my daughter into my arms. I refused to take her for fear I'd commence to shake violently and drop her. An experienced nurse solved the dilemma by simply thrusting the infant into my arms and withdrawing.

Eighteen months later, while suffering some common childhood ailment, my daughter's fever reached such a degree that she went into a febrile convulsion. My wife was with her in the nursery when it happened at about 11:00 p.m. on a bitter cold night in February. I was down the hall, lying in bed reading, dressed only in boxer shorts. When I heard my wife scream, I ran into the nursery and seized the baby off the bassinet. Somehow mindful that precautions must be taken to prevent a person having convulsions from chewing their tongue, I thrust the index finger of my right hand into my daughter's mouth, and she clamped down on it with her four teeth, two on top and two on the bottom. I phoned my father for transportation to the hospital, since my wife was paralyzed with fear. When he arrived I flew out of the house and into the car with her still cradled in my arms. Upon arriving at the emergency room I created a substantial disturbance in demanding better services for the baby than were being provided. Short of being taken into custody by hospital security guards, I calmed down and took a seat in the waiting room.

It was then that I felt cold vinyl on my back and my legs and realized that I had been out in the February weather of minus ten degrees with no clothes on other than my shorts. Later, about 3:00 a.m., I would feel pain for the first time in my finger, which had been broken.

All of this occurred when I was quite sober. Yet, the following day, try as I might, I could not force myself to enter the hospital and journey up to the second floor pediatrics to visit my child. I was obliged to first go to the bar to drown the awful guilt. I remember later going up the elevator to make my visit but I don't remember seeing her.

I functioned like that. I functioned like that throughout her and my son's childhood. I was never a father to them during the first decade of their lives. I try to be now during their teen years. I visit them a lot. My long bout with alcoholism and the subsequent sobriety has made me more introspective, more silent, and much more of a listener. When we visit, my kids and I hurt much inside for the years I missed but I marvel too at the continuing miracle of recovery. God, I'm grateful for that! Grateful especially that I can see and appreciate the beauty and love of my children.

SUMMARY

What we learned from these seven stories is that alcoholism exacerbates even mild feelings of insecurity. To the alcoholic, threat comes in many forms, in situations, events even as children. Indeed, an innocent newborn we learned, can be the catalyst that precipitates the most outrageous of behaviors.

We also learned that alcoholism can make a person insensitive and indifferent to the needs and feelings of others. Once alcohol is entered into the equation of human relationships that equation can never be balanced. Its lopsided effect is invariably to hurt and demean, often to destroy. The reason for this is that the alcoholic's low self-esteem is lowered further and the self-esteem of all those identified with the alcoholic, especially family members, is also lowered.

Inebriation, we learned, gives a person an even darker view of one's own self and invariably of others. This darker view of self invariably is characterized by strong feelings of self-hate and loathing.

Too often this is projected onto those near and once dear to the alcoholic. The long and short of it is that the alcoholic and his family are steeped and live with much, much pain.

Finally, we learned something else, too, something very hopeful. Even the most hard-core of alcoholics can stop drinking, can get on the road to recovery. Seven of them told us so.

TOPICS FOR
DISCUSSION AND REFLECTION

1. What are the effects of alcoholism on one's sense of security?

2. How does inebriation affect feeling accepted?

3. How does living alcoholically affect accepting others?

4. Reflect on the self-esteem of the principals of the seven stories. What were the specifics which kept and maintained it low for all seven?

5. How specifically did inebriation influence perception of self and others?

6. What did addiction to alcohol do to the trust of one's self and of others?

7. How did addiction affect others; outside the family? Within the family?

8. Reflect on the pain each of the principals experienced. Of the seven whom did you feel described it most vividly? Why?

9. Reflect upon the pain inflicted upon others. Do you believe it can ever be effectively resolved?

10. Some counselors believe it requires courage to achieve and maintain sobriety. Why do you think they believe so?

PART III
TREATMENT

THE THERAPIST

How effectively therapy proceeds will be determined in considerable measure by the personality which the therapist brings to the session. Quite apparently, the therapist's self-image and the image which is projected to the client will influence interaction in counseling. How secure or insecure the therapist is personally, how confident or anxious, how tolerant or judgmental will affect client reactions, responses, and outcomes.

This author's view is that the critical ingredient in the therapist's personality is the motivation to grow and learn. Trite but true, every client is unique. Ergo, every counseling session can and should be viewed by the therapist as a potential learning experience and as another opportunity to grow.

The person who cannot or will not take such a view ordinarily does not find reward in doing therapy. Such a person should give second thoughts to becoming a therapist. If such an individual is functioning in the therapist role, he/she should quit. Why? Because the effective, competent therapist knows and feels that he/she does more than fill a role. *The effective therapist finds reward in serving another person.* If the therapist does not find reward in serving, he/she will not find reward in doing therapy. Most assuredly, such a therapist will "burn out."

RESEARCH FINDINGS

Therapist's Perception

How therapists perceive themselves influences significantly how they are perceived by their clients. Long, Floyd-Walker, and Foreman (1989) found that a strong correlation exists between selfevaluation by the therapist and the client's evaluation of the therapist's ability. A question that many practitioners have asked for a long time about their perception of clients has to do with client appearance. Simply put, do the client's looks influence how therapists perceive them? The answer is yes. Sussman et al. (1990) found that body appearance influences a therapist's view and the client's face appearance affects how a therapist approaches and behaves toward the client. The more attractive the client is, the more positive the attitude, and the more enhancing was the behavior of the therapist.

Therapists' perception of alcohol is critically affected by their backgrounds. For example, Waller and Casey (1990) found that those prospective therapists who were adult children of alcoholics needed special attention while learning about alcohol and its treatment.

Therapist's perception and attitudes are strongly influenced also by the therapist's expectations. For example, Geller, Faden, and Levine (1990) found that prospective psychiatrists had a much higher tolerance level for ambiguous outcomes of their work than did other colleagues who intended to go into other medical specialties. A therapist's tolerance for expectations and outcomes is of considerable importance in work with alcoholics. Optimism, however, is even more valuable. For example, Leake and King (1977) found that therapists who perceived a client's outcomes optimistically affected positively the outcomes of therapy. What these researchers found in a study of disadvantaged alcoholics of skid-row status was that those therapists were the most successful who adhered to the most optimistic expectations of their clients' recovery. These findings are proven in a study by Talbot and Gillen (1978), who researched a comparable client population and by Skuja (1981), who sampled counselors who were themselves recovering alcoholics.

Values according to Hertzman and Mitnick (1978-79) are a critical factor in alcoholism programs. They have recommended that ethics be included in the curricula of alcoholism training programs because value judgments are necessarily involved in every aspect of the training and evaluation of the counselor and in the treatment of the client.

Personal and Professional Qualities

Studies in the field of therapist effectiveness indicate that the counselor's personal qualities are a more valid and fruitful area for research than are education, training, or theoretical orientation. Wrenn (1960) found that a therapist's ability to respond effectively to his/her client has little to do with the theoretical school followed. Strupp (1957), in an earlier study comparing the psychoanalytic with the client-centered approach, found the same data. He felt that Wolberg, an analyst, and Rogers of the client-centered approach "were both warm, accepting, and noncritical." In short, both were comparably effective.

In another earlier work, Perez (1985) indicated that the effective therapist is one who meets important personal needs when he/she does therapy. Prime among these needs, according to Munson (1961), is nurturance—that is to shelter emotionally and to take care of people. Mills and Abeles (1965) found that the need to like people was as important to a therapist as the need to be nurturant. In a later study with two others, Mills, Chestnut, and Hartzell (1966) found that therapists also are concerned with being "warm and passionate, intuitive, and psychological penetrating."

A study by Valle (1981), which dealt with personal qualities of the therapist, found that therapists who related easily and well, who find it easy to be empathic, and who are basically genuine and straightforward, have a lower rate of recidivism among their alcoholic patients than therapists who are not as interpersonally competent.

One of the more comprehensive studies in the area of therapist characteristics was done by Menne (1975). With the help of 75 experienced therapists, he drew up a questionnaire which listed 132 counselor qualities. More than 350 therapists responded to this research instrument. The four highest ranked qualities concerned:

1. **Professional ethics.** The therapist's personal conduct in the therapeutic relationship was given number one priority.

2. **Self-awareness.** This quality particularly as relates to competency, attitudes, prejudices, and limitations ranked second.

3. **Personal characteristics.** These were ranked third. These qualities focused upon maturity, flexibility, respect for clients, and intuitiveness.

4. **The ability to listen and communicate.** That this quality should rank so high reflects this therapist's conviction about its importance. These findings may be interpreted to mean that the effective, professional therapist is a person of conscience and that ethics are an integral part of conscience is obvious. If one reflects upon the other three findings by Menne (1975), they too, are aspects of conscience. Why? Because they all reflect the extent to which one is emotionally identified and concerned with others. Self-awareness, as defined in this book, is premised upon interpersonal relationships as is respect, maturity, and even, perhaps especially, the ability to listen and communicate.

Another way to interpret these findings is that the therapist is one who finds reward in giving and in helping others. Apparently by helping others, the therapist helps himself/herself (Rakos & Schroeder, 1976).

SELECTED COUNSELORS' RESPONSES

Studies are critical because they provide data that are detached and authoritative. At the same time the counseling process itself is quite the opposite. It is warm, dynamic, and more often than not, emotional. This is especially true when one counsels the alcoholic.

In order to inject some warmth, even human interest into the discussion, the author asked five experienced, practicing counselors of alcoholics to respond to the following questions:

1. What are the most important qualities which make for an effective counselor of alcoholics?

2. How do you perceive the alcoholic?

3. What personal qualities do you seek to exhibit when you counsel the alcoholic?

4. What professional qualities do you deem to be most important when you counsel the alcoholic?

Responses received from the five counselors are provided.

Alice, Counselor, Female, Forty-two Years Old, Ten Years Experience, M.A.

I see the alcoholic as a person suffering from an incurable illness which can be arrested if the use of alcohol is discontinued.

This can be done. I know it because I've seen alcoholics recovered. I also bear in mind that he/she is a very sensitive and fragile person who needs to develop a balance in his/her life to cope with feelings.

I try to show my clients that I know about the deviance of alcoholism. I try to show them that I accept them but not their drunkenness. I stay in touch with their feelings. Mostly I show them that I am nonjudgmental. Alcoholic clients have been judged enough, especially by themselves.

I've always believed that to have communication with an alcoholic client you must show your wholeness as a person and you must share in appropriate terms your own self. I share. I share my thoughts and my experiences.

Myron, Counselor, Male, Fifty Years Old, Ten Years Experience, Recovering Alcoholic

(This counselor preferred to be interviewed rather than to write his responses. The material is derived from an edited tape.)

I deal with drinkers, not alcoholics. A person comes in because he has a drinking problem not because he is an alcoholic. I hate labels. But that's not the reason I differentiate between a person who's uncomfortable with his drinking and an alcoholic. The word alcoholic terrifies people, especially one who got the courage to walk in here. Why scare the person away, and I would if I saw and referred to him/her as an alcoholic. So I see each person who comes in as a person who's got a drinking problem, and how bad the drinking problem is has got nothing to do with how often I see the person or how often he/she wants to see me. All that doesn't mean much, in fact I think it's irrevelant. When I counsel I'm totally honest (I like to think I'm like that all the time). There's no bluff in my counseling. The counselor who bluffs will get nowhere. That counselor might just as well close shop. See, a bluffer is the easiest guy to con. And drinkers, my friend, are masters of the con.

I learned a long time ago that I do my best counseling when I share my own story. I'm very direct and I don't soften my words, but what I never do is put the person on the defensive. I never attack. I never judge him/her. What I try to communicate is two things: (1) like that person, I'm trying to beat the booze, I'm in the same boat; and (2) it's a life-time battle.

Professional qualities—the two most important ones are empathy—let the person know that you share the same world, yeah, you've walked in his/her moccasins;

and also listening. I mean listening—you know God made two ears but only one mouth. The counselor should listen twice as much as he/she talks. The counselor should always let the client identify his/her problem. To try to do that for the client is the surest way I know to drive the person away.

Fred, Counselor, Male, Twenty-four Years Old, Seven Years Experience, M.A., C.A.G.S.

I perceive alcoholics as individuals who are in much pain. A person who feels completely hopeless and who has lost touch with own values, who's thinking is distorted and does not know why.

The behavior that an active alcoholic displays is behavior that often times is in direct conflict with his/her values. This, I believe causes an astronomical amount of guilt and remorse.

Because I believe the previous statement, I feel the most precious, most fundamental quality that is needed by an alcoholism counselor would be that of complete acceptance. An active alcoholic, a person who is "new" to treatment (booze free) feels "bad," guilty, and involved in behaviors that seem to have no rational explanation. They need to be accepted, not judged; they are their harshest judges anyway. Compassion is vital. Then after these traits have been established guilt reduction ensues and value clarification can follow. In time, the recovering alcoholic can then learn to accept his/her illness, thus begin to see the rewards that come from values that are clarified. This hopefully keeps alcoholics sober.

I feel I most need to remain compassionate yet detached, congruent-consistent, yet empathic. These qualities I try very hard to display to the alcoholic. I constantly must be aware/be cautious of over-identification with the alcoholic. This is difficult because it is much easier to be human and to display human qualities than be a professional trying to reduce pain by the professional guidelines. The two, human compassion and professional sensitivity, have a fine line separating them. Nonetheless, it is a boundary which must be adhered to for maximum effect.

Beth, Counselor, Female, Thirty-Nine Years Old, Ten Years Experience, M.A. in Psychology, L.C.S.W.

The most important qualities which makes for an effective counselor are empathy and acceptance of the client where he/she is. The ability to give guidance through options open to the client and in an in-patient setting to provide a positive role is critical as a counselor is more visible in his/her humanness.

While a college degree with a major in psychology is useful, I feel that empathy and a counselor's own personal growth is essential in counseling the alcoholic as in other counseling. While the need is to be objective, also a need is for genuine compassion. It is important that the counselor not be controlling but accepting.

These clients need, as do other clients, to be viewed in a holistic manner—spiritually, physically, and psychologically. Value clarifications are important for some clients and for others the issue is around sexuality, some ask for spiritual guidance. It is a "no no" generally in the field of psychology to deal with the spiritual realm, but A.A. talks of "Our Higher Power" and feels that sobriety is based on giving over their disease to God. Some are not ready to deal with this; others want to understand.

As counselors, I feel we must help these individuals find their own answers as to how they can relate to their God. There is no need to go into depth. There are others in the religious life who can be of assistance in that area. It has to be understood that alcoholism, because of the nature of the disease, leaves clients with a loss of values and habits that they would never have chosen sober. This leaves them with a tremendous amount of guilt and self-anger. It cannot be ignored.

Along with this, a client needs to be treated with respect and supported in building a more positive self-image.

They need to be provided with as much information on the disease as possible along with available resources for support in the community. A counselor should look at the client's positive points and build on these. You may find a great deal of artistic talents. Many are highly intelligent and creative people. Looking at their recreation and past hobbies is also important. Many have lost sight of a healthy balance in their work and play life, lost their job skills or are in need of guidance for the future.

Vocational counseling is essential for those who have lost their job skills or are in need of guidance for the future.

Socially, they either have lost the knack or never had it in the first place. They need to see that it is a basic need for all of us, and they need to begin work on interpersonal relationship. Those are essential for survival in the real world without alcohol.

For some the sexual drive has been affected, and they may need reassurance and understanding in this area. Others may need further professional help.

Again, the whole person must be treated but as an "individual" with individual needs. The family also has needs and Al Anon is most effective. There are times when out-patient care should be considered for the alcoholic.

The twelve steps of A.A. are a beautiful way of life not only for alcoholics but also for all of us as human beings. I feel alcoholics who seek treatment for their disease are the most courageous human beings. They find the need and face the dark side which we all possess in order to begin the process of completely changing their lives. They painfully have to accept their disease, possibly change their environment, friendships, life-styles, and behaviors almost immediately and simultaneously. They live with the fear of death should they again pick up that one drink. They see the poor recovery rate and wonder if they are gong to make it. They are told they have to attend A.A. weekly, that there are no simple answers to maintain sobriety. There are other options but the success rate is much poorer. They find their families are possible enablers, that they too have become sick in living with the alcoholic. They need to know that their attitudes can change the relations and attitudes around, that the "glass is half full."

Each patient I work with, as Sheldon Kopp says, is a journey for me into another world. It is a privilege and obligation for me to do the best I can. Therefore, I as the counselor have an obligation to stay healthy and to grow emotionally, as well as intellectually. I believe also that you must, as the Indian Prayer says, be aware that you do not know someone unless you have walked in their moccasins.

It is important for me to see the patient through his/her eyes and assist him/her in building up his/ her fragile ego. That's primary to treatment. The program in which I counsel is thirty days in length and is scheduled in eight sessions. It is difficult to go beyond secondary withdrawal and confusion. Some patients can get into insight work, others not. I look for most clients to seek further treatment through out-patient work and/or halfway house and A.A. Support. Their strength is obvious in their incredible ability to have survived thus far and their courage to try ONE MORE TIME, A DAY OR A MOMENT AT A TIME. When I think of the tremendous energy needed for me to change one negative behavior in my life and then see the alcoholic attempt so many more, I cannot help but be in awe of the "Spirit of the Individual."

Wayne, Counselor, Male, Fifty-Nine Years Old, Thirty-Four Years Experience, M.Ed.

There are many teachers, few Socrates. There are many physicians, few Schweitzers. There are many religious, few Luthers or Mother Teresas.

I guess what I'm trying to say is that in alcoholism counseling, the most effective therapy begins in the nail-beds of the counselor's and client's toes and spreads thence to every cell of the body—physical, mental, and spiritual. It is true holism, wherein something greater than the sum of the parts is hoped for.

Quite obviously, love, genuineness, and empathy must be internalized realities of the therapist's substance. Unfortunately empathy is best learned in the street, by feeling the pain of an empty belly and the slow dying of hope. Yet it is from this human condition that the indigent drug abuser frequently comes.

Lofty intellectualism has little or no place in working with the disenfranchised and disenchanted alcoholic. It is an added slur to his/her desperate deprivation, alienation, and isolation. Squalor neither sees an exquisite sunset nor experiences the joy of a Goya hung in the local museum. This sort of thing is better left in the hallowed halls of learning.

I don't mean to imply that a solid working knowledge of psychological theorists is not desirable; it is indispensable. Also of indispensability is a solid working knowledge of the Fellowship of Alcoholics Anonymous, historically perhaps the most available, inexpensive, and effective therapy since alcoholism began to emerge from the dark-ages of ignorance and bias a mere 50 years ago.

It has been this writer's experience that needs of the patient are best served if both ongoing counseling and A.A. participation are utilized concurrently rather than sequentially. Assisting the patient to identify, assess, better understand, and then modify unhealthy emotions which frequently contribute to the development and/or perpetuation of addiction is essential and traditionally the role of the counselor, psychologist, or psychiatrist. The philosophy, teachings, and activity of Alcoholics Anonymous provide daily availability and continuity of community, socialization, nonjudgmental support, *compassion, and role modeling. The process of recovery should be hastened by making available to the patient the "best of both worlds" (hopefully), professional as well as paraprofessional.*

P.S. I always counsel with this thought feeling:

Humble love, and not proud science
keeps the door of heaven.

Young

The previous five responses reflect a number of common denominators in perception and in personal and professional qualities.

An Analysis-Therapist Perception

Therapists, like subjects in research findings, tend to perceive optimistically. They believe alcoholics can recover. They focus on positive qualities and "build on these." Alice, the first therapist, noted that the illness "can be arrested if the use of alcohol is discontinued" and went on to say, "This can be done. I know it . . ."

Therapists perceive realistically too. Thus two therapists, Alice and Fred, observed that the alcoholic is a fragile person "who is in much pain. A person who feels completely hopeless and who has lost touch with own values, whose thinking is distorted . . ." What this all means is that an optimistic and realistic perception are needed if a therapist is going to be effective.

The therapist's perception is characterized also by a need to share the client's perception. These counselors know that they can't change the alcoholic by themselves. He/she must want to change. The starting point for this change, they feel, is in communicating to the client that they want to share his/her view of the world.

Therapist Personal Qualities

Therapists recognize that they can accomplish change if they *share* themselves. The first therapist, Alice, put it very succinctly "I share. I share my thoughts and my experiences." The second therapist, Myron, put it just as aptly another way, "What I try to communicate is—[that I'm] like that person, I'm trying to beat the booze, I'm in the same boat." Emotional sharing to this author means emotional investment. It is when he/she is able to communicate these feelings that the effective counselor feels that dividends are received from their emotional investment. And what are the dividends? They are rich and precisely, the counselor's knowledge that the client no longer feels alone in despair and threat that he/she perceives.

What other qualities do these therapists deem important? **Authenticity** seems to be among the top ones, "When I counsel, I'm totally honest . . . There's no bluff in my therapy." Complete **acceptance** of the alcoholic person is another. This acceptance seems to stem from another quality, namely: **compassion.** These therapists seem able to incorporate both qualities because they've learned to distinguish between the person of the alcoholic and the behavior. They accept him/her, not the drinking. Inextricably interwoven with these qualities is a strong penchant for **nurturance.** Nurturant therapists are those who are interested, who care, and who are motivated to help.

Professional Qualities

Despite these personal qualities of nurturance, compassion, acceptance, and sharing, therapists believe that the effective therapist is one who must remain **cognitively detached** from the counseling. When one remains so, the therapist is able to listen and to respond better. Equally important, only by maintaining this detachment will the therapist be able to maintain an appropriate perspective of the counseling relationship. This quality is what one therapist, Fred, was referring to when he wrote, "I constantly must be aware/ be cautious of overidentification with the alcoholic." What this therapist recognizes is that when he/she overidentifies with the client, he/she is responding to his/her own needs and not those of the client. When the therapist becomes overidentified with the client, **he/she is in danger of destroying the therapeutic relationship.** When overidentification occurs, therapists invariably fall prey to their own feelings. They become overwhelmed by the client's emotions and demands. They lose the ability to listen and interpret the true meaning of the client's feelings. Their perception becomes so clouded that the person of the client becomes major for them, the behavior (alcoholism) minor, or they become unable to distinguish between the two at all. To meet therapist needs (perhaps justify the feelings of supposed love for the client), the counselor often lets himself/herself be sucked into the client's psychological defenses, denying or rationalizing the client's alcoholism. Under circumstances such as these, the therapist's perception becomes so distorted that he/she loses sight of the basic purpose of the counseling—to meet the needs of the client. In sum, if therapists are not careful about maintaining their cognitive detachment, they risk losing their integrity both as therapists and as persons.

Finally, the quality, personal-professional, which seemed to transcend the personalities of these five therapists, was their **pensiveness.** These are thinking people, who unquestionably have a bent for introspection. Consider some of their lines, ". . . you must show your wholeness as a person" (Alice). "It is much easier to be human and to display human qualities than to be a professional trying to reduce pain via professional guidelines" (Fred). "When I think of the tremendous energy needed for me to change one negative behavior in my life and then see alcoholics attempt so many more; I cannot help but be in awe" (Beth). "Squalor neither sees an exquisite sunset nor experiences the joy of a Goya hung in the local museum" (Wayne). Thoughts like these are an important ingredient in functioning as an effective therapist.

TRAINING OF THE THERAPIST

Not enough can be said about the value of training for the alcoholism counselor. Kahn and Stephen (1991) found that a prospective therapist's self-esteem, not only as a therapist but as a person, goes up commensurate with the level, quality, and duration of training. The training the therapists in the sample received induced them to stay in their jobs longer and contributed toward a more tolerant and optimistic perception of their clients. McDermott et al. (1991) found that prospective alcoholism in therapists significantly increased their objective knowledge about the treatment process. Their conclusions were that specialized training in counseling programs for alcoholism therapists was a dire need.

Therapist training is as important as his/her personal and professional qualities. While the literature abounds with statistical research about the latter and about the nature and treatment of alcoholism, only a few studies, statistical or even descriptive, have been concerned with the training of the counselor of alcoholics. What this author learned, however, is that the paucity of reporting does not reflect what's happening. Indeed, what he discovered by telephone and mail is that training programs are conducted in virtually every institutional setting where alcoholism is treated. Most institutions in which alcoholism is treated view therapist training as an integral part of their total activity. These training programs vary in scope and depth and at all treatment levels. Many institutions offer intense orientations for volunteer therapists. Even more offer regularly scheduled classroom didactic work for paraprofessionals during their working shift. These didactics frequently are offered in conjunction with or to supplement courses offered by private colleges, state colleges, or university extension services. Many institutions offer intense orientations for volunteer therapists. Even more offer regularly scheduled classroom didactic work for paraprofessionals during their working shift. These didactics frequently are offered in conjunction with or to supplement courses offered by private colleges, state colleges, or university extension services. Many institutions have visiting lecturers come several times each month for the professional staff.

The variance of offerings reflects the prevailing view about alcoholism counseling; namely, it is an ongoing process where fresh useful research about its nature and treatment constantly is being uncovered for all types and levels of counselors. In alcoholism counseling there does seem to be a veritable myriad of types and levels of counselors.

They come from all the helping professions. Thus, in most institutional settings for alcoholics, one will find nurses, psychologists, physicians, social workers, school guidance counselors, and teachers. Some of these professionals have impeccable credentials in counseling. Some have few, if any. Then too, many work with alcoholics who have relatively little formal education or formal backgrounds in counseling. In no area of mental health is there more disparity in education and training than in alcoholism counseling.

This author does not view this situation with alarm or even with concern. Rather he views the issue of the professional counseling background of counselor of alcoholics in the same way Haley (1971) viewed the family therapist's background. On this topic Haley (1971) once wrote, "A therapist is now often judged on his merit—the success of his therapy—not upon his professional background." This view seems especially appropriate for the counselor of alcoholics. For generations, alcoholics were treated most successfully not by professionals from medicine, psychology, social work, or education, but by counselors from Alcoholics Anonymous. Figure 6.1 provides some interesting data about the make-up of Alcoholics Anonymous. It also reflects the very considerable impact that A.A. has made upon alcoholism counseling.

Alcoholism counselors have come from a kaleidoscope of vocations and, in many instances, vocations which had little to do with mental health. Many of these nonprofessionals knew what the professionals refused to accept or even to see, that alcoholism is uniquely different from any other form of mental health illness. The recovering alcoholics, who served as counselors, knew that generations ago. Even though they might have been lacking formal education or training in counseling, their perception of the illness and of the client served to mitigate any professional deficiencies. Why? Because they knew they could establish rapport more quickly and empathize far more effectively with the alcoholic than any professional nonalcoholic because they had themselves **experienced** the client's illness. What is most surprising to this author is that the research supporting the recovering alcoholic therapist's view is startlingly recent. Argerious and Manohar in a 1978 study found that recovering alcoholics were far more effective with young drinkers than were nonalcoholic therapists. Lawson (1982) substantiated these finds with a study published four years later. He found that a history of alcoholism in the therapist promoted the therapeutic relationship. Invariably the alcoholics rated this therapist higher than the nonalcoholic therapist.

An important note is that these studies do not mean a nonalcoholic cannot be an effective therapist of alcoholics. Perhaps the most important meaning to be derived from these studies is that a recovering alcoholic has an advantage over a nonalcoholic therapist precisely because of what has always been known about therapy in general. *The more positive the client perceives the counselor; the more productive the therapeutic relationship will be.*

Research Findings

Whatever one's position might be regarding the counselor's professional counseling background, a uniform view by institutional staffs and administrators is that ongoing inservice training is beneficial (McDermott, Tricker, & Farna, 1991; Rutter & Hagart, 1990). Other studies which show this include one by Skuja, Schneidmuhl, and Mandell (1975). They studied the effects of an intense training program upon 41 alcoholism trainees after 7 weeks and again after 14 weeks. At the seventh week juncture and again after 14 weeks, these researchers found a significant increase in trainee competence, and in utilization in alcoholism work, personal involvement, responsibility, and overall job performance. Hoffmann and Bonyge (1977) did a study with 16 female alcoholics who entered a nine month training program to assess the effects of the program upon their personalities. They found that the nine months of training (the emphasis was upon personal confrontation and selfawareness) helped these female counselors to become more task oriented and accepting of sympathy from others. Wehler and Hoffman (1978) compared the scores of 14 female alcoholism counselors on the Personal Orientation Inventory before and after a nine month training program. These women scored significantly higher after the program in such areas as spontaneity, capacity for intimate contact,

(Continued on page 134)

Alcoholics Anonymous 1989 Membership Survey

1 Length of Sobriety

29% Sober over 5 years
37% Sober between 1-5 years
34% Sober less than 1 year

Average sobriety of all members is more than **four** years

About A.A.

A.A. can be found almost everywhere, almost all the time—in more than 87,000 groups throughout the world. We welcome opportunities to cooperate with others in providing help to alcoholics. Look for A.A. in your phone book or write: Box 459, Grand Central Station, New York, NY 10163.

2 Sex of Members

All Members:
  35% Women   **65%** Men

Age 30 and Under:
  40% Women   **60%** Men

3 Meeting Attendance

The average member attends **three** meetings per week.

In 1989 more than 9,000 A.A. members from the U.S. and Canada participated in a carefully designed, random survey of the membership. Such studies have been conducted every three years since 1968 by the General Service Office.

The purpose of the survey has been to keep A.A. members informed on current trends in membership characteristics, and to provide information about Alcoholics Anonymous to the professional community and to the general public as part of the effort to reach those who still suffer from alcoholism.

4 Introduction to A.A.

Factors most responsible for members coming to A.A. (two responses permitted).

Through an A.A. member	**34%**
Treatment facility	**30%**
Self-motivated (on my own)	**27%**
Family	**19%**
Counseling agency	**10%**
Doctor	**7%**
Employer or fellow worker	**6%**
Non-A.A. friend or neighbor	**4%**
Al-Anon or Alateen member	**4%**
Newspaper/magazine/ radio/TV	**3%**
A.A. literature	**3%**

Figure 6.1. Alcoholics Anonymous 1989 Membership Survey. Reprinted with permission.

Figure 6.1. Continued

5 Ages of Members

Under age 21	3%
Ages 21 through 30	19%
Ages 31 through 40	30%
Ages 41 through 50	25%
Ages 51 through 60	14%
Ages 61 through 70	7%
Over age 70	2%

The average age of an A.A. member is **41** years.

6 Members' Occupations

Professional/Technical	23%
Labor	17%
Manager/Administrator	13%
Sales	6%
Homemaker	5%
Craft Worker	5%
Office and Clerical	5%
Student	4%
Retired	8%
Unemployed	6%
Disabled	3%
Other	5%

7 Group Membership

88% of the members belong to a home group

8 Sponsorship

85% of members have, or have had, a sponsor. **72%** of those got their sponsor within 90 days.

9 Additional Help . . . Before

Before coming to A.A., **68%** of the members received some type of treatment or counseling, such as medical, psychological, spiritual, etc. **80%** of those members who received treatment or counseling said it played an important part in directing them to A.A.

10 Additional Help . . . After

After coming to A.A., **60%** of the members received some type of treatment or counseling (other than A.A.) such as medical, psychological, spiritual, etc. **85%** of those members who received treatment or counseling said it played an important part in their recovery from alcoholism.

11

In addition to their alcoholism, **42%** of the members said they were addicted to drugs.*

Alcoholics Anonymous' primary purpose is recovery from alcoholism.

12 Relationship with Doctors

70% of members' doctors know they are in A.A.

self-regard, and feeling reactivity. Also a stronger bent existed for personal self-actualization among the subjects after the training program.

Functional Programs

Manohar (1973) described a program for training volunteers. It involved ten weeks of classroom work and fifty weeks at forty hours a week of work in an alcoholism clinic under professional supervision. During the forty hour week the trainees also attended seminars and staff meetings. In a previous journal report Wilson (1968) felt that alcoholism training programs need to employ not only the traditional counseling one-on-one approach but should also train counselors in psychodrama, group therapy, and videotaping.

These two reports reflect the trend toward competency-oriented programs because of the acute need for counselors. Brammer and Springer (1971) have described just such a program, designed and implemented in Washington state. In this program, performance objectives are developed and described. The counselor applies and is assessed. The decision is then made whether to recommend him/her for certification or a skill training program. If he/she is certified, the counselor continues into "Lifelong professional development." If the counselor chooses to enter the skill training program, he/she does so and is subject to reassessment at the end of it and presumably state certification.

A Recommended Program

The previous two programs and the dozens of unpublished ones which the author has studied have commonalities. They include both theory and practice. Not all, however, assess their applicants at the current level of functioning in either theory or practice. The author's conviction is that an assessment period would be ultimately beneficial to both the trainee and the institution. Criteria and length of training would be determined by needs of the setting. Ideally the program should be counselor centered and its curriculum and length determined by the counselor's performance.

Stage One—Theory. Readings, discussion, and assessment in the following areas:

- Personality Theories—Freud, Jung, Adler, Rogers

- Abnormal Psychology

- The Alcoholic Personality

- Selected Theories and Techniques of Counseling

- Group Dynamics

Stage Two—Practice. This period could begin concurrently with Stage One or many weeks after the onset of Stage One. The variable would be the entering level of trainee sophistication in Stage One.

Purposes of Stage Two are two-fold:

- To increase the trainee's own sense of awareness.

- To teach him/her counseling skills.

Accordingly, at Stage Two experiences would include:

- Doing individual counseling under videotaping. If this is not possible, then by tape recorder. Recordings would be discussed with a mentor supervisor.

- Role-playing with the mentor supervisor. The trainee could alternate roles between the alcoholic client and the counselor.

- Working as a co-facilitator with a staff member experienced in group dynamics.

THE NEW COUNSELOR

Counseling is a very personal and private enterprise. To a very great extent it is a function of personality. How it is done finally is up to you, the particular therapist.

All foregoing research findings, explanations, and therapists are presented for your critical examination. What implications they have for you and your counseling is dependent upon you. Quite apparently, they can be accepted and injected into your developing counseling system or they can be reflected out of hand—your choice. The ultimate criterion for what you accept or reject has to be what fits and works for you. For in your counseling, **you are the ultimate technique.** This is a heavy responsibility because for your client, at least, you are the personification of the counseling process.

To live up to your client's expectations and more importantly, to your own, you will need to strive for excellence. Striving for excellence in counseling is a life-long process and it involves constant self-examination. If you are going to strive for excellence in your work, you will need to operate from a solid frame of reference so that you will be able to articulate, to yourself and, if need be, to others, your philosophy of counseling process.

The following list of questions are intended as guidelines to help you develop your own philosophy.

Guidelines for Developing a Personal Philosophy of Counseling

1. What is your definition of counseling?

2. What are the appropriate goals of therapy?

3. How would you define your own role as a helper?

4. What are the most important functions of a therapist?

5. What are the personal qualities that make for a competent therapist?

6. What makes for a therapist's excellence? What distinguishes a mediocre from an outstanding therapist?

7. What are the main values you live by? How did those values become yours? How might those central values influence you as a helping person?

8. What are some of your beliefs and attitudes about

   a. religion, politics, women's liberation;

   b. sex outside of marriage, abortion, marriage, alternative life-styles; and

   c. neglect of the aged, welfare, using drugs.

9. How can any or all the previous items in Number 8 help or hinder your work?

10. How would you define or describe "the good life?"

11. Why are you selecting work in one of the helping professions? What is in it for your personally? What needs of yours are being met by being a "helping person?"

12. How do you view your own level of functioning? What makes you think you can be of value in assisting others in resolving their struggles?

SUMMARY AND CONCLUSIONS

Counseling will proceed productively when the counselor is able to view each session as an opportunity to grow and to learn. The effective counselor is one who finds reward in serving another person.

Research indicates that therapists perceive their clients optimistically. Therapist expectations and values influence the outcomes of therapy.

Education, training, and theoretical orientations of a therapist seem to have little impact on therapist effectiveness. Personal and professional qualities, however, seem to be of critical importance. Chief among these are conscience from which are derived a sense of ethics, self-awareness, respect, maturity, and the ability to listen and communicate. Counselors find reward in giving probably because by giving to others they also help themselves.

The perception, personal, and professional qualities of five practicing therapists seem to gibe with the research findings. Thus, these therapists are perceived optimistically but realistically too. They seek to share the client's perception of the world so that he/she won't feel alone in the despair and threat which he/she perceives. Authenticity, acceptance, compassion, and nurturance are also the important qualities which these counselors incorporate into their personalities.

The most salient professional quality of the therapist is cognitive detachment. Only by remaining so will the therapist be able to maintain a healthy perspective of the counseling relationship. Should he/she lose this detachment and become overidentified with the client, the therapist will jeopardize his/her professional and personal integrity. The therapist also reflected a healthy penchant for introspection.

The paucity of research on the training of alcoholism counselors does not reflect what is really gong on. Most institutions treat training as an integral part of the total activity. Quite rightly, training is provided at all counselor levels and training seems to have a more positive effect on the treatment of the alcoholic than do the credentials of the therapist.

An effective training program is one which includes both theory and practice. The theory should include traditional clinical didactics and the practice should focus on developing the trainee's sense of awareness and provide him/her with the opportunity to develop basic counseling skills.

Counseling is a very personal and private enterprise. What new counselors finally accept for theory and technique will be determined by what fits and works for them. All developing counselors should operate from a frame of reference so that they can articulate especially to themselves their personal philosophy of counseling.

TOPICS FOR DISCUSSION AND REFLECTION

1. Describe and explain how you perceive an alcoholism client.

2. What image do you believe you project toward clients? Is the image you project determined by the sex of the client? If so, how?

3. What personal qualities do you possess which will enhance your work as a counselor? Which will limit or obviate the kind of success you seek?

4. Do ethical concerns play an important role in your day to day life? Will they be of practical importance in your work as a counselor?

5. Among the professional qualities described as desirable was that of cognitive detachment. Do you possess that? If not, do you seek to develop it? Why? Why not?

6. Are you a pensive, introspective type? Do you feel this quality is important in the counselor? Why? Why not?

7. Are there specific skills which you seek in a training program? If so, what are they?

8. Do you believe that a strong grounding in the theory of personality and counseling is important for a prospective counselor? If so, why? If not, why not?

9. Do you believe that you are the ultimate technique in your counseling? Is it healthy or unhealthy to take such a view?

10. What makes for therapist excellence? What contributes to therapist mediocrity?

CHAPTER SEVEN

THEORETICAL CONCERNS

As noted in Chapter 6, the effective counselor is the one who finds reward in serving another person. Unfortunately, this valuable quality is sometimes mitigated in the new counselor by a Florence Nightingale-like zeal and expectation that he/she will cure all clients.

The beginning counselor should know that experience will teach him/her very early, that no cure in alcoholism counseling exists; however, a recovery process does exist. This process can be both effective and productive if the client stops drinking. **The stopping is done by the client,** not the counselor. The counselor must bear in mind constantly that the choice to stop drinking is the client's. No amounts of badgering, condescension, haranguing, or pep talks by the counselor will accomplish that. Only the client can do that.

TREATABLE AND UNTREATABLE

As many reasons exist as to why alcoholics stop drinking as there are alcoholics. All these reasons have this common denominator. Namely, they are born out of sense of desperation.

Bottom

Among alcoholics a phenomena exists termed **high bottom, low bottom,** and even **middle bottom.** Alcoholics "bottom out" when they find a drink no longer provides any solutions for the desperation. At this junction most alcoholics perceive only two alternatives—death or treatment.

Each alcoholic arrives at his/her "bottom" differently and for different reasons. For example, the middle class housewife who is still very much intact materially feels she has lost love and respect of her children. She seeks help—a "high bottom."

Another example is a male executive who loses not only his children, but his spouse, his friends, and all his material possessions. One day he finds himself on skid-row or awakens in a state hospital "loaded up" on thorazine. He seeks help— a "low bottom."

While the level and nature of the "bottom" varies with the person, it always embraces the alcoholic's entire dynamic system. Perception, defenses, and values are always affected. Despite these variances from person to person, a common denominator prevails for all alcoholics in "the bottom"—it is the beginning of treatment.

Only when alcoholics experience their private "bottom" (and of course not all do) can they appreciate their own cry *"Help me!"* Only when an alcoholic says to the counselor "help me" and the counselor *believes him/her,* only then is the client ready to start the psychotherapeutic journey to sustained recovery.

Recognition needs to be made that some alcoholics are not good candidates for psychotherapy. These include

> the hard core sociopath who is incapable of trust,
>
> the person afflicted with Korsadoff's syndrome,
>
> the individual who is so deficient intellectually that he/she cannot retain cognitive or affective meaning from session to session,
>
> the psychotic who suffers from flattened effect, and so forth.

Such alcoholics are the exception. The author's conviction is that "bottomed out" alcoholics can profit and mightily, from emotional self-examination by way of psychotherapy. How effective this self-examination will be is a function of the counselor's technique and skill. To these concerns Part III of this book is addressed.

GOALS

Goals are a basic issue in counseling. Wolberg (1954) believed that they are critically important because the success or failure of the counseling can be assessed only in terms of the understood objectives. Patterson (1963) believed that the general goal of counseling is for the client to become "responsible, independent, and self-actualizing." Rogers (1961) believed that the prime purpose of counseling is to help clients become "more similar to the idea which he/she has chosen." Goals which Kanner (1963) deemed appropriate for children apply to adults too. The goal of counseling he believed is to "relieve, relate, release, relearn, and relax." On reflection they seem especially apt for the alcoholic.

Primary Goal

The primary goal in counseling alcoholics is achievement of a continued sobriety. In addition to the primary goal are secondary goals that are important because they facilitate the process toward the primary one and equally important, help the alcoholic adhere to the primary goal.

Secondary Goals

1. To help clients learn as much as possible about their alcoholism. For motivated clients this is achieved fairly easily because the objective is primarily cognitive in nature. Regular attendance at A.A. meetings is basic of course. Reading, discussion with the counselor and others, lectures and seminars also are helpful.

2. To help clients restructure their perception both of selves and of environment. The focus of this effort would be to help alcoholics see that their sense of victimization is of their own thinking and doing. The author has found that many of his clients are surprised to learn that the feeling of being a victim is virtually universal among other alcoholics.

3. To help clients structure their life so they may learn to find reward in sharing and giving. In his own counseling the author has usually found this goal the first one achieved. For whatever reasons, alcoholics almost instinctively seem to find their future health and well-being lies in giving to others by sharing their own experience. Much complementary support to achieve this goal comes from Alcoholics Anonymous. This idea is the premise upon which A.A. is structured.

4. To help clients gain insight into those defenses which keep them persevering in their "stinkin thinkin." Most often these include denial, rationalization, projection, and intellectualization.

5. To help to evaluate their self-esteem by helping them to see that failure is part of the human experience. Just as important here is to help clients structure their lives for experiences, vocational, interpersonal where there is a high probability of success. The cornerstone of the client's self-esteem is continued sobriety and the counselor should bear in mind that the alcoholic client constantly is beset by the anxiety of a relapse.

Periodic Reevaluation of Sobriety

The best way to deal with this anxiety is to help the client discuss feelings and symptoms indicative of the alcoholic's latent but constant emotional nemesis, the phenomenon termed BUD, **B**uilding **U**p to **D**rink. These discussions must be interspersed and concurrent with the pursuit of secondary goals if the primary goal is to be achieved and maintained. The symptoms of BUD often come in combination and are as follow:

- Periods of silence in the usually talkative and cheerful client,

- Machine-gun like monologues by the client who usually speaks deliberately, slowly quietly,

- Uncharacteristic irritability and/or hypomanic-like movements and activity,

- Unexplainable, acute fatigue,

- Listless, apathetic behavior in the usually active person,

- Focus and perseverance on depressed talk, and

- Euphoric-like over confidence in the client's talk about he/she adhering to his/her sobriety.

If the client is unwilling to admit or to discuss these symptoms when the counselor sees him/her, the client invariably lapses into drink. What this counselor has observed is that symptoms usually become even stronger after the alcoholic begins drinking. In most cases, however, the lapse can be obviated if the client is helped to discuss symptoms, both those apparent to the counselor and those felt by the client.

The reader might want to complement his/her reading of this section with a rereading of the section entitled ALCOHOLISM—THE RELAPSE which is in Part II of this book.

Two Illustrations of Goal Setting

The following two illustrations exemplify two approaches to counseling the alcoholic. The first is termed *directivist* and the second, *nondirectivist.* Both counselors are vitally concerned with the client's achievement of sobriety and both leave the responsibility of attaining it to the client but there the similarity ends.

The directivist is assertive, confrontative, at times harsh, and quickly responsive to the client's rationalizations and denials. At times he/she seems even harsher in his/her attack upon those defenses.

The nondirectivist is reserved. He/she does not give advice, believes rather the client should decide upon his/her own way. The counselor approach is to help the client come to his/her own realizations about the nature of his/her distorted perception and the futility of his/her "stinkin thinkin." The counselor focus is on developing a healthful positive relationship. Subsequent illustrations will include both approaches. The reader will decide for himself/herself which approach is more effective and may decide to incorporate aspects of each into his/her own counseling.

Counselor as Directivist.

CO = Counselor   CL = Client

CO: *Ah, John good to see you come in, come in and sit.*

CL: *Thanks, I'm sorry I'm late.*

CO: *You were the first time we met too, You're nervous about seeing me?*

CL: *Maybe a little.*

CO: *Yeah, I appreciate that, but being late doesn't make me go away. You still want to see me, right?*

CL: *I guess.*

CO: (Chuckles) *Not sure, eh?*

CL: *I want to see you.*

CO: *I know I'm not exactly loveable. I'm abrasive even. But I'm here John—all the time—and my job is just one, to help you stay sober. You want to stay sober?*

CL: *I wouldn't be here if I didn't.*

CO: (Nods). *Saying it's good. Important even. But if you were on time, maybe even a little early even that would show me you really mean it.*

CL: *I got held up at breakfast.*

CO: *That's cause you were late there. You were coming in when I was going out. John, let's not bluff each other. Like I said yesterday, all the cards are on the table. Otherwise my friend all we're going to do is shovel seaweed against the tide. I don't like to shovel. I got a bad back. Did you go to A.A. last night?*

CL: *Yeah.*

CO: *How much did you read of the book I gave you?*

CL: *About a hundred pages.*

CO: (Smiles) *That's good, man.* (The counselor asks him questions about the reading.)

CL: *How come all these questions. Don't you trust me?*

CO: *I don't know yet. Once you start opening up I'll know better how much I can trust you. Actually it doesn't matter if I trust you or not. What matters is that you trust yourself to do all the things you have to do to stay sober, A.A., the readings, opening up to me, and working on the weekends like you're supposed to.* (Counselor chuckles.) *Yeah, and it would help if you trusted me.*

CL: *Why are you badgering me?*

CO: *I prefer to call it bird-dogging. I'm gonna bird-dog you 'till you don't need me.*

CL: *I don't know how that's gonna help me. That's been my problem all my life, my boss, my wife, everybody badgers me—in fact everybody shits on me.*

CO: *If they shit on you it's cause you let them. People treat you the way you let them. It's up to you how they treat you.*

What we saw in this brief excerpt is a hard-nosed counselor who makes it clear to the client what his goal responsibilities are and will be with respect to meeting time, A.A. attendance, reading, and self-disclosure.

Counselor as Nondirectivist.

CO: Ah, Tom good to see you.

CL: Sorry I'm late.

CO: Only a few minutes. It happens. These first few sessions make most new people a little anxious.

CL: (Nods.) I know.

CO: So what do you want to talk . . .

CL: I went to the meeting. I really enjoyed it. Listening to that speaker made me realize a lot.

CO: Tell me.

CL: Well for one thing. I've really been a bastard to a lot of people for a long time.

CO: Haven't we all?

CL: What do you mean?

CO: Just that all of us from time to time are selfish, petty, we lie, cheat. Those sins aren't peculiar to you.

CL: No?

CO: No. What matters is where we go from here. The past, Tom, is a canceled check. What matters is the future.

CL: I don't see too much of a future; I don't even have a job anymore.

CO: *You'll get one.*

CL: *I know, but will I be able to keep it?*

CO: *I honestly don't know that. Only you do. Only you can determine that.*

CL: *That scares me. I just don't have any faith in myself for anything, leave alone getting and keeping a job. I mean what am I going to tell them when I apply, that I'm a drunk?*

CO: *You don't want to tell them you're a drunk?*

CL: *Christ no!*

CO: *Hmmm.*

CL: (Laughs.) *But I have to, huh?*

CO: *Your decision.*

CL: *How do you tell somebody you're a drunk?*

CO: *Didn't the speaker do just that last night?*

CL: *Yeah, but that was A.A.*

CO: *In front of what, forty, fifty people?*

CL: *Yeah, I get your drift. If he can do it with so many, why can't I with one?*

CO: *You already have. You told me.*

CL: *You knew about me.*

CO: *But this is the first time you actually said it.*

CL: *This is different, you're supposed to understand. It's your job. Besides, you're an alcoholic yourself. How does it make you feel to tell people?*

CO: (Laughs.) *Honest. It makes me feel honest.*

CL: *I never feel like that.*

CO: *Well?*

CL: *I should try it, huh?*

CO: *Your choice.*

CL: *Don't you ever give advice?*

CO: (Shakes his head.) *Not usually. Life's hard enough without living it according to somebody else's opinion.*

This counselor while he alludes to goals, gives minimal direction, preferring to let the client carry the counseling ball. His focus, if you examine the excerpt, is the relationship and letting the client choose his own way.

RAPPORT

Definition, Research, and Discussion

As in the French language from which rapport is borrowed, it, in general, has to do with accord and affinity in a relationship. In counseling, rapport means that warmth and trust exists between the counseling participants, an emotional give and take, critical to counseling. Two researchers found that its establishment inevitably facilitates the resolution of interpersonal problems. At least one study concluded that if rapport cannot be established, then the client should be referred (Cheng & Hsin, 1973; Katsuhiko, 1969).

Qualities which make for an effective therapist, explained in Part II of this book, facilitate the establishment of rapport. Briefly, those included an optimistic perception, authenticity, acceptance, nurturance, and compassion. Axelson (1967) found that the counselor quality which establishes rapport most quickly and effectively is an **empathic disposition.** Although the word empathy has been used in other contexts a number of times, perhaps taking a closer look at it might be profitable because of its close relationship to rapport. Empathy is derived from the German Einfuhlung which means "feeling into." One of the more complete explanations of the meaning of empathy in counseling was given by Arnold Bucheimer (1961) in an address to the American Personnel and Guidance Association (named changed July, 1992 to American Counseling Association). In this he described five aspects of empathy.

1. **Tone,** which has to do with harmony and mutuality with which the counselor and client interact;

2. **Pace,** which has to do with the timing with which the counselor leads the client;

3. **Flexibility,** which has to do with the counselor's ability to adapt to new climatic moments and ignore and discard previously thought out procedures;

4. **Frame of reference,** which has to do with becoming attuned to and gaining an understanding from where the client is coming and then rephrasing, reflecting, and getting at the essence of what the client is communicating; and

5. **Repertoire of leads,** which has to do with the counselor's ability to respond to both verbal and nonverbal contexts of the client's consent.

One can rightly conclude then from Bucheimer's (1961) thoughts that the counselor's ability to establish rapport is closely allied with his/her ability to empathize effectively.

When the client comes for the initial contact, the emotional climate may be strained. This strain is understandable. The client is meeting a stranger with whom he/she is obligated to share thoughts and feeling which until that moment have been viewed as supremely private. Add to that all the characteristics associated with the alcoholic personality as outlined in Part I of this book, it becomes transparently clear why the initial moments may be strained. Then the counselor has the obligation to relax and relive the initial strained moments. Some counselors believe that the best approach is to open with a neutral topic like the weather. Others believe the neutral topic approach is a waste. Counseling finally is not a social chit-chat. Moreover, chit-chat sometimes leads to even more tension if the counselor has not developed a more communicative approach. In his/her opening remarks the counselor should focus on why the client is in his/her office. After the initial greetings and amenities the counselor may make these kinds of comments, *"I'm glad you're here, tell me how I can help." "I'm your counselor. This is your hour." "The fact that you're here tells me that you want to start back to something better."*

More often than not the counselor has access to client records regarding background and family. These data should be examined before the first session so that the counselor can ask open-minded questions. Questions about work usually are appropriate, i.e., *"I understand you're a cop. Tell me what it is like." "I understand you were just promoted to foreman. How is it different from being on the line? "You're a teacher, I understand. What is it like?"* When delivered with a casual appropriate tone, comments and questions such as these facilitate communication. They are meaningful questions to the client because they are about him/her and unlike social chit-chat they are forthright because they focus on the reality of the client's presence.

At the same time, recognize clearly that rapport is more than just relaxing a client and getting underway. It transcends the whole process of counseling. It is constant. It continues from initial contact to termination and is characterized by cordiality, confidence, and cooperation. The working relationship between counselor and client is and needs to be unique, far different from most other relationships that the client has.

The author asked a directivist and a nondirectivist to express their views on the subject of rapport. Both responses were tape-recorded.

Directivist View of Rapport

Edwin—Male, Forty-One Years Old,
Eleven Years an Alcoholic Counselor,
Ed.M. in Counseling, and a Recovering Alcoholic

What can I tell ya? I think rapport is important. Course it's important. Who would say otherwise? But to be honest with ya, I don't myself focus on it. I focus on the purpose, the goal— sobriety. Rapport has to do with being liked. To be frank with you, I don't care whether my patients like me or not. I'm not running a beauty contest. There's one issue and one issue only— the patient's sobriety.

When a patient comes in to me that first day I tell him/her plain and simple, **"I'm not your nurse maid, I'm not even your friend. I don't know you yet. I am your counselor. I'll help by listening and if asked, I'll answer straight forward. I expect the same."** *I don't like patients who make like they're Spanish athletes, ya know, throw the bull. Only one way a patient can make progress and that's if he/she is completely honest, right to where it hurts him/her and hurts badly. Before my patient can do that I gotta' do the same thing. So I do it. I tell him and if it's a her I tell her too, about me and my booze. By the time I'm through, takes about three sessions, I usually have my rapport. At least they know me. And that's where it's at in this game. If you want rapport, patients have gotta feel they know you, before they can trust you. And in this business trust is where it's all at. Once patients trust you, they will let you take the first step with them down that awful long road back to life.*

Nondirectivist Views of Rapport

Loretta—Female, Thirty-two Years Old,
Six Years a Counselor, the Last Three with Alcoholics,
M.A. in Clinical Psychology

Rapport is critical. It is the foundation of the whole process. Without it, you have no counseling, you can't because you have no trust. Prior to my coming here I worked with mentally handicapped, retarded children. Rapport was so easy there. They loved me immediately. It's very difficult here. The nature of the problem makes it so. Alcoholics are paranoid to begin with. Their defenses revolve around projection. I've noticed that it's especially bad when they're coming off the booze. Somebody really should do a study to see what the relationship is between guilt and projection. That's what I find in my first contact— guilt and projection. I suspect that's why I find obtaining rapport difficult. It takes me several sessions to begin to feel we have it. I could do like most of my colleagues and confront, confront, confront, but I won't. My training and convictions are that all clients, even alcoholics, have the capacity to help and heal themselves to the extent they can and to which they want. Confrontation does not hurry that process I don't think. Anyway, my way toward rapport and toward help of the alcoholic might be a little slower but I think it's sounder.

Obstacles to Establishment of Rapport

Some obstacles effectively can block the establishment of rapport. These include

- a lack in counselor's ego strength,

- unmotivated client,

- client's negative perception of counselor, and

- personality clash.

Counselor's Ego Strength. Deficiencies in the counselor's ego can interfere with the establishment of rapport. In counseling he/she does need to have an ego that is strong—strong enough to focus, attend, and adhere to the client. The counselor should be disciplined enough to prevent and block irrelevant and distracting thoughts from interfering with the ability to meet needs of clients. In short, when doing therapy, the counselor should be able to keep personal life compartmentalized, and the healthful ego should be in total control of his/her personality.

Unmotivated Client. Sometimes the counselor finds himself/ herself with a client who genuinely is not motivated, a client who has not "bottomed out," but who is at best conflicted in his/her self-referral, or worse who has been mandated into the therapy, a not uncommon phenomenon, especially with recent drinking and driving legislation.

To establish a meaningful productive rapport under a mandated referral is especially difficult, if not impossible. The length of time for counseling usually is fixed and the client, of course, knows it. More often than not, such clients present themselves as victims. Not uncommonly, they are resentful, hostile, and sometimes do not even try to hide their boredom. At best, such clients attempt to manipulate the counselor by putting on a deferential, even submissive manner so that they can fulfill their obligations, "serve their time," and get the note for the judge which will let them drive—and drink again. Counseling under these conditions is an exercise in futility.

Client's Negative Perception of Counselor. Rapport establishment is often difficult when the client perceives the counselor negatively. This negative perception usually has nothing to do with the counselor's competencies or credentials but has to do with the needs and perception of the client. For example, the counselor may be years, decades, even a generation younger than the client. Under such circumstances the client's view might be "What can a counselor who's young enough to be my son/daughter do for me?" Or again the client may be well aware of the fact that some available counselors are themselves recovering alcoholics. Such clients are convinced that their nonalcoholic counselor can't help them. The competent, knowledgeable counselor must learn to take situations in stride. Even so, the recommendation is that the counselor should hold several sessions with the client, if possible, and assess the situation. If in good conscience he/she feels that meaningful rapport has not been established, then the client should be referred to another counselor.

Personality Clash. Sometimes rapport cannot be established because of a personality clash. For the counselor this should be a very rare occurrence indeed. The truth is however that counselors also have their own idiosyncratic dynamics. As a result, each counselor will find he/she has difficulty in working with some clients for whatever reasons. Even so, the counselor should be perceptive and honest enough to know the potential for an ineffective relationship by the end of the first session—certainly by the second. Then, after discussing the problems honestly and kindly, the client should be referred. To delay referral will result in communication of a personal rejection later—something no alcoholic needs. Just as bad, it may result in little or no progress in the counseling.

SETTING

Counseling Room

The conclusion can be drawn from research that physical setting influences how people perceive each other. In a study by Maslow and Mintz (1956) and another by Mintz (1956), people perceived more optimistically when the room in which they were situated was more attractive. Conversely they perceived more pessimistically when the room was shabby. On the basis of these studies, time, energy, and money should be invested in making the counseling room attractive and comfortable. Pictures and draperies should be hung, rugs laid, and flowers or plants added. The validity of such efforts is reflected in a study by Chaikin et al. (1976) who found that the more positively a client perceives the room, the positively he/she will relate to the counselor. In short, a room decorated with care can only enhance the counseling process.

Haase and Dimattia (1970) did a study to determine what kind of seating arrangement counselors and clients preferred most. The arrangement they found to be the most popular was the one which is used most, the client sitting at the side of the desk. Widgery and Stackpole (1972) found that the position of the desk influences the counselor's credibility. Those clients who were binding much anxiety rated counselor credibility higher when no desk was present. Those with low anxiety rated it higher when a desk was present.

Space

The effect of space upon the counseling process has been investigated. Haase and Dimattia (1976) have found smaller rooms tend to inhibit the length and duration of self-reference talk. In another study Haase (1970) found that which sex a client is does not influence the distance preferred between counseling participants. Both males and females indicated that between 30 and 39 inches was about right. Research in social and familial settings indicates that this is the distance preferred by spouses and by intimate friends. Interestingly, clients feel that the same kind of distance is best for counseling.

COMMUNICATION

In a previous work Perez (1979) the author explored a system of communication which he termed **Avenues of Communication.** What the author has learned in the intervening years is that his approach to an understanding of communication is especially apt for describing interaction among alcoholics in general and especially in the alcoholic family. The system, revised and modified in light of his experience with them, is presented here.

The avenues of communication common to many are

1. condemnation,

2. submission,

3. indifference, and

4. congruence.

Condemnation

Condemnation is characterized by an interpersonal stance that is generally demeaning. Nagging, hypercriticism, and belittling are common aspects of it. It is the way of the individual who feels threatened, of the individual who perceives a hostile, threatening world. It is the way of the person who seeks to distance from others. It is the way of the individual termed a loser. It is a fairly common way for the alcoholic.

People familiar with this avenue have self-esteem problems. Their emotional rationale seems to be that one's bigness is a function of the other person's smallness. Their interpersonal demeaning style becomes constant and inured, a veritable core aspect of their personality.

Alcoholics who follow this road are usually dictatorial. People, problems, and situations are perceived in black and white. They are quite unable to tolerate grays. Even though they have a strong penchant for argument they will themselves brook none from others.

Such behavior can be understood as defensive, a reaction formation to a loss of control. Among the harsh realities of addiction to alcoholics the harshest has to be the loss of control over their lives. By travelling this avenue of condemnation and engaging in its ancillary behaviors they are able to feel that they are in control of others, of their environment, and of themselves.

Submission

The personality trait most salient among people who relate submissively is guilt. Alcoholics are usually laden with it and so are enablers. More usually still, people so laden have an acutely low self-esteem just like the condemner types. The reason submissive types communicate in a diametrically opposite way is that they are beset by an insatiable, all-consuming need to be liked. So insatiable is this need that they have surrendered to their environment. More often what they believe, indeed their very convictions, are fleeting and transitory—a function of whom they are talking to at the moment. For them being liked is the issue, not convictions. The effect of such an interpersonal stance only reinforces and confirms low self-esteem.

Manifestly, "nice guys and gals" submissives seem also to be givers and enhancers. When asked to give of time or money they cheerfully give far, far more than asked of both.

The inevitable effect of such giving is that it alienates people because it makes them feel obligated. The resultant wrong is, that the submissives all consuming basic motive is totally confounded. People don't like them. People stay away. More ironically still, such behavior by others only fuels the submissive alcoholic's and/or enabler's perception that people do not like them!

The final wrong and the saddest has to be that people inclined toward submissiveness frequently find and marry condemner types. The why of this might be that one or both perceive what the other is like or can be and want the relationship. It might be simply that they meet each other's perverted needs at the outset or again, that they cultivate and unconsciously nurture each other's potential disposition. Whatever the reason, condemners and submissives do seem to find each other and in the alcoholic milieu the problems of each are only exacerbated.

Indifference

Among the avenues this is one to which alcoholics gravitate and adhere. Aloneness and emotional distancing fit with their need. Among the avenue of communication it is the most unhealthy because it communicates total unconcern, if not meanness. Unfortunately it is used most often with those to whom alcoholics are closest, i.e., family or persons with whom they work because it is most effective with them.

Indifference can never enhance but only demean. It is precipitated by hostility, fear, and the abiding alcoholic's need to manipulate.

Indifference can be communicated in different ways. One is **silence,** another might be termed **quasi-indifference,** and a third way is by **avoiding behaviors.**

Quite apparently, one can communicate anger or any other negative emotion by simply not talking—**silence.** The anger can be communicated even more apparently if at the same time the nontalker slams drawers, cabinets, and glares. Such behavior can be long or short lived, its duration being dependent upon the intensity of the hostility or the reason for manipulation. Sometimes alcoholics and/or enablers especially are silent because they just don't want an emotional scene. Not infrequently it's because of embarrassment precipitated by guilt. Probably the most common reason among alcoholics is the most obvious, the simplest— they don't care.

Quasi-indifference refers to a method fairly common in alcoholic homes. For example, the alcoholic who has not uttered fifty words over the course of a week dutifully brings home his paycheck, leaves it on his wife's pocketbook, and goes another week not uttering fifty words.

Avoiding behaviors involve talking in flat monotones, without effect and without looking at one another. If forced into interaction, for example at a meal, the topics are always safe ones, i.e., the weather, current foreign news events. Everyone scrupulously avoids being together for no reason. If three rooms are in the apartment, each of its three inhabitants manages to stay most of the time alone in one of them.

Congruence

This is the healthy avenue of communication. The object of counseling, be it individual or group, is to hope the client learns to travel this avenue of communication.

One communicates with congruence when words, emotions, and behaviors all meld. One communicates with congruence when soft words ride on soft tones and facial and body expression fit with both. Similarly at those rare times when anger is in order, angry words are expressed in tones and with a face and body stance which match.

People who communicate by this avenue say and emote what they mean and do so comfortably. While they are able to express what they feel and usually when they feel so, they are able to do so tactfully. Tact, they have learned, is a function of the tolerance derived from their healthful levels of security, acceptance, and self-esteem.

Via Body and Emotions

DeRivera (1977) is one who believed that emotions and body are very much woven together. His work has led him to conclude that emotions ". . . both influence the body and reflect the condition of the body." This view is comparable to one expressed earlier by the noted psychiatrist Thomas Szasz (1961) when he wrote that most of our bodily symptoms are no more than "cries for help." The alcoholic, who when sober, is too often perspiring profusely, who is constantly complaining of headaches and a variety of ailments may be saying only, *"Help me, I'm in trouble." "I want to talk about me."* Unfortunately, what he/she wants to talk about are physical ailments. Note that these ailments can indeed be a starting point for what should be the focus—the emotional dysfunctions which have precipitated the client's addiction.

Communication occurs in a variety of ways, with words, with tones, with behaviors. When these are congruent, the message is simple, clear, and direct. Communication becomes garbled, however, when words, tones, and emotions do not gibe and they do not often with many alcoholic clients. *"Damn it, I'm not mad,"* spits out the client; or again, *"No I wasn't hurt, at least not that much, when he called me a drunken slob,"* she says wiping her eyes.

Levels of Communication

Human communication is too often complicated. Communication becomes especially intriguing when it occurs on different levels, the unconscious as well as the conscious. Freud (1959) was the first to point out this phenomenon. He explained in a convincing way that at times people let their ego relax, give vent to id strivings, and by the verbal slip, memory loss, or behavior let their true feelings come forth. Such emissions are unconscious but should be taken seriously as they have the greatest meaning. Thus he wrote, "the slip itself makes sense" and should be viewed "as a valid mental process following out its own purpose."

Resorting to unconscious messages is of course a sad commentary upon human interaction. That they do so, however, reflects the frustration, intense need, and determination which all people have to reach out, express themselves—in a word communicate. Nowhere is this seen better than in the alcoholic. Most alcoholics feel that their messages are not received, that no one is listening, that no one even cares to listen— ergo alcoholism. Their alcoholism can quite rightly be understood as a message—a message that they have given up and surrendered to a cruel environment.

Via Double Messages

The confusion and fear which alcoholics experience in trying to communicate are due in no small part to the lack of learning and mislearning they underwent during the critical childhood years. Many of them never learned how to communicate in a congruent fashion (words, tones, behavior gibed) because they weren't exposed to such communications in their families. They were exposed rather to double messages, i.e., *"Of course I love you darling and you know how much I do too. But I'm really, really sorry I just can't come to the play this morning. It's that awful migraine again. I'll make it next time. Promise. Come, give mother a big kiss. Hurry now, or you'll be late for school."* Messages such as these have a devastating effect upon a child. They split him/her in two emotionally. Which message does the child accept? Desperately he/she wants to believe and accept the words of love punctuated with a kiss. Yet there's the other message, too—a message of rejection brutally exemplified in an absent mother with the perennial migraine. The conflict for the child necessarily becomes more acute, especially when the child begins to learn that gin is simply not an appropriate medicine for migraine. The conflict and confusion inevitably result in a latent, constant depression when the child begins to feel (children simply don't intellectualize) that mother loves booze more than him/her. In any case the home where a pattern of double messages is the communicative style is a home that breeds confused and too often uncommunicative people.

Via Body Language

The body is a prime vehicle for communication. How a client takes care of it, spaces it, and uses it tells the counselor much about the client.

The client who comes in looking impeccably well groomed simply does not have the same self-view of the world as one who comes in smelling and looking like he/she needs a bath. Quite apparently the former communicates a strong concern for self, perhaps for counseling. Conversely the latter person is on the skids and doesn't care. Self-care is a reflection of self-love and self-esteem and is demonstrated physically in one's appearance.

This author has found it useful to have at least a couple of alternative chairs available for the client. Where the client sits in relation to the counselor also reflects something about his/her interest and motivation to communicate. Accordingly, this counselor makes it a point to sit in his chair first and lets the client choose his/her seat, one being farther away from the counselor (about five feet) and the other (about three feet). The distance a client sits from the counselor affects process as has been supported in research data. Knight and Blair (1976) for example, found that the distance between counselor and client affects client comfort. Stone and Morden (1976) found that when clients sat too close or too far from the counselor, they were more inhibited about their self-disclosures than if they sat at an intermediate distance.

The language of the body motion has been the topic for research and discussion now for almost three decades (Ekman & Friesen, 1969; Kendon, 1972), and quite rightly so. On the whole, a relaxed person sits casually. In the protected, emotionally charged climate of counseling, most clients display their feelings by their bodies, on their faces usually, or with a leg that swings, a hand that drums, or a general shifting and reshifting of their bodies. Even the immobile, stone-faced clients are telling the counselor something—they are hidebound by their denial and/or intellectualization defenses. In sum, the perceptive counselor is one who is sensitive to the body movements of his/her clients. If appropriate, the counselor will react and deal with them.

Via Defenses

The clinical roots of communication are found in psychological defense. Another way to understand the communication system of the alcoholic, then, is to approach it through his/her defense system. The most salient defense in the alcoholic's repertoire is denial. Rationalization, intellectualization, and projection are used too, usually to support denial.

Denial. The refusal to acknowledge one's behavior and the effects of it upon oneself and others invariably engenders guilt. Not uncommonly the guilt effects changes in the alcoholic's personality, i.e., submissiveness or passivity; or again the guilt may precipitate behaviors at the other end of the behavioral continuum—fits of anger or temper tantrums. One of the more insidious aspects of denial is that too often it seems to infect others close to the alcoholic. They too begin to deny. They joke about the alcoholic's drinking, tolerate it, even protect him/her in it. Not uncommonly, after a time they begin to see the drunkenness as part of the general personality. Communication, if at all, focuses on irrelevancies. Any occasional attempt by a friend or family member to confront or even broach the subject of drink seems futile. Compounding the problem further is the fact that often the alcoholic becomes positively creative in thwarting such attempts. This response to what is perceived as an attack upon his/her denial may be a humorous quip, indifference, anger, or worst of all, a stony silence.

Rationalization. Communication with rationalizers is almost impossible. They neatly justify what they do, even what they themselves think. Rationalization is an important prop for denial. Alcoholic rationalizations are all too familiar. "I only drink beer, never the hard stuff." "I never drink before noontime," or again, "Only on weekends," "I just don't drink that much, a pint of gin a day just isn't that much, besides I haven't missed a day's work in almost two months."

Intellectualization. Often a prop for the alcoholic's denial is intellectualization. With the highly intelligent person, intellectualization is especially difficult to break down. The reason for this difficulty is that the intellectualizer talks and seems to function as if he/she has no emotions. He/she behaves as if joy, rage, and despair are not part of his/her ken. This lack of emotion combined with a refined ability to think, reflect, and analyze makes any meaningful communication difficult.

The best way to deal with intellectualizing alcoholics is precisely not to intellectualize, not to duel with them intellectually, with logic, or with analyses. The weak link in their armor is emotion. They refuse to acknowledge their own emotion, and are more often than not befuddled if not terrified by the emotion exhibited by others. Thus, they belittle emotion, scorn it, or react indifferently to it, because they do not know how to deal with it. Accordingly, the counselor's responses should be inflected with feeling tones and all comments and questions should focus on the client's emotions. The following illustrations might prove helpful.

Counselor as Directivist—
Illustrative Excerpt of Intellectualization

CO: *Now let me get this straight. You mean to tell me that your wife had half of your pay legally attached and deposited in her account? She actually did that?*

CL: *Yeah, she did that.*

CO: *Wow!*

CL: *Actually, I can understand her doing that.*

CO: *Okay, you can understand it, but explain to me how did it make you feel? I mean in your gut? How did it make you feel?*

CL: *Well, to be honest, I'm not sure. What was important was what to do. I thought about it and went to my lawyer.*

CO: *John, weren't you angry, upset?*

Counselor as Nondirectivist—
Illustrative Excerpt on Intellectualization

CO: *Your wife had your pay attached.*

CL: *Yes.*

CO: *How did that make you feel?*

CL: (Shrugs.) *I'm not really sure. I did check with my lawyer. It was legally appropriate.*

CO: *Did the legality assuage any possible feelings of anger you might have had?*

CL: (Pause.) *To be honest about it, I'm not sure.*

CO: *You said your drinking increased dramatically after the attachment.*

CL: *That's true.*

CO: *And what might that tell you, John?*

Both counselors are following their convictions about the approach. The directivist is himself more emotional. The nondirectivist, it should be noted, gets into a little dueling with his client, manipulating him, almost trapping him into admitting he had to feel anger at the attachment. Both counselors however focus on the real issue, the intellectualizer's apparent alienation from his feelings about the matter.

Projection. Communication with alcoholics who project stretches a counselor's patience to the limit. The essence of the problem is that projectors perceive people as being basically hostile or selfish or unconcerned with them. People don't like them. (These feelings, of course, are ones which they harbor about themselves.) In any case what projecting alcoholics do is test people. They make demand upon demand until people react negatively thereby confirming the alcoholic's basic perception that people don't like alcoholics.

In counseling, problems are considerable. As has been observed, the essential ingredient for counseling to proceed is rapport founded on trust. The projector finds this intolerably difficult. Testing of the counselor may take a variety of forms, i.e., late appointment, self-disclosing little bombshells a few moments before the end of the hour to extend it, cynical comments about counseling, and so forth. The most effective way with this client is firmness and adherence to agreed upon ground rules. For example, if the client comes late, he/she gets only the balance of the scheduled hour, cynical comments are ignored. The counselor cannot permit manipulation by this type of client for a moment. Rapport will not be obtained that way for the obvious reason that trust cannot be obtained in a relationship where there is manipulation.

TRANSFERENCE

Definition

Transference is the process of redirecting feelings and desires, especially those unconsciously retained from childhood, toward the therapist. Briefly, the transference occurs because of two dynamic phenomena—repression and identification. The client who was exposed to parental rejection in childhood and/or was not permitted to express his/her true feelings toward parents represses these feelings. These repressions stultify emotional development and invariably result in problems in sexual identification.

In the emotionally sheltered climate of counseling, the client who develops rapport with the counselor identifies with him/her and inevitably goes into transference; that is, the client attaches feelings repressed in childhood toward the rejecting parent(s). The parent figure(s) and the therapist unconsciously blend for him/her, and they may do so even if the rejecting parent figure and the therapist are of different sexes.

The transference can be positive or it can be negative. Whichever, it is dependent upon the nature of childhood repression. Thus if in childhood the client was too terrified to express dissatisfaction or hostility, then in the transference (negative) the client will vent these feelings upon the therapist. If as a child the client was not able to attach feelings of love, then the transference is characterized by these kinds of feelings for the therapist.

By working through the transference with the counselor, the client gains insight into the cause of the problem. The alcoholic gains insight into what his/her true feelings about himself/herself and others, the counselor included.

The reader should know that transference is a phenomenon dealt with by the psychoanalyst. Many, perhaps most counselors, do not deal with it as the lead-in to insight but treat it lightly, if at all. Three of the most renown among these are Carl Rogers—the exponent of client-centered therapy, Albert Ellis—the exponent of rational emotive therapy, and Joseph Wolpe—the advocate of conditioning therapy.

This author, who is not a psychoanalyst, tends to agree with Thorne (1950) (who is not an analyst either) that ". . . it is necessary for the counselor to understand its nature since it may be anticipated that such relationships tend to develop automatically if the counseling process reaches deep emotional levels of personality." Wolberg (1954) a renowned analyst, feels that transference is inevitable. "Sooner or later a patient will 'transfer' past attitudes and feelings into the present relationship."

Manifestations

Whatever one's position may be on the issue of transference, the author believes that the counselor who is oblivious of its nature will be at a disadvantage in dealing with his/her client. To obviate this disadvantage, some manifestations of transference are outlined.

Positive Transference

1. The positive attitudes expressed by the client increase, i.e., "I like you. I feel you really understand me," and so forth.

2. The client begins to ask questions about the counselor's personal life. "Are you married? Are you from around here?" and so forth.

3. The client begins to sit closer.

4. The client may seek to touch the counselor.

5. The client who initially arrived a little late for appointments begins to show up promptly, even early.

Negative Transference

1. The client begins to express negative attitudes, if not about the counselor then about the counseling, i.e., "I think this is really a lot of crap. I'm not sure you're helping me. Did you really have to go to school for this?"

2. The client begins to sit farther away.

3. The client, initially talkative, may fall into protracted periods of silence.

4. The client begins to arrive late, may even begin to cancel appointments.

Treatment

The alcoholism counselor has a variety of options.

1. The counselor may, as many do, simply ignore the dynamics of the transference and focus on the alcoholic's behaviors.

2. The counselor may focus on those aspects of the transference which seem especially pertinent to the client's life now or which threaten to thwart progress already made. Fore example, if the client is of the opposite sex and feels he/she is in love with the counselor, the counselor may feel that an explanation of the dynamics might be in order. This author feels

that such an explanation would be prudent. Without such an explanation a client could interpret the counselor's responses as being cool, uninterested, and essentially rejecting. Interpretations such as these would probably terminate the counseling at a critical juncture.

3. The counselor could pursue an analytic approach seeking to work through the transference by probing with questions focusing on the client's childhood.

COUNTERTRANSFERENCE

Definition

A countertransference occurs when the counselor attaches repressed feelings to the client. (See discussion under Professional Qualities, Chapter 6.) However, it should be pointed out that the counselor can effectively prevent a full blown countertransference if he/she is acutely sensitive to all of its symptoms.

Symptoms of Positive Countertransference

The obvious positive symptoms of countertransference may include one or more of the following. The counselor

- is attracted sexually to the physical aspects of the client;

- is obsessed in off-hours about the client;

- looks forward to sessions with the client;

- spends more time in physical grooming for the sessions than typical;

- probes, during sessions, into aspects of the client's life and habits which are at best only tangentially related to the alcoholism problem; and

- does for the client what he/she ordinarily does not do with others, i.e., helps the client on and off with coat, offers coffee, brings doughnuts, and so forth.

The symptoms of a positive countertransference are transparent. The reader should know that too often they are not so to the counselor who is suffering it. The ethical, competent counselor suffers it indeed. A few years ago this author received a call late on a Friday night from a colleague, a 37 year old single woman with a flawless reputation for both competence and ethics, who counsels in a local clinic. She was very distraught and wanted to talk. She came to this author's home and told him how she had agreed to a date for the next night with a 45 year old divorced client, who was in her professional judgment a recovered alcoholic. She had had five sessions with him once a week for the past five weeks. The woman, who dated seldom and who could fairly be described as "average looking," when queried about the client described him as a handsome and once successful lawyer who was practicing again. When asked why she had come to talk, she replied embarrassedly that she wanted confirmation that the date she'd made was okay, wasn't it? The author who felt pompous, even sanctimonious doing it, told her he felt it was inappropriate, even unethical, and that she was in a classic countertransference. She left, kept the date, went through a stormy love affair with him, which terminated recently. She is still a practicing counselor. The lawyer is still sober and still single.

What the reader should conclude from this is that a countertransference can happen to the very best of counselors. No guaranteed way can be given to prevent one. The best, the only prescription to minimize its happening, is for the counselor to know what his/her weaknesses are with respect to other human beings.

Symptoms of Negative Countertransference

The symptoms of a negative countertransference are easy to detect but even more easily rationalized. The counselor

- is irritated by client's speech, manner, dress;

- discusses the client with colleagues in a disparaging way;

- dreads sessions with the client;

- is uninterested, inattentive, and bored during the sessions;

- forgets an appointment, cuts it short, even cancels appointments; and

- will be making minimal progress if at all.

A negative countertransference can happen but it should happen very rarely. Again, the best prescription for its prevention is a strong counselor sense of self-awareness.

INSIGHT

Many counseling theorists believe that achievement of insight is an indispensable requisite to the whole counseling process. According to Munroe (1955) "the crux of the therapeutic process is the development of insight." Wolberg (1954) believed that insight is basic to counseling despite school or approach, "Insight on some level is fundamental in all therapies." Sustained change toward a more healthful life, these therapists argue, is not possible without insight achievement. Some counselors disagree with this view. Skinner (1956) in one paper and Hobbs (1962) in a later one have both questioned the importance and significance of insight in bringing about change.

Definition

What exactly is insight? This author defines it as an intellectual understanding and an emotional appreciation of the why of the problem(s) which led the client to seek counseling. Both the intellectual and emotional levels of appreciation are critical. An intellectual understanding without concomitant feeling is simply not enough. This counselor has sat many times with alcoholic clients who explained, analyzed, and interpreted the why of their own behavior. They sounded positively insightful doing so. Then they went out and got drunk. Intellectual understanding is not enough.

Importance of Insight

When both an intellectual understanding and an emotional appreciation about the *why* of drinking exist, the question remains, can a guarantee be given that the alcoholic will achieve his/her sobriety? The answer is no. Guarantees as one wag put it are found on boxes of soap powders. Simply put, none are in human dynamics. This too, must be said, however, that while the client may not stop drinking because he/she has achieved insight, he/she definitely will not stop drinking if he/she has not achieved it. In short, the counselor can conclude that helping a client to achieve insight has merit.

TERMINATION
Uniqueness in Counseling the Alcoholic

Ordinarily the counseling process has a period of time devoted to terminating. This period is considered important by most counselors. It prepares the client to integrate what he/she has learned about himself/herself, to rid the self of any vestiges of dependency, and prevent any depression over the sense of loss about ending a unique relationship. Commonly, termination generates a measure of anxiety in the client.

None of these termination activities need to be true in counseling the alcoholic. The author's conviction is that formal terminating in alcoholism counseling is inappropriate. Even when a prolonged and healthful state of sobriety has been reached, the door should be left open for subsequent contact. No alcoholic is ever cured of the anxiety associated with taking a drink. This knowledge has led this counselor to do what he never does with clients suffering from other types of illness— he calls his alcoholic clients periodically to learn how they are doing. More than a few times these calls have resulted in added counseling sessions. The latent anxiety this counselor feels about terminating his clients is shared by other counselors. Goodyear (1981) in a provocative paper observed that termination is a loss experience for the counselor as well as the client. Counselors, he pointed out, often have anxieties about client competence and may suffer feelings of guilt and sadness when their clients are leaving. This counselor has experienced these feelings about his clients generally and about his alcoholic clients in particular.

SUMMARY

Among alcoholics the phenomena termed high, low, and middle bottom exist. Each alcoholic arrives at his/her bottom differently and for different reasons. The level and nature of the bottom varies with the person and always embraces the alcoholic's entire dynamic system. Meaningful, effective counseling can occur only when the alcoholic experiences his/her private bottom.

Goals are basic issues in counseling. The primary goal in counseling the alcoholic is the achievement of **continuing sobriety.** The secondary goals are important too, as they facilitate the achievement of the primary goal. Periodic reevaluation of the client's sobriety is critical if it is to be maintained because most alcoholics experience the BUD phenomenon.

Rapport has to do with accord, affinity, warmth, and trust in a relationship. Tone, pace, flexibility, frame of reference, and repertoire of leads are all integral aspects of rapport. Rapport transcends the whole process of counseling. Counselor ego strength, an unmotivated client, a client's negative perception of his/her counselor, and a clash in personalities are all potential obstacles to the development of rapport.

The setting in which counseling is done can affect it. The size of the room and the seating arrangements bear important consideration. Time, energy, and money need to be invested in making the counseling room attractive.

Communication between counselor and client is the essence of the counseling experience. The avenues of communication common to many alcoholics are condemnation, submission, indifference, and congruence. Clients communicate also by body and emotions, on unconscious levels, by double messages, with body language and by defenses.

Transference is a function of repression and identification. The transference can manifest itself both positively and negatively. The counselor can ignore it, focus on those aspects which are pertinent to the client's life, or can pursue an analytic approach.

As is the case with transference, countertransference has both positive and negative symptoms. The best prescription for minimizing the occurrence of a positive or negative countertransference is for the counselor to have a full appreciation of self.

Some believe that achievement of insight is an indispensable requisite to the counseling process. Achievement of insight by the alcoholic as to the why of his/her addiction is no guarantee that sobriety will be achieved, but the alcoholic will definitely not stop drinking if insight is not achieved.

Formal termination in alcoholism counseling is inappropriate because alcoholics live with a constant latent anxiety that they will relapse into drink. Accordingly, periodic check-ups by counselors of their clients is appropriate.

TOPICS FOR DISCUSSION AND REFLECTION

1. Why are some bottoms reached quickly (a matter of months) and some never?

2. Articulate what are for you the primary goals for your professional counseling?

3. Which approach has more merit for you—the directivist or the nondirectivist approach? Why?

4. What personal and professional qualities do you harbor which will facilitate and/or hinder rapport with clients?

5. What body language habits do you possess which facilitate and/or hinder communication with clients?

6. What needs do you have which may be conducive to a countertransference?

7. How can counselor awareness and sensitivity to the transference phenomena help the client? The counselor?

8. What is your definition and/or criteria for achievement of client insight?

9. The author's position is that an alcoholic can not achieve sobriety if he/she does not develop insight. Do you agree with this? Why? Why not?

10. Do you agree with the author that formal termination of alcoholism counseling is inappropriate? Why? Why not?

CHAPTER EIGHT

PRACTICAL TECHNIQUES

The practical techniques which are explained in this Part will be employed more effectively if the counselor has an understanding of the frame of reference with which many alcoholics operate. By frame of reference the author refers to where the alcoholic is coming from emotionally, spiritually, and intellectually.

A FRAME OF REFERENCE

Without doubt the organization which has been most effective in helping alcoholics to achieve and maintain sobriety has been Alcoholics Anonymous. A couple of recent studies have shown this: one with physicians (Galenter, Talbot, & Ballegos, 1990) and one with the general population (Kaufman, 1990).

For many the achievement and maintenance of sobriety are living and identifying with the *Twelve Steps of Alcoholics Anonymous.* More often than not these Steps are the alcoholic's frame of reference and not uncommonly, provide initial topics for explanation and discussion in counseling.

The prospective counselor who is a recovered alcoholic knows the Steps, has reflected, meditated on them, and lived with them.

The counselor who is not a recovering alcoholic may not be familiar with these steps. The author's conviction is that the effective counselor, recovering alcoholic or not, is one who knows what these Steps are and is concerned with what they mean to the client. Quite generally, the counselor who has an intellectual and emotional appreciation of the Twelve Steps finds that rapport with the client invariably comes early. More importantly, once the counselor has learned how the client interprets these steps, the counselor has obtained an invaluable window into the client's system of thought and emotional life too.

These twelve steps are provided in the material that follows. For the first five the author has provided his interpretations. Hopefully, counselors, who are familiar with these Steps and have developed their own interpretations, will find more food for reflection. Counselors who are not familiar with these Steps are encouraged to explore other interpretations and finally develop their own subjective meaning.

Step One

"We admitted we are powerless over alcohol, that our lives had become unmanageable."

Taking this first step is critical if one is to change and redevelop his/her personality. The view here is that a healthy nonalcoholic personality can be built only upon a foundation of a vowed human weakness. The person who is not able to admit to a lack of control toward drink cannot expect to recover in any substantial way. A person who is unable to attain a meaningful sobriety is precisely one who has not been able to admit to innate powerlessness.

Acceptance of this first step is excruciatingly difficult because it is an admission that one has lost control over one's own self. Many cannot accept this first step because by doing so they feel that they become "losers" in their own eyes. This first Step can best be understood as an avowed, external admission of long time internal feelings of weakness and ineffectuality. The denial and rationalization defenses have kept these internal feelings from surfacing. In most cases an acute sense of desperation is what tears them down. The process of restructuring and altering these defenses is an important focal point of the early counseling session.

Step Two

"Came to believe that a Power greater than ourselves could restore us to sanity."

This step is conducive to restructuring of defenses. Why? Because with acceptance of this Step, the alcoholic begins to perceive a whole new world. He/she comes to understand that physical and emotional energy need not be directed inwardly or focused upon personal inadequacies and failure, but rather, can be directed externally. By this step the alcoholic comes to understand that the investment in one's fellow human, God, in whatever context, or the cosmos generally can reap rich and enhancing dividends. Implied in this Step is that every individual must have an object upon which to attach faith. Without such an attachment, self-esteem and a continuing self-enhancement are not possible.

Implied too, in this Step is that the alcoholic, who comes to accept this step, admits to an emotional life in shambles and a distorted system of thought. Simply, the alcoholic admits to a life which has been lived insanely. Previously, energies have been channeled into maintaining that insanity. With acceptance of this second Step the alcoholic is able to return to a sane life.

Step Three

"Make a decision to turn our will and our lives over to the care of God as we understand him."

Steps One and Two lead the alcoholic away from an exaggerated concern with one's self and encourage physical and emotional energies externally. Both Steps are meditative, reflective, and oblige only acceptance. Step Three obliges the alcoholic to act on the acceptance of the first two Steps.

The key to acceptance of Step Three is motivation. The alcoholic who is motivated toward investment in God will be successful. The definition and interpretation of God are left to the particular individual. For many this definition is the fellowship of Alcoholics Anonymous. To this fellowship many submit their will and their lives.

By this Step then, the individual becomes dependent on A.A. Such a dependence he/she comes to believe results in an independence of spirit and a more emotionally relaxed life. What this author has learned is that clients who have accepted the third Step develop a more optimistic perception of problem situations. More importantly, people are viewed more tolerantly and interaction with the alcoholic invariably becomes rewarding.

Step Four

"*Made a searching and fearless moral inventory of ourselves.*"

The desire to fully achieve this Step leads many alcoholics into counseling. The traditional A.A. interpretation of this Step is based upon an understanding and control of the basic human instincts. In the A.A. view instincts unbridled are conducive to self-destruction.

The author has utilized the client's interest in this Step differently. Thus, the counselor has encouraged the client to focus on those aspects of his/her personality which are of special concern. This counselor has found that general and basic psychological needs—security, love, self-esteem, and self actualization—have provided an effective framework in which to help the client better understand his/her specific concerns and anxieties and those instincts from which they spring. What the author has found, too, is that the alcoholic penchants for excess, guilt, and mood swings stem from a lack of understanding of the basic human search for satisfaction of these needs. This Step Four seems to be best achieved by clients when they come to have a clear understanding of what self-esteem means to them.

Step Five

"Admitted to God, to ourselves, and to another human being the exact nature of our wrongs."

The A.A. view here is that "confession is good for the soul." Such a view not only promotes the counseling enterprise but may even facilitate rapport. The author's experience has been that clients who are strongly identified with this fifth Step are positively eager to "spill their guts." These clients seem especially eager to explain in graphic detail those incidents where they inflicted pain upon others.

For such clients the counseling session is perceived as an opportunity for an emotional catharsis, and it is. Clients at the end of a draining session usually feel better. (A positive byproduct is that rapport and the client-counselor relationship are almost always strengthened.) The counselor should be very much aware that catharsis, while beneficial, is not in itself the end-all of the counseling process. Catharses are at best temporary. Their value lies in precipitating insight and in turn, change. Very often clients, especially alcoholics, have shared their most intimate experiences and conflicts and even convincingly explained to the counselor the why of their drinking. Then they proceed to engage in the same destructive behavior! In short catharsis, even catharsis complemented with insight, is no guarantee of positive changes especially in the alcoholic client. Only when the client genuinely finds reward in change will he/she be and stay on the road to recovery.

NOTE: Steps Six through Twelve are reproduced verbatim for the benefit of those counselors who are not familiar with them. They were not interpreted because the author felt that their content was not conducive to any meaningful interpretation of the counselor-client process. The A.A. interpretations can be obtained from the manual *Twelve Steps and Twelve Traditions*, Alcoholics Anonymous World Services Inc., 468 Park Avenue South, New York, N.Y. 10016.

Step Six

"We're entirely ready to have God remove all these defects of character."

Step Seven

"Humbly asked Him to remove our shortcomings."

Step Eight

"Made a list of all persons we had harmed, and became willing to make amends to them all."

Step Nine

"Made direct amends to such people wherever possible, except when to do so would injure them or others."

Step Ten

"Continued to take personal inventory and when we were wrong promptly admitted to it."

Step Eleven

"Sought through prayer and meditation to improve our conscious contact with God, as we understood Him, praying for knowledge of His will for us and the power to carry that out."

Step Twelve

"Having had a spiritual awakening as the result of these steps, we tried to carry this message to alcoholics, and to practice these principles in all our affairs."

REDIRECTING AND RESTRUCTURING DEFENSES

As noted in Part I, helping the alcoholic client to restructure his/her system of defense is a critical task of the counselor.

In many of the illustrations which follow, notably confrontation, the reader will be able to see that this process typically is woven together with other client issues. Examples which follow are simulated to focus specifically on the issue of defense. The counselor style depicted melds directivist with nondirectivist.

Denial and Rationalization

These two defenses are treated together because they often occur in tandem with rationalization as a support for denial. A common phenomenon among newly recovering alcoholics is the refusal to acknowledge their competencies. Such is the case here.

Counselor Shawn.

CL: *I think I've decided not to take the office supervisor job.*

CO: *Oh?*

CL: *I honestly don't think I'm ready for it.*

CO: *I'm confused.*

CL: *Why?*

CO: *Yesterday you said you were going to take it. You told me you were looking forward to going back to it.*

CL: *I changed my mind.*

CO: *What changed it?*

CL: *I'm just not ready for it.*

CO: *I was under the impression you were a supervisor for almost twenty years.*

CL: I was and look what happened! I became a drunk.

CO: *You became a drunk because you were the office supervisor?* (A hint of incredulity in the tone would not be inappropriate.)

CL: *Well, it contributed to it. People, women especially, are a bitch to work with. If I were a man I wouldn't hesitate—women respect men more.*

CO: (Grinning) *It's because you're not a man that you can't be a supervisor at this time. You don't feel you command enough respect.*

CL: *You think I'm making excuses don't you?*

CO: *Aren't you? Janice, the reality is that you functioned for twenty years as a supervisor and the last five you were drunk a good part of the time.*

CL: *And if I did it drunk, I can do it sober, eh?*

CO: *What do you think?*

What the counselor does here is to focus on the client's denial, repeating, and rephrasing. The counselor always is focusing on what the client is saying. This helps the client see her vacillation is founded upon the plain fear that she can't do what she's already done for a couple of decades.

Displacement

Occasionally, clients will ventilate anger. More often than not, this counselor's response has been simply an acceptance of the client and his/her feelings. To respond with anger is grossly inappropriate. The view is that the follow-up session to the ventilation, sometimes during the same session if clients are feeling remorseful, is the more critical point in the therapy. What the counselor has to communicate to clients is that while anger is a legitimate emotion, when displayed it doesn't serve to enhance personality. What the counselor has to communicate, too, is that what angry clients usually feel is a function of other disquieting and troubling circumstances of their lives. More importantly, that they have to deal with those people and situations which have endangered that anger.

Fantasy

What clients daydream about, what they wish for is important. Fantasizing can be more than a simple escape from boredom or harsh reality. It can be a springboard to creativity. Certainly fantasy does not have to be destructive as it may have been for alcoholics during their drinking days.

Alcoholics, particularly those who seek to share their fantasies, need to hear those ideas. When they begin talking about some of their wishes and dreams, the sensitive counselor will do more than listen. He/she should help clients to evaluate the feasibility of translating fantasies into reality.

Projection

The suspicious client is not easy to deal with and many alcoholics are very suspicious. Too often it is a major aspect of alcoholic's make-up. The best counselor antidote for suspiciousness in alcoholic clients is reliability and trustworthiness. A promise or appointment should never be made with the clients unless the counselor knows full well that he/she can keep it. Authenticity and candor also are excellent antidotes. Nothing feeds and expands this defense as much as game playing.

Clients who project are exquisitely sensitive to verbal nuances, body movements, a simple sigh. If a usually engaging client asks the counselor if the latter is anxious to terminate an interview when he/she is, the counselor can answer honestly, *"I am but it's got nothing to do with you. I found out a half hour ago that I'm the one who has to pick up my son at the sitter's because my spouse got hung up in town."* An honest explanation punctuated with a chuckle and even a compliment, *"I thought I was hiding my nervousness. You're very perceptive,"* will help the client to see that his/her perception is accurate and to express it under such circumstances is perfectly O.K.

Regression

Regression as was noted in Part I is characterized by immature behavior and is often manipulative. The counselor's task is to communicate that the behavior affected by his/her defense is seldom attractive and more often than not will alienate other people. The illustration which follows exemplifies a situation which has occurred a number of times with the author.

Counselor Ralph.

CO: *I'm sorry, John. I can't do it. I'm not going to serve as your job agent. You'll have to make the call yourself.*

CL: *What's the big deal?*

CO: *It's a big deal. You'll have to set up the interview yourself.*

CL: (Yells) *I thought you were here to help me.*

CO: (Quietly) *I am. I'm here to help you help yourself.*

CL: (Sulking) *What a crock this place is. All they tell you here is that they want to help. You ask for help and you get a lot of horseshit explanations.*

CO: *Not horseshit. It's true. We're, I'm here to help you help yourself.*

CL: (Cries out) *So! Help me!*

CO: (Quietly) *John, a man who whines like a baby does not endear himself to people.*

CL: (Grimly) *Man, you can take this place, your psychology too, and roll it up into a big fat ball and shove it, man, shove it.*

(Slams out)

Next day

CL: (Sheepishly) *I made the call. I got an interview at two o'clock today.*

CO: *Good!*

CL: *I'm scared, man, I'm scared.*

CO: *Aren't we all. Let's talk.*

Repression

Repression is the defense which clients may well have employed immoderately in their past. Too often the effect has been to leave them scared, immature, and unsure of themselves. Rather than attempt to deal with the whys and whens of the repression, this counselor has found it more productive to help the client build other defenses. Two defenses which seem to address themselves to the debilitating effects of repression are **compensation** and **sublimation.** In the former, clients are encouraged to look for and identify with situations, hobbies, events where they can find some reward and demonstrate some measure of success to their own selves. Similarly, sublimation involves directing energy in the service of others and one's own healthy self. Alcoholism programs especially provide ample opportunity for the development of both defenses.

Silence

Silence is often threatening to counselors, even thoroughly competent ones. They became anxious, seeing a protracted pause as a symptom of their ineptitude. Not understanding the many excellent reasons for it, they break it clumsily and thereby communicate their anxiety and in turn increase the client's discomfort.

Why Silences Occur. Silences may occur for various reasons. The following seven reasons are the most common causes.

1. Embarrassment is a major reason silences occur especially at the initial contact. Clients do not know what to say. The initial contact with the alcoholism counselor may well be their first experience with counseling. The most alcoholics know, and this in a dim way, is that they are supposed to confide and

share innermost feelings, fears, and fantasies. Clients might be willing to do this, but do not know how. Simply, they are too embarrassed to begin.

2. Resentment, hostility, and anger are all reasons why silences occur. This is especially true in the mandated referral. The counselor is perceived as an agent of the person making the referral. What the alcoholic sees is that he/she is being victimized by the court, the parole office, or whomever. The client then releases his/her hostility in a passive way—by keeping mum.

3. Testing of the counselor is another reason for silence. The alcoholic, it will be remembered, often has a disposition toward paranoia. The silence may well be a response to that. By keeping silent, letting the counselor do the talking, the client can size up the counselor better. In addition, the client can evaluate the counselor's reaction. This client knows that he/she has some kind of responsibility to talk and share. The client knows that the silence can precipitate a variety of reactions in the counselor: impatience, anger, embarrassment, etc. So he/she tests the counselor. This interpersonal stance by the alcoholic may well be habitual and not even conscious.

4. Conflict is another reason for silence. More often than not, alcoholics are emotionally betwixt and between. They don't know what to say, where to start, precisely because they have so much to say. So clients sit tongue-tied and helpless, victims of their emotional conflicts. Such clients often perspire, fidget, twitch.

5. Fear is a major reason for silence, especially at the initial contact. The counselor finally is just another stranger. Typically, alcoholics have learned that most people are simply not that caring. Moreover, at some level all clients understand that a purpose of the counseling is to change them, and note, no human being ever delights in that idea. On the contrary, most people are scared by any potential change in themselves. They know what they have. Who knows

what change will bring? This kind of feeling is a major reason alcoholics persevere in their drinking.

6. Integration by the client of what he/she or the counselor has said. Counseling can be painfully emotional, even traumatic at times, and some clients need time to absorb it all. A silence for some clients is simply a manifestation of that need.

7. The end of a topic may produce silence. Sometimes a silence occurs because the counselor and the client have finished a long discussion. A pause may occur while the client searches for a relevant topic.

Handling the Silence. Once the counselor understands that the silence is a product of complex client dynamics it should be less threatening. In any case he/she should be better equipped to deal with it. Some of the specific reasons for a silence (at times several reasons may exist) are easy to discern. Others are more difficult. The counselor's ability to fathom and deal with these more indiscernible reasons will test both his/her clinical skills and perceptual sensitivity. Following are some suggestions for dealing with differently motivated silences.

1. ***Embarrassment*** is easy to detect. Confrontation usually aggravates it. The better approach is a comment or question manifestly unrelated to the client's alcoholism but about the client and/or his/her interests. (A look into his/her background before the first session is always helpful.) The question might focus on a hobby, his/her work, family, and so forth.

2. ***Resentment, hostility,*** or ***anger*** is very apparent. A gentlelike confrontation is appropriate. In the case of the mandated referral, a comment like this might be helpful: *"John, I know you were sent here and quite apparently you're not happy. Just know that I'm here to help, if you want it. And I know real well I can't make you open up if you don't want to."* When a mandated referral is not the reason, confrontation is still appropriate. *"John, you're not happy. I'm sorry*

for that. Just know that I'm here to help if you want it . . ." and so forth.

3. **Testing** of the counselor can occur for various reasons. This motive for silence is not always easy to detect. When the counselor genuinely is puzzled as to the why of the silence, probing with neutral comments is in order, i.e., *"Sometimes it's tough to talk,"* or *"You're quiet today. Do you know why?"* Under no circumstances should the counselor launch into chit-chat. If the counselor concludes because of the client's facial expressions, body language, and just feelings that the client's silence is a function of hostility, then the counselor should lean back, smile appropriately, shrug, and say to the client, *"Whenever you're ready is okay with me."* The idea is to communicate patience and receptivity.

4. **Conflict** is very apparent. Reassuring comments delivered softly with warmth are usually beneficial and ultimately move the client to talk.

5. **Fear,** once detected and it's not difficult to do so, is dealt with in much the same fashion as one would deal with conflict.

6. **Integration** by the client of ideas, concepts, insights, and personality components often produce silence. This silence is best left alone as the client is in the process of absorbing what he/she is feeling or has just learned. A comment by the counselor serves no purpose. A question would be even worse.

7. The **end of a thought** expressed by the client may cause silence. The author has let this silence go on with the new client hoping he/she would break it and thereby assume more of the responsibility for the counseling. He has not let it go on if the client was becoming embarrassed; nor has he let it go on when the rapport and progress are solid. Under these latter circumstances this counselor breaks silence with a comment like, *"Well, what thoughts are you having?"* If the client responds with none, the counselor

will break the silence by referring to something the client said previously.

LEARNING ACTIVITIES

The following activities on learning to deal effectively with silence and those which come immediately after each of the subsequent techniques illustrate activities which the prospective and inservice counselor can utilize to both learn and upgrade counselor skills. These activities are in outline form and can be modified, expanded, or revised to meet local training needs. Any alterations, however, should retain the requisite elements of any effective learning exercise. These are

justification,

purpose,

objectives/outcomes,

specific activities, and

evaluation methods.

STUDENT ACTIVITIES FOR LEARNING TO DEAL EFFECTIVELY WITH SILENCE

Justification

Protracted pauses may generate anxiety in the counselor and/or the client. Learning to deal with the silence can abate that anxiety and facilitate counseling.

Purposes

1. To expand the student counselor's theoretical knowledge about the element of silence in counseling.

2. To develop and sharpen the student counselor's practical skill to deal effectively with silence.

Outcome

Student counselor demonstrates that he/she can indeed handle silence.

Specific Activities

1. Student counselor obtains verification that he/she knows theoretical reasons why silences occur in counseling.

2. Student counselor obtains verification that he/she knows possible and varied ways to handle silence.

3. Student counselor views video demonstrations on how to handle silence.

4. Student counselor views live demonstrations by mentor on how to handle silence.

5. Student counselor engages in role-playing with the mentor.

6. Student counselor views videotaping of himself/herself during a counseling session with a new client.

Evaluation

1. Feedback is obtained from mentor and student colleagues.

2. Activities continue until student counselor and mentor are mutually satisfied with student counselor's performance.

LISTENING

Prefatory Comments

Moustakas (1966) has observed that "When we are listened to, it creates us, makes us unfold and expand." Most alcoholic clients have never learned how to unfold and expand precisely because they feel that no one ever really listened to them. This feeling has contributed much toward their suspiciousness, their anger, and their penchant for testing others. The counselor who listens, in a word, enhances. Such a counselor provides the alcoholic with a rare opportunity to unfold and expand.

Patterson (1959) believed that listening is "the basic, most universal, most important technique in counseling and psychotherapy." If listening isn't the most important technique, it is certainly critical. Without this ability the counselor will find that meaningful rapport is impossible.

Effective listening is sometimes difficult even for competent, experienced counselors. In the emotionally charged climate of counseling, easily conditions can cause the counselor to ask inappropriate questions; to offer unasked for, unneeded advice; to interrupt with an irrelevant interpretation; or to supply a well intended but unnecessary supportive remark. Behaviors like these communicate a lack of interest, tell the client that the counselor is not listening, and that the counselor is one who is meeting his/her own needs, not those of the client.

Aspects of Listening

The listening counselor not only hears the client's words but also is exquisitely sensitive to his/her feelings, tones, and sounds made. **Feelings** and **tones** carry the real meaning of words and reflect the emotions of the client. Such tones Westcott (1966) has termed **phasis.** The counselor who is finely attuned to the phasis in client talk is the one who can get close. Thus in his/her responses the counselor can, should address the emotion the client is feeling as well as the verbal content expressed, i.e., *"I believe you, Bill. That crackle in your voice tells me real well how angry you really are."*

The counselor also should be fully aware of **sounds** which a client makes, like finger drumming, hand clapping, even making the chair squeak with his/her constant shifting. Westcott (1966) has termed such sounds **strepitus.** They speak much about the client's internal anxiety. To respond to them or not would be dependent upon the quality of rapport existing between the counselor and alcoholic. If the rapport is good, a comment whimsically made might be very appropriate; i.e., *"That's a regular tattoo you're doing there. It's even got a regular beat."* In sum, a response to feeling tones, to sounds made by the client demonstrate in a concrete way how well attuned the counselor is to the client's presence and to everything about him/her.

Listening Techniques

For the counselor to listen is not enough, he/she also needs to communicate his/her motivation to do so. Following are some practical suggestions to accomplish this communication.

1. How the counselor **sits** communicates much about motivation to listen and is really a function of personality. Some counselors are more formal or casual than others. Simply, one should sit so he/she is comfortable. Counselor comfort will communicate and set a comfortable tone for the encounter. The counselor should sit, of course, so the client can be observed directly. This author who leans back and puts his feet on top of the desk has never been able to appreciate Freud's method to sit behind the head of the lying down client.

2. The counselor should structure the counseling hour so **no interruptions** occur. A phone for incoming calls should be programmed for transfer to another phone. If this isn't possible, a feasible procedure might be to have the phone put on a jack so it can be pulled out for the counseling hour. Hanging out a "Do Not Disturb" sign is eminently appropriate. All these procedures will serve to communicate to the client his important idea—you are the focus of my attention.

3. To listen at his/her best, the counselor should develop the ability to **isolate distracting** thoughts. This idea was explained fully in Part III under "Obstacles to

Establishment of Rapport." A rereading of that section might be helpful.

4. The counselor will not be able to listen attentively if he/she is not fully cognizant of **topics and words** which precipitate a negative reaction internally. Certain words and subjects are emotionally laden for some people and counselors are no exception. This fact was illustrated in dramatic fashion to this author about a year ago. The alcoholic at the very first session told this counselor an ethnic joke, followed with another about Blacks. The counselor overlooked them figuring they were a function of the client's anxiety, perhaps some kind of testing, and so forth. At the next session, the client opened with a particularly tasteless story about Blacks. This counselor let down his guard and winced. The client became embarrassed and asked if he had been offensive. When told he had been, the client became angry and left. He returned later that day and apologized, finished with the rationalization, *"We're all different."* However, he never made another racial slur.

In this instance it all worked out okay. However, had the author better known what his feelings were he would not have winced, would not have had to say he was offended, and thereby come near to losing the client. However strong one's feelings might be regarding the obscenity and foolishness too, of prejudice, the counseling session is simply not a forum for instruction in healthier race relations.

5. The counselor who asks focused, pertinent **questions** will demonstrate that he/she is listening. The questions should always be derived from the client's comments and should never introduce a new topic. Questions unrelated to what the client is discussing ordinarily reflect inattention, boredom, and general uninterest. This whole topic of questioning is developed more fully in the next section.

ACTIVITIES FOR LEARNING
LISTENING SKILLS

Justification

Counseling is not possible if the counselor does not know how to listen. Effective counseling is enhanced mightily by a counselor who is a skilled listener.

Purposes

1. To increase the student counselor's theoretical knowledge about listening in counseling.

2. To develop and increase the student counselor's practical listening skills.

Outcome

The student counselor demonstrates that he/she has acquired listening skills.

Specific Activities

1. The student counselor obtains verification that he/she knows reasons why counselor listening can be blocked.

2. The student counselor obtains verification that he/she knows how effective listening can be enhanced.

3. The student counselor views video demonstration of counselors who are effective listeners.

4. The student counselor views live demonstrations by mentor counselor.

5. The student counselor role-plays with mentor counselor or colleagues.

6. The student counselor views himself/herself on video tape.

Evaluation

1. Student counselor obtains feedback from mentor, colleagues, and clients.

2. Activities continue until mentor and student are mutually satisfied that the student counselor is an effective listener.

QUESTIONING

Problems

Questions, especially with alcoholics, may have certain problems. Questions by their very nature are designed to elicit information, information which the client can consider too private to share. They may touch on areas which engender fear. In short, a basic problem with questions is that they probe into the unknown.

Questions for some counselors too often lead to more questions. Too often, the counselor takes on the spectacle of a courtroom with the counselor playing the role of a prosecuting attorney. A barrage of questions can turn counselor and client into adversaries.

Questions have another potential disadvantage. Clients may become conditioned to think in terms of answering questions, not in terms of sharing, expressing voluntarily, self-examining. In short, their sense of responsibility for counseling may become stultified.

Finally, questioning per se has another major disadvantage—too often it focuses upon the cognitive domain rather than upon feelings. Cognitive understanding is helpful, even desirable, but without emotional appreciation the cognitive understanding has little value for the client. Under such circumstances, meaningful insight is simply not possible.

Positive Aspects

Despite these limitations, thoughtful questioning can be helpful and facilitative. It can serve as a lead into productive discussion. Clear, succinct, gently toned questions ordinarily are not inappropriate if the counselor derives them from the client's comments and discussion.

Questions posed should always be open-ended. After posing the question, the counselor should wait for the client's response. Therein will lie the validity and fruitfulness of the counselor's query.

Following are two illustrations. In this scene the client has been talking nonstop for almost ten minutes.

Counselor Myrtle—
Inappropriate Use of Questions

CL: . . . anyways like I was saying I know I have to take each day at a time and I'm doing that but I think I can start making plans to get out of here. I've been sober for two months now and I want to thank you. You've really helped me.

CO: Why are you banging on the table like that?

CL: (Laughs) I'm nervous.

CO: Why are you nervous?

CL: (Shrugs) I don't know, the way you're looking at me makes me nervous, makes me feel like a goldfish in a bowl . . . (Client's talk continues aimlessly for several minutes.)

CO: Why are you talking so much today? And why are you banging on the table again?

CL: Like I said. I'm nervous.

CO: You're getting ready to blow it aren't you?

CL: *You know damn well I'm not.*

CO: *Then how come I didn't see you yesterday?*

CL: *I told you about that.*

Comments on Counseling Excerpt

This counselor broke the rules of good questioning. His/ her questions were not founded on client comment. He/she asked a second question before he/she got an answer to the first. He/she sounded a little bit like an anxious but determined prosecuting attorney. Even his/her observation of client table drumming sounded more like accusations than gently toned comments designed to communicate an accepting confirmation of the client's hyperactive behavior.

Counselor Rosemary— Appropriate Use of Questions

The following scene opens exactly as the first did.

CL: *. . . anyways like I was saying I know I have to take each day at a time and I'm doing that but I think I can start making plans to get out of here. I've been sober for two months now and I want to thank you. You've really helped me.*

CO: *That's why I am here. To help. How exactly have I helped?*

CL: (Drumming hand on the desk) *Well you're not like some of the other guys around here, always on your back, buzzing around, asking questions, trying to get into your head. Al's got a counselor like that, always asking him if he's building up to drink.*

CO: (Smiles) *Should I ask you that?*

CL: *Sure, ask.*

CO: (Seriously) *Are you building up to a drink?*

CL: *No!* (Slams the desk)

CO: *Would you say this beating your giving this desk today is the you that you were a week ago?*

CL: (Silent for a moment. Sighs.) *You know, huh?*

CO: (Nods) *I know.*

CL: *I'm dying, Doc.*

CO: (Smiling) *Let's talk about it.*

Both counselors are very aware that the client's behavior was symptomatic of BUD. The second one's use of questions aimed at letting the client know of her awareness without making him defensive and getting him to talk. In sum, a counselor's questions should not be merely a reaction to a client's specific comment. They should have an ultimate purpose too. In this instance it was to get the client to discuss his craving.

ACTIVITIES FOR LEARNING QUESTIONING SKILLS

Justification

The counselor, who questions effectively, demonstrates interest in the client, reinforces rapport, and generally facilitates the counseling progress.

Purposes

1. To increase the student counselor's theoretical knowledge about the technique of questions.

2. To develop and sharpen the student counselor's questioning skills.

Outcome

Student counselor demonstrates that he/she has the ability to question effectively.

Specific Activities

1. The student counselor obtains verification that he/she is familiar with the theory of positive and negative aspects of questioning.

2. The student counselor obtains verification that he/she knows appropriate and inappropriate use of questioning.

3. The student counselor views examples of effective counselor questioning.

4. The student counselor views live demonstrations of effective questioning.

5. The student counselor role-plays with mentor or colleagues.

6. The student counselor views video tape of himself/herself questioning in counseling session.

Evaluation

1. Student counselor obtains feedback from mentor, colleagues, and client.

2. Demonstrations continue until counselor and client are mutually agreed that the student is an effective questioner.

REITERATION OF CONTENT

Definition

Reiteration refers to a literal restatement or rephrasing by the counselor of what the client said. When the counselor does this restatement, he/she is telling the client that he/she understands. Ordinarily when the counselor reiterates, no attempt is made to interpret the meaning of what the client said.

Explanation

Reiteration as a technique serves many useful purposes. It immediately puts the counselor into an accepting role, thereby facilitating both rapport and communication. It invariably elicits client feelings conducive to better cognitive understanding. Reiteration helps clients to focus and delineate their thinking. It can help clients reconsider both thinking and viewpoint, i.e., when the counselor reiterates with an inquisitive or honestly puzzled look. Another prime value of reiteration is, then, to help clients crystallize their thoughts.

The following two examples illustrate this technique. The client is an alcoholic wife and mother in her early thirties. This excerpt was taken from a tape and was edited by the author.

Counselor Greg, Directivist—
Illustrative Excerpt

CL: *You can't help me, not in this.*

CO: *When you open like that I know you want to talk. So talk and try me.*

(Pause)

CL: *He's having an affair.* (She starts crying.)

CO: *Your husband's screwing around on you.*

CL: *Yes. Bastard. When I really needed his support. Instead of help, I get degraded.*

CO: *The bastard degraded you.*

CL: *God, it's enough to make me want to blow it.*

CO: *You want to get blind, stinking drunk.*

CL: *(Screams) I won't! I won't!*

CO: *You won't if you don't want to.*

CL: *I want to. He said his life was hell when I was drinking. God knows I want to make his life hell again for what he's done to me.*

CO: *You want to make his life hell for degrading you. Drinking will punish the bastard.*

CL: *And it will too!*

Counselor Joel, Nondirectivist— Illustrative Excerpt

The following illustration is a simulation of the preceding excerpt.

CL: *You can't help me, not in this.*

CO: *You don't feel I can help you. You may be right. I'm here to try if you want me to.*

(Pause)

CL: *He's having an affair. (Cries.)*

CO: *John is having an affair.*

CL: *Yes. Bastard. When I really needed his support. Instead of help I get degraded.*

CO: *Right in this time that you need support the most, he degrades you.*

CL: *God, it's enough to make me want to blow it.*

CO: *It's enough to make you want to return to drink.*

CL: *I want to. He said his life was hell when I was drinking. God knows I want to make his life hell.*

CO: *You want his life to be hell for what he's done to you.*

Comments on Illustrative Excerpts

Both counselors did a credible job. Joel, the nondirectivist, as usual is a little less blunt, a little less emotional, and little more literal in his reiteration. Greg, the directivist, tends more toward colorful rephrasing, is more inclined toward the supportive remark, "You won't if you don't want to." Both did well to focus and respond to the client's statement and neither did any interpreting.

ACTIVITIES FOR LEARNING HOW TO REITERATE CONTENT

Justification

The counselor who can reiterate well is one who facilitates both rapport and communication.

Purposes

1. To heighten the student counselor's awareness of the effectiveness and benefits of the reiteration technique.

2. To sharpen the student counselor's ability to reiterate content.

Outcome

Student counselor is effective in ability to reiterate content in an actual counseling session.

Specific Activities

1. The student counselor obtains verification that he/ she knows theory underlying when and how to reiterate content.

2. The student counselor views excerpts of model counselor reiterating on video tapes.

3. The student counselor views live demonstrations of reiterating.

4. The student counselor does role-playing with colleagues with or without mentor observing.

5. The student counselor observes self reiterating on video.

6. The student counselor demonstrates ability to reiterate in live counseling sessions.

Evaluation

1. The student counselor obtains feedback from mentor, colleagues, and so forth.

2. The student counselor continues activities until counselor and mentor are both satisfied with performance.

REFLECTION OF FEELING

Definition and Value

Reflection of feeling is closely allied to the concept of empathy. When counselors reflect feeling they communicate that they understand and perceive what clients are experiencing and feeling.

Reflection of feeling is among the least threatening of counselor techniques because the focus is on emotions and not intellectual content. It involves no questioning, no verbal pushing, the counselor merely mirrors tones and feelings exliciting and clarifying self-referenced emotion.

Counselors who reflect feelings effectively invariably lead the client into self-confrontation. Clients who hear and feel feelings come back at them are made to realize that their feelings are important, legitimate, and not crazy at all. Why? Another human being has understood and mirrored them.

The major benefit of this technique is not only in clients crystallizing their feelings but in understanding their feelings in relation to people. Feelings which trouble the most, of course, are those which have to do with relationships.

Alcoholics who come for counseling are usually very confused about relationships. They are laden with anger, guilt, and/or fear about them. As their feelings become clarified, self-understanding, in relation to others, becomes more ordered, more logical, and more healthful. The change, though gradual, is usually discernible as it is reflectd in clients' talk, general manner, even appearance.

Language

The counselor should try to use the language easily understood by the client. This counselor's preference is to use the same words as the client, varying only to avoid sounding like "Little Sir Echo." In any case, pretentious terminology always should be avoided.

Client Enhancement

Clarification of feelings enhances the client in two important ways. When feelings are reflected to them, clients come to see that feelings more often than not are causes of much dysfunctional behavior. Frequently client's ultimately see something more important—that they can cause their behavior, that they do not have to be victims, and, if they are, the reason is that they choose to be. The development of this way of thinking is vital if the alcoholic is to begin to recover.

The counselor can be most effective when reflecting feelings if certain points are kept in mind.

Feelings Hide Feelings

The counselor should address only the feelings presented by the client. At the same time, the counselor should bear in mind that the obvious feelings are not always the most important ones. Many clients mask their more debilitating feeling with other ones. The author recalls a female alcoholic, for example, who punctuated every third sentence with a sharp, nervous laugh to mask her anger and guilt.

Timing

Too often counselors wait for a client to finish a rather lengthy verbalization and miss much important affect. Feelings should be reflected as soon as possible after they are expressed.

Once the client has come to see that feelings cause behavior, he/she invariably begins an examination of precipitating motives. Such an examination can only lead to a better self-appreciation.

Clarification of feeling is essentially a technique of the Rogerian nondirectivist school. The illustration which follows is by a follower of that school. The edited excerpt is drawn from four sessions. These tapes are from a colleague's library.

Counselor Toni—
Illustration of Reflection of Feelings

CL: *I'm going to have to stop drinking. I know it.*

CO: *Your tone says that you don't want to.*

CL: *I do. It's just that my husband and my daughter . . . but they're right, I know they are.*

CO: *They're pressuring you, making you feel guilty.*

CL: *Yes, especially my daughter. My daughter had such a look of horror on her face when she caught me pouring a drink.*

CO: *And so the guilt. You wanted to die.*

CL: *Yes, I did. And I made it worse. I screamed at her for tip-toeing. I've got a tip-toer for a daughter. She never wears shoes in the house only those damn slipper socks. It's like she haunts the house, always materializing out of nowhere.*

CO: *She tip-toes around, materializes out of nowhere, and makes you feel guilty and angry 'cause you can't have a drink whenever you want.*

CL: *My husband's worse. He just lectures me. I have to account for every damn penny now. It's hard saving money for booze out of the grocery money. And he lectures me right in front of her. How do you think that makes me feel?*

CO: *Humiliated and then angry too, I'll bet.*

CL: *Yes, and the humiliation is hurting my daughter, too. I've told him that. I've told him I've got to want to stop myself and he's only making it worse with his damned sermons.*

CO: *He makes you so mad that you want to keep drinking.*

CL: *Yes. Honestly, sometimes when I'm alone and drinking I feel like I hate the two of them for what they're doing to me.*

CO: *Drink makes you feel you hate them.*

CL: *I'm not so sure it's the drink that does it. Sometimes even when I'm sober I hate them. Like right now.*

CO: *Right now you feel you hate them.*

CL: *I think like that a lot. Really it's why I started. I'm convinced of that. You know that old line about being driven to drink? It's not so crazy, not so crazy. They drive me to drink, the two of them, him with his sermons and her watching me like a hawk.*

CO: *I can appreciate how being watched like a hawk would make you angry. It would me.*

CL: (Crying) *God I was so awful. I made a real ass of myself.* (Pause) *We went to our annual family reunion and I got drunk. The whole thing's a blur for me. I don't remember too much only that I tried to dance on a picnic table while people ate and I fell off. I remember looking up and the looks, the awful looks, and a woman's voice saying, "She's a drunken bum." The last thing I remember is driving home in the car and my daughter was sobbing. Right then I wanted to die. I had humiliated my husband, my daughter, and me. Drunk, drunk as I was, I cried. Believe it or not for the first time in my life I got a good look at myself in the awful looks, in that woman's sneer, "She's a drunken bum," and in my daughter's tears. You have to know she never cries. I made her cry.*

CO: *Her tears made you see yourself better.*

CL: (High pitched voice) *It's not them I hate. It's me. I hate me and what I'm doing to them and to me. I hate myself. I hate myself for how I look, too puffy in the face, too big in the stomach—all vodka and gin. It's me I hate, not them.*

Comments on Illustrative Excerpt

To fully appreciate this or any effective counselor by the printed word is very difficult. On the tape the counselor's tones gibed perfectly with those of the client. The reader can still learn from this excerpt though. The counselor didn't use the stereotypic lines "What your feeling is . . ." or "You feel . . ." Instead the counselor focused on the client's feelings and her words by rescuing them, paraphrasing them, and by reinforcing the validity of her dramatic self-confrontation. Probably a fair assumption would be that the counselor's knowledge and exquisite sensitivity probably convinced him at the outset that her avowed hate of both husband and daughter was only a mask for her own self-hate and a prop for her denial of the love she really felt for them.

ACTIVITIES FOR LEARNING
HOW TO REFLECT FEELING

Justification

The ability to reflect feeling effectively is a critically important skill in counseling because through this technique the counselor is able to communicate empathy.

Purposes

1. To heighten and reinforce the student counselor's awareness of the importance of emotional communication in counseling.

2. To sharpen the student counselor's ability to reflect feeling.

Outcome

The student counselor demonstrates his/her ability to reflect feeling effectively in a real counseling session.

Specific Activities

1. The student counselor obtains verification that he/she is thoroughly conversant with the theory behind reflection of feeling.

2. The student counselor views video excerpts of professional counselors as they reflect feelings.

3. The student counselor views live demonstrations of feeling reflection.

4. The student counselor does role-playing with colleagues and with mentor.

5. The student counselor demonstrates ability to reflect feeling in live session.

Evaluation

1. The student counselor obtains feedback from mentor, colleagues.

2. The student counselor considers progress of his/her real clients.

3. Activities continue until the mentor and the student counselor are satisfied with performance.

ROLE-PLAYING

Requirement

The basic and only requirement in role-playing is that the participants talk, do, and try to feel as the other whose role they are playing.

Value

The author has found role-playing to be an especially valuable tool in alcoholism counseling. When this technique is utilized, alcoholics have an opportunity to become the object of their very own denials, rationalizations, and projections. This technique provides a unique learning experience for them because they see and hear in a dramatic way how they are perceived and how they relate to others. In turn, they act out the feelings they know others have toward them.

The technique should be used by counselor and client only after rapport has been established and participants feel that they know each other well. Role-playing is a novel and even exciting alternative to the regular counseling session. It is especially instructive and emotionally illuminating for the alcoholic when this technique is used with other family members. Alcoholics usually seem to be astounded to learn how much they know about a wife's, husband's, and child's feelings and interpersonal stance. More often than not, the alcoholic and his family usually seem to be emotionally rocked by the experience. Clients have found no technique more effective in promoting cognitive understanding and emotional appreciation of their problems and of the other person's too.

ACTIVITIES FOR LEARNING
THE ART OF ROLE-PLAYING

Justification

Once the counselor has mastered this technique, the alcoholism counselor can help the client to experience feelings which he/she has denied, projected, and rationalized. Also through this technique, the client experiences how he/she is perceived and can come to understand why people relate to him/her as they do.

Purposes

1. To heighten feeling awareness in the student counselor.

2. To facilitate the student counselor's identification with clients (people) and thereby promote flexibility in counselor personality.

Outcome

The student counselor demonstrates his/her ability to role-play effectively.

Specific Activities

1. The student counselor obtains verification that he/she is well grounded on the theory behind the role-playing technique.

2. The student counselor does role-playing with colleagues under mentor observation.

3. The student counselor does role-playing with a mentor.

4. The student counselor does role-playing with a real client with mentor observing or a video-tape of a role-playing session with a client is made for self and mentor evaluation.

Evaluation

1. The student counselor obtains feedback on previous four activities from a mentor.

2. Activities continue until the mentor and the student counselor are both satisfied that skill has been attained.

RECAPITULATION

Many alcoholics have a talent for delivering long discourses. This is true especially in the initial sessions but generally abates as the relationship strengthens and they become healthier.

Why the Long Discourse?

The long discourses are usually a function of the usual alcoholic ailments—fear, suspicions, and unbridled anxiety. By giving a long discourse, alcoholics are able to keep the counselor at a distance while they evaluate him/her; or again, the discourse may be nothing more than a camouflage for insecurities. No matter. Whatever the reason, long monologues are not uncharacteristic of alcoholics in their initial sessions. What can the counselor do? He/she can recapitulate.

Definition

The counselor who recapitulates responds with a focused, succinct synopsis of the client's discourse. Recapitulation then is a cognitive, intellectual activity. When counselors recapitulate they should try to use the client's words and phrases.

Value

Recapitulation has three benefits:

- It helps to build rapport because it shows the client that the counselor is listening.

- It helps the client to focus thoughts and keep to a point or theme.

- It reinforces the counselor's own understanding.

The illustration which follows is simulated but serves to exemplify this simple but valuable technique. The client in this illustration is a blend of several alcoholics whom the author has treated. The counselor is a directivist. The session is the initial contact.

Counselor Michael—
Illustration of Recapitulation

CL: *Why do I drink? It's easy. No big mystery. My life stinks. I got a boss who's a prick, a wife who's a nag, and five kids that are driving me bananas. That's why I drink. All those tests I took, I could've saved you the trouble. Should've asked me. It would have been simpler. So I get bombed, big deal. Everybody's entitled to once in a while. I did. It's not the first time and it won't be the last. What else have I got? I mean what have I got? I feel like I'm being eaten alive and my bones picked clean. My wife's just not the wife I married. Everytime I turn about it's, Jim, we need this, and Jim, we need that. I make a good pay and it's not near enough. I wanted to stop after two kids. She has this crazy idea about big happy families. We got a big family all right but it ain't happy lemme tell ya'. Well she learned. Now we don't even sleep in the same bed. Twin beds. I'm in dry dock, nagged to death cause she can't stand her big happy family and blames me besides. Me who never wanted the goddamned kids. No I'm not an alcoholic, I'm too realistic to be an alcoholic. If I'm drinking too much, it's cause my life stinks. That's all. What're you thinkin'?*

CO: (Laughs) *I'm thinking that you didn't leave too much out. Your life stinks, a nagging wife, five kids who are driving you crazy, no sex life. You feel your bones are being picked clean. So you get bombed once in a while. The only thing is you never really finished telling me about your boss. You just said he was a prick and sort of left it at that.*

CL: *Like I said, he's a prick. Hounds me. Nags me. In fact he reminds me of my wife and she reminds me of him. Different sexes, same people, and they both get their jollies screwing me. That son-of-a-bitch. You know what that prick does? He comes looking for me in the john. I mean Jesus! I can't even take a crap without worrying about him. People go when they gotta' go and I gotta' go every day about eight. Bastard comes lookin' for me. And I put out more work that anybody on that floor. Everybody knows that, even he knows that, but the bastard will never admit it. Never. Christ who wouldn't drink. I need a couple of quick ones at lunch once in a while. Two days ago I really had it so I didn't come back. I got absolutely stinko. I woke up in detox yesterday morning. So I'm here.*

CO: (Nodding) *You said your boss reminds you of your wife. He hounds you like she does. He even comes looking for you in the john even though you put out more work than anybody which he'll never admit. But tell me was it all worth it? Waking up in detox?*

Comments on Illustrative Excerpt

The counselor here is building rapport by showing the client he's listening. He lets the client vent even more by returning to an undeveloped theme, the boss. By recapitulating so effectively he reinforces the client's understanding.

ACTIVITIES FOR LEARNING
THE TECHNIQUE OF RECAPITULATION

Justification

Alcoholism counselors who can recapitulate effectively build rapport, help the client to focus thought, and thereby facilitate the counseling process.

Purpose

To develop counselor ability to recapitulate.

Outcome

The student counselor will be able to incorporate this technique into his/her repertoire of techniques.

Specific Activities

1. The student counselor obtains verification that he/she accepts "justification" previously.

2. The student counselor does role-playing with colleagues, under a mentor's observation.

3. The student counselor will do role-playing with a mentor while focusing on recapitulation.

4. The student counselor will make audio tapings with one or more clients.

Evaluation

1. The student counselor will obtain feedback from the mentor.

2. Activities continue until the mentor and the student counselor are satisfied that the skill has been attained.

CONFRONTATION

Research

The research indicates that confrontation as a technique is both valuable and productive. In a study by Kaul, Kaul, and Bednar (1973), clients found that confrontation led them to explore their inner feelings.

Kelly (1975) has expressed that confrontation is more effective and productive than is reflection of feeling. Use of confrontation, he felt, increases self-awareness for both client and counselor and is the technique which most effectively can lead to a client's commitment to change. Koeppen (1972) viewed confrontation as a threatening technique because pain is given and received but she pointed out, a promise to help and grow is in this technique too.

Discussion

The counselor who confronts, threatens. More often than not the alcoholic is scared by confrontation. Why? Because at some level he/she knows that it potentially can tear down defenses and alter not only the distorted perception of self but the perception held of others too. Herein lies the promise to which Koeppen alluded. For only when defenses and perception are righted can the alcoholic get back on the road to recovery.

Confrontation is an art. It's effectiveness will be determined by the counselor's emotional astuteness and competence in discerning the correct moment to confront.

Critical in any confrontation is concern, concern which springs from an honest belief that in the threat of the confrontative remark there does indeed lie a potential for enhancement. The most effective confrontative remarks are those which communicate that concern.

To accomplish this communication, the counselor should introduce confrontative questions with words that are neutral and tones that are gentle. For example, with the alcoholic who shows symptoms of Budding, the author has found such comments as these following appropriate.

> With the silent alcoholic who's usually talkative. (Chuckle) *"Seems like I've been doing more than my share of talking today. What's happening?"*

> With the irritable alcoholic. *"We all have our irritable days, but seems as if you've really been bitten today. Can you tell me about it?"*

> With the overconfident, euphoric alcoholic. *"You feel like you're definitely recovered. What do you think that means?"*

The real artistry in the previous confrontative remarks lies in the counselor's ability to have affect gibe with words. The counselor must be and sound unaffected and must know the client. The counselor must feel confident that confrontative remarks will not alienate the client but will indeed enhance the relationship.

The following two excerpts illustrate this confrontation technique.

Counselor Roselyn, Nondirectivist— Illustrative Excerpt

CL: *The doctor thinks I ought to go on antabuse.*

CO: *Oh? And what's your feeling about that?*

CL: *I don't want to.*

CO: *You don't want to.*

CL: *No.*

(Pause)

CO: *You want to tell me why?*

CL: *Jesus. If I haven't learned anything else, I've learned I've got to do this thing myself. I don't want to get hooked on something and I don't want to lean on any crutch. Besides I don't believe in taking any pills. Like I said I got to do this by myself.*

CO: *You don't want to lean on anything or anybody. You want to beat the booze yourself.*

CL: *You got it.*

CO: (Smiling) *You don't want to lean on anybody. Correct me if I'm wrong but essentially what you're saying is that you don't feel that you need any help?*

CL: *I'm not saying that.*

CO: *You're not?*

CL: *No. There's a difference between leaning and getting help.*

CO: (In an honestly bewildered tone) *What's the difference?*

CL: *Well, I meant like there's a difference between pills and people. You lean on pills, you get help from people. You're a person I get help from because you're a person.*

CO: (Grinning) *Seems like I haven't helped all that much now, have I?*

CL: (Grinning back) *You mean just cause I blew it twice in the past month?*

CO: (Nodding) *Yeah.* (Pause) *Do you feel the doctor's a person?*

CL: *He's okay.*

CO: *I guess what you're saying then is that you want my help but not his help.*

CL: *No, what I'm saying is that I don't want pills. (Eyes wide) They're dangerous. They can kill you.*

CO: (Nodding) *Or at least make you damn sick if you drink.*

CL: (Sheepishly) *Yeah.*

CO: *Maybe what you're saying is that you still want to be able to choose to get drunk when you want to.*

CL: (Stonily) *What I'm saying is that I don't want to get hooked on a pill.*

CO: (Grinning) *Are you saying that you prefer to be hooked on alcohol?*

CL: (Loudly) *No I'm not saying that.* (Sighing) *Right now I guess I don't know what I'm saying. Let me think about it okay?*

The previous simulated excerpt is an example of the kind of approach to confrontation which this author prefers. The nondirective confronts but does so gently, at times deferentially, but hangs on doggedly, occasionally even dueling intellectually with his/her client in order to adhere to the main point, helping the client to dismantle his/her denial defense and rectify his/her perception.

Counselor Danielle, Directivist—
Illustrative Excerpt

CL: *The doctor thinks I ought to go on antabuse.*

CO: *What do you think?*

CL: *I don't want to.*

CO: *Why not?*

CL: *Jesus. If I haven't learned anything else, I've learned I've got to do this thing myself. I don't want to* get hooked on something and I don't want to lean on any crutch. Besides I don't believe in taking any pills. Like I said I got to do this by myself.

CO: *What you're telling me is that you don't think you need any help.*

CL: *I'm not saying that.*

CO: *So what are you saying?*

CL: *There's a difference between leaning and getting help.*

CO: (Candidly) *What difference?*

CL: *Well, I mean like there's a difference between pills and people. You lean on a pill, you get help from people. You're a person. I get help from you because you're a person.*

CO: (Seriously) *Doesn't seem like it's been all that much. You got drunk twice in the past month.*

CL: *Yeah, but I've been dry now for over a week.*

CO: *What are you saying? Maybe that you're not sure you want to stay dry too much longer.*

CL: *Christ no! I'm not saying that.*

CO: *So what's all this about helping and leaning? Doctors help like they know how, with prescriptions. Me, I help by listening and talking. People help how they can and how they know how. So what are you saying.*

CL: (Stonily) *What I'm saying is that I don't want to get hooked on a pill.*

CO: (Seriously) *You'd rather be hooked on booze?*

CL: *Christ I hope not.*

CO: *Okay, let's go over it again . . .*

This approach is blunt. At times, it is harsh. There is no intellectual dueling. The counselor's affect is serious and reflective. Her genuine concern is reflected in final comment, *"Okay, let's go over it again."* What the counselor means is that the client's denial defense needs to be attacked again.

Which of the two approaches is better? That is for the counselor to decide. The most important criterion is that the counselor must be comfortable with the method employed. Directive, nondirective, or somewhere in between, the method must fit with the counselor's personality if he/she is to confront with artistry.

ACTIVITIES FOR LEARNING
THE CONFRONTATION TECHNIQUE

Justification

Confrontation is conducive to self-exploration and heightened self-awareness by the client. Its special value in alcoholism counseling is that it can serve as a catalyst to restructure defenses.

Purpose

To develop the counselor's competence to confront.

Outcome

The student counselor will be able to demonstrate an effective use of the confrontation technique.

Specific Activities

1. The student counselor obtains verification that he/she accepts and is conversant with the theory behind confrontation.

2. The student counselor makes an observation of video tapes or listens to audio tapes of counselors who use this technique effectively.

3. The student counselor does role-playing with colleagues or mentor.

4. The student counselor demonstrates ability to confront with real client (live or on video tape).

Evaluation

1. The student counselor obtains feedback from the mentor.

2. Activities continue until the mentor and the student counselor are satisfied that the skill has been attained.

SUMMARY

The frame of reference for many alcoholics is derived from the Twelve Steps of A.A. The counselor who has understanding of these steps finds that rapport comes more easily. Once the counselor has learned how the client interprets these Steps, the counselor gains a valuable window into the client's system of thought and emotional life.

An important task of the counselor is to help the client to redirect and restructure his/her defenses. Explanations and/or illustrations were provided for denial, rationalization, displacement, fantasy, projection, and regression. Repression is a defense better left alone. Its best antidote would seem to be establishment of other defenses like compensation and sublimation.

Silence is threatening even to competent counselors. Silence occurs because of embarrassment, resentments, testing, client conflicts, fear, client need to integrate, and the end of a client counselor topic. A variety of techniques exist to handle the silence.

The counselor's ability to listen is critically important if progress is going to be made in counseling. He/she needs not only to listen to words but also needs to be exquisitely sensitive to the client's feelings, tones, and sounds. The counselor's motivation to listen is communicated by how he/she sits, by obviating interruptions, by isolating distracting thoughts, by being fully cognizant of those topics and thoughts which can block counselor ability to listen, and by learning to ask focused, pertinent questions.

Questioning as a technique has innate problems because

- it probes into the unknown,

- it can lead to more questions,

- it may cause the client to become conditioned to think in terms of questions and thereby lose his/her sense of responsibility to share more fully in the counseling, and

- questioning focuses upon the cognitive rather than upon feelings.

At the same time questioning also can be facilitative as it can lead into productive discussion, especially when the questions are open-ended and avoid the noted dangers.

Reiteration refers to a literal restatement or a rephrasing of what the client says. Reiteration is valuable because it puts the counselor into an accepting role, elicits client feelings, and helps the client to delineate and reconsider his/her thinking.

The counselor who reflects feeling communicates that he/she understands and perceives what the client is feeling and experiencing. The values of reflecting feelings lie in helping the client to crystallize his/her feelings and in understanding those feelings in relation to people. When reflecting feeling, the counselor should use simple language and be concerned about timing. This technique enhances the client by helping him/her to learn that feelings cause behavior, that feelings hide feelings. The ultimate benefit of such knowledge is to help the client explore the motives of his/her behavior.

Role-playing involves talking, doing, and trying to feel as the other whose role one plays. Role-players become the object of their own denials, rationalizations, and projections. Role-playing is an especially valuable technique in counseling the alcoholic intrafamilially.

The counselor who recapitulates responds with a focused, succinct synopsis of the client's long monologue. Recapitulation helps the client to build rapport, to focus thoughts and to keep to a theme. Recapitulation also reinforces the counselor's own understanding.

Confrontation is a valuable and useful technique as has been reported by researchers. The counselor should be fully aware that confrontation can be and often is threatening. Counselors can mitigate this threat if they are emotionally astute, if they genuinely are concerned and can communicate that concern, and if they introduce their confrontative remarks with neutral words and gentle tones. In addition, they must be and sound unaffected, know their client, and feel confident that their remarks will ultimately enhance the counseling relationship.

TOPICS FOR
DISCUSSION AND REFLECTION

1. Articulate your position on the Twelve Steps of Alcoholics Anonymous.

2. Do you believe that your penchant will be toward the directivist or toward the nondirectivist?

3. Which of the alcoholic defenses do you believe will be most difficult to restructure?

4. With which of the techniques described do you feel you will experience the most difficulty? With which the least?

5. Do you find client silence a threat? If so, reflect on the why of it.

6. Is the ability to listen to both tones and words part of your make-up? If not, do you feel the need to develop such an ability?

7. Are you one who can mirror feelings? Do you agree with author on its importance?

8. Role-playing involves a "let's pretend" attitude that often becomes very reality oriented. Do you expect to role-play in your work with clients?

9. Confrontation with some clients can be embarrassing. Will you be able to do it?

10. Learning practical techniques in counseling requires the expenditure of much time and energy. How willing are you to do so?

CHAPTER NINE

GROUP APPROACH TO ALCOHOLISM COUNSELING

The basic and general goal of counseling alcoholics in a group is the same as counseling the individual, namely, ***to help the alcoholic achieve and maintain sobriety.***

While purpose and goal for both are identical, counselor interaction with the group (from six to ten individuals) is substantially different from interaction with one person. The nature of group counseling will be described under these topic headings:

Benefits

Behaviors of Alcoholic Group Members

Functions of the Group Alcoholism Counselor

Stages and Techniques

BENEFITS

Counseling the alcoholic group has inestimable value. In group, alcoholics can derive the following benefits:

1. learning to become a helper,

2. learning to accept help,

3. learning about self,

4. learning interpersonal skills, and

5. learning tolerance, of others and self.

Learning to Become a Helper

The physical presence, nearness, and emotionally intense sharing through talk and behavior in group, invariably lead alcoholics to give of their own selves. This is in the best tradition of alcoholism rehabilitation. Indeed, upon this very idea Alcoholics Anonymous was founded; upon this idea A.A. is able to maintain its remarkable popularity.

Like it or not, and initially members do not, the mere act of listening in group becomes a sharing. As they tell their own stories they find themselves actually giving. Wondrously they learn to find reward in this giving. Nowhere does the ancient dictum that it is in giving that we receive have more pertinence than in counseling the alcoholic group.

Learning to Accept Help

Most alcoholics are quite unable to accept help from others. Their suspicious, if not paranoid perception, simply will not permit it. In their view, people have an ulterior purpose for everything they do and want. Their conviction is that nobody gives anything for nothing. Everybody's got his/her little bag, visible or not, because everybody's trying to sell something. Everybody's a manipulator.

Cynical as this view of others might be it should be remembered that most alcoholics have not been the happy recipients of selfless giving. More typically as children, adolescents, and even as adults, they have been the objects of neglect, indifference, and the manipulation they so abhor and fear. The irony, of course, is that they themselves harbor a remarkable penchant for manipulation.

Learning About Self

For most alcoholics the inevitable effect of learning to give and accept help from others is to learn about their own selves. In the emotionally receptive and caring climate of group, alcoholics learn that their addiction is due not to external forces or manipulating but to their own mislearnings and dysfunction.

As they listen to the moving and authentic self-disclosure of peer alcoholics and their own and as they question and are in turn questioned, they learn to look inside. They learn to do this with the new-found need to learn about the workings and control of their own selves instead of the narcissistic preoccupation which precipitated and maintained their alcoholism. They learn that their mislearnings and dysfunctions are not unique or strange but are part of the alcoholic condition. They learn that their problems stem from within and not without, from their own choices and judgments and not external manipulation. In short, alcoholics in group learn to do what they have never done—to take responsibility of their own selves.

Learning Interpersonal Skills

While true some alcoholics behave warmly, expansively in small and large groups, the truth is that few indeed feel comfortable or able interpersonally. The apparent warmth and expansiveness which some are able to show in most cases are nothing more than a veneer.

Beset by a latent but constant nag that people can not be trusted, alcoholics are quite unable to let others get close emotionally. Those alcoholics who frequent the same neighborhood bar or lounge to be with others, and even, perhaps especially, those who have an inordinate need to be the focal point of attention, seldom share or relate anything meaningful about themselves. Their interpersonal method and style are "to keep it light." Typical and favored topics include the weather, headlines, sports teams, and/or celebrities—all external, all noncontroversial, all "safe." Serious self-disclosures are not part of their emotional ken.

This inability to talk about themselves keeps them emotionally and interpersonally stunted. At some level, of course, they know it, and that knowledge breeds a fear that were they to share themselves they would necessarily display fool-like qualities. This distorted thinking among alcoholics fuels their need to distance and even isolate themselves.

In group counseling, alcoholics are not able to do either. Membership obligates participation and participation militates against distancing. Ergo, as alcoholics proceed to give and accept help, as they explore the wonder of their own selves, they learn how to relate with increasing comfort and satisfaction.

Learning Tolerance of Others and Self

The inevitable derivative of the four benefits previously described is the development in alcoholics of a trait alien to them—namely tolerance. As noted in prior context alcoholics are beset with a conscience which could fairly be described as scrupulous. The common effects of scrupulosity are obsessiveness, hypercynicism, a nagging disposition, and a general intolerance. In short, people, any and all, are a constant and fair game for criticism at best, playfully ironic, not uncommonly with a sarcasm vitriolic.

If any specific learning accelerates and facilitates the acquisition of this trait of tolerance in the new alcoholic members, it has to be finding out that their peers in the group suffer, experience, and display many of the foibles and weaknesses which harass them. Such learning even though usually known, albeit timely, is a positive revelation. More often than not, this revelation precipitates or at least facilitates the giving and loving of self by new members. Please note. This giving and sharing by these new members are not motivated exclusively by feelings of altruism, but are generated, and understandably enough, by the need to understand and become comfortable with their own respective selves. Whatever the motive, the effect is enhancing both for these new members and their peers.

BEHAVIORS OF ALCOHOLIC GROUP MEMBERS

Group sessions are characterized by both healthful and unhealthful behaviors. The healthful behaviors are those which facilitate the emotional growth progress of the venter and/or of another member. The three most important among these are

1. attending,

2. sharing, and

3. facilitating.

The unhealthful behaviors are all those which are self-destructive, which emotionally stultify another member, or which impede the collective progress of the group. Among those behaviors are included

1. hostility,

2. nonparticipating,

3. absenteeism,

4. buffoonery,

5. psychologizing,

6. assaulting,

7. housekeeping,

8. manipulating, and

9. seducing.

Healthful Behaviors

Attending. The critical ingredients of attending are **listening** and **communicating.** When we feel we are listened to, we are enhanced. Conversely when we feel no one is listening, we feel demeaned.

Most alcoholics feel that no one listens to them. They are probably right. They have lost credibility because of broken promises, procrastinations, and elusive and cynical ways. For whatever reasons, being a member of counseling group affords a wonderful opportunity to feel listened to, with a consequent sense of importance previously unknown.

As is true for most human behaviors, listening is learned. In a group the counselor is in the best position to teach it. Leader words, actions, and general demeanor are invariably modeled by members.

Posture and expression tell the speaker whether they are being listened to or not. In a group, the effective counselor sits as if he/she is motivated to hear everything said by everybody. Face and body bent tell members who are talking not only that they are being heard but their words are being processed. The counselor can accomplish that easily by reiterating member comments, by questioning, and by *not* introducing new thoughts or ideas, i.e., thoughts and ideas not addressed by group members.

By adhering strictly to these ideas of the listener role, the counselor lets members know not only that they are important as people but also that a behavioral model is present with whom members can identify.

Group members communicate when they talk *to* and *not* about each other. Very little ever occurs in human interaction which is more awkward or stilted than to hear oneself being discussed. This is true even when the talk is complimentary. Please note. In a group, this is often not so. Accordingly, an important first issue with all new group or with new entering members into the ongoing group is to simply inform them **any and all talk about another is to be addressed to that member.**

In a group, members communicate when their words, their emotions, and their body language all fit together. Most people find it difficult to process the meaning of words per se. Words in and of themselves can be and often are boring. For most *the emotion upon which words ride is what makes them interesting, even captivating.* Most people are more likely to laugh uproariously when they hear funny dialogue than when they read it. Students are more likely to be bored by a monotone-like delivery than with one filled with affective peaks and valleys. In sum, *most people are not touched by the cognitive (words) alone but by a blend of words and emotions.* When the words and emotions gibe with the speaker's body language then their attention is indeed "grabbed." Their attention is grabbed for the very simple reason that the message delivered *communicates*—its words, emotions, and body stance fit and complement each other. Such are the requirements of authentic communication.

When appropriate, effective group therapists model these ideas. Members should see that it's not only O.K. but desirable to smile a happy or complementary thought. When members accompany an angry statement with a glower or when they lacrimate a sorrow, the counselor's reaction should tell them such reactions are perfectly O.K.

Sharing. Sharers in a group are those who have come to trust. Trust is a rare trait among newly recovering alcoholics. It is even rarer among alcoholics who are drinking. Their paranoid perception militates against its development.

New members, more often than not, are newly recovering and have had no experience with group counseling. They are fearful and suspicious of a process which obligates trusting especially as their learning is that they can't trust anybody.

Non-trusting alcoholics can be understood as being still in the throes of projection and denial. Not having been exposed to situations or experiences where they could or had to learn it, they do not know sublimation. Put another way, they have not yet been able to learn to find reward in giving or that the road to health can be eased much by the development of emotional relationships. Sad but true, in the giving of self and in interpersonal relations in general, **alcoholics function with the emotional wherewithal of children.**

In a group, trust comes to the newly admitted only after they have had an opportunity to become acclimated. As they begin to identify with the talk and behaviors of individual members and of the group collectively they begin to sense the warmth and mutuality which are the essentials of rapport. Of course this new found rapport precipitates the trust needed to get on with one's own rehabilitation.

Once alcoholics begin to find emotional reward in trusting others, they show it—in their talk and in how they look. Why? Because trusting raises self-esteem, both of the trusted and the trustee.

A principle obstacle to learning to trust is confidentiality. Group members have to know, alcoholic members especially, that anything and everything said in the group is inviolate. It behooves the counselor to explain and reiterate this to the whole group whenever a new member is admitted. The author's explanation always includes the idea that confidentiality is an indispensable prerequisite to group process. My line delivered with conviction is that, *"If there is no confidentiality there can be no group."* My sense is that group members have always honored the confidentiality dictum. In no case can I recollect an instance where it has been violated. My sense, too, is that the group's apparent respect for confidentiality has facilitated trust in the newly entering member.

Group leaders would do well to let new members know that they recognize the difficulties involved in trusting a number of strangers. A statement in this regard can only be helpful as it confirms and reinforces what new members know albeit dimly—that participation in group is premised upon trust.

Trust leads to self-disclosure which ironically in turn, promotes more trust. This promotion and expansion of trust in a group is probably why counselors find that group members invariably reward and often do so generously that first fumbling attempt at self-disclosure by newer members.

The wonderful thing about self-disclosure is that once alcoholics have come to trust, they learn to do it quickly. A very strong, positive correlation exists between self-disclosure and improvement of emotional health. The more alcoholics share and confide their most acute anxieties, frustrations, and past embarrassments, the healthier they become. Their self-perception and perception of others becomes more optimistic. Their ability to listen improves and increases. Thus they are able to share the anxieties and frustrations of other members.

With increased self-disclosure the defenses with which alcoholics insulate themselves—projection and denial—begin to crumble. As they share more and more, these defenses are replaced slowly but inevitably by sublimation.

The author is pleased most when self-disclosure comes at the beginning of a session. What he has learned is that if alcoholics have time to mull over what a member has shared, they are likely to be moved themselves to share. Self-disclosures early in a session generally precipitate self-disclosure by other members. These subsequent precipitates can be understood as supportive statements to the initial discloser. Whatever the reason, the effect is usually a happy one. Interaction invariably becomes warmer and more tolerant.

Facilitating. Initially the counselor is the prime facilitator. As the group progresses, facilitating behavior becomes the choice behavior for most members. A point to note is that not uncommonly, alcoholism counseling groups include one or more members who because of prior group experience are quite knowledgeable about facilitating. Not uncommonly too, some members because of disposition and/or inclination are natural facilitative types. The danger with these last, discussed under the heading "Unhealthy Behavior, Psychologizing," is that some members might be facilitating consciously or unconsciously at the expense of their own needs. Such facilitators are of course in denial. That is, they are facilitating to avoid dealing with their own problems. Member facilitators not psychologizing but who are themselves progressing toward health and termination from group can be understood as being in accelerated recovery. The especially active member facilitators are usually those who have most recently discovered the emotional pleasure to be found in the sublimation defense.

Alcoholics find special reward in facilitating because they learn, and quickly, that it is not purely an altruistic activity. What they learn is that the feeling effects of facilitating enhance the self as much as they enhance others.

Facilitators move group members toward health. They do this by listening like they mean it. They respond only to what is said and question and probe with nothing more threatening than authentic concern and curiosity. Their words, their effects, and their body language when they do all this **communicates** a need to help—sans strings.

Indigenous to facilitating is giving feedback. When a group leader or a member gives feedback, he/she focuses on words or behavior of a particular member. The one giving feedback tells own feelings about what the member has said and/or done. Giving feedback never involves nagging, carping, or criticizing. Rather, its cardinal rule is that it be couched in deference, if not humility, and its emotional by-play are tact, diplomacy, and simple kindness. The author tells his group that giving feedback is a purely subjective process. I am very fond of saying that, *"What is true in a group depends upon who is lookin'."* Ergo, feedback has value only if the recipient thinks and feels that it's so. **Feedback finally is one person's reaction to another. Feedback is not objective truth.** With these statements as a frame of reference then the one giving feedback should preface the words with *"My personal feeling is that . . ." "I'm not talking for anyone else when I say that . . ." "My reaction and mine only is that . . ."*

Such prefaces not only make it clear that feedback is just one human's opinion to another, but they inform and elucidate. More importantly, they minimize the risk of hurt.

Feedback's most important effect is to expose the recipient of it to another view of himself/herself. Couched with good will, only the feedbacker's view is usually accepted thereby enhancing the member's and the group's movement toward growth.

Unhealthful Behaviors

Hostility. As has been noted in this text in a variety of contexts the prime defenses for many alcoholics are denial and projection. The effect of denial usually is to put one on a different emotional and perceptual wave length from those with whom he/she comes in contact. More often than not, the effect of all this on alcoholics is bewilderment and anger, compounded typically by the fantasy defense.

Fantasy in alcoholics is characterized usually by a sense of victimization. It is this sense which helps to develop and cultivate tableaus in male alcoholics where they can seek and achieve violent revenge. These tableaus are a too frequent source for the interpersonal stance which they assume not only with family, with those with whom they work but with perfect strangers too. Please note, that when they first enter the alcoholic group, it is composed of perfect strangers!

Every alcoholic displays his/her hostility differently not only because of the generic uniqueness of human personality but for the obvious and simple reasons that hostility varies from person to person in kind, amount and intensity. Even so, among alcoholics in group counseling there are certain commonalities in which it might be useful to delineate and describe. These are

1. humor,

2. rudeness, and

3. testing.

Hostile alcoholics, especially newcomers to group are seldom funny. Their **humor** is usually personally directed rather than generalized, sarcastic rather than ironic, and demeaning instead of enhancing. Such humor relaxes no one including the jokester. It does however, increase tension and anxiety.

Now, what should the response be to such "humor?" Laughter, even embarrassed smiles are undesirable as they could be interpreted as some kind of reward and rewards of any kind are potential fuel for future hostile humor. The best response to the newcomer's initial hostile jokes by the group leader is no response. The leader will find that group members will follow suit should the humor continue, disparaging looks are not inappropriate. Sometimes a curt interjection of unfeigned displeasure will let the person know that hostile humor is simply not appreciated in the group. Occasionally a remark albeit, not a "put down," may be necessary.

The behavior of a disproportionate number of hostile alcoholics is characterized by **rudeness.** Their behavior is so, not because of reasons outlined above (denial, projection, and fantasy) but for the reason that many of them simply never had a model who taught them how to behave in socially appropriate ways. Put simply, these alcoholics never learned how to be "nice." This is one aspect of hostility which is mitigated fairly easily and will lessen as the newcomer learns to identify with the acceptance, warmth, and trust generated by the group.

An unfortunate aspect of the hostile alcoholic is the need to **test** all strangers. Testing can best be understood as one of the more salient symptoms of the alcoholic's suspiciousness if not paranoia. Its rationale while simple can be most exasperating. Central to the testing is the alcoholics' perverted idea that how much hostility a person will tolerate from the hostile person is a measure of how much they care. The testing can take any of a variety of forms—vitriolic teasing, temper tantrums, mimicry, etc. As is true with the humor, the more people put up with the abasements, the more they fuel the hostility. If and when they do react with anger, the hostile testing alcoholic has a ready response, *"I always knew you didn't care!"*

The only happy note about testing in a group is that it declines rapidly as members become acclimated to each other (and pass each other's tests)!

No specific or simple techniques can be outlined for dealing with alcoholic hostility. Confrontation in any form is not a good idea as it reinforces the alcoholic's basic notion that hostility is justified because everyone else is hostile. The best way for the therapist to mitigate hostility in a group is to communicate to all the members that they are all accepted and unconditionally. Therapists can best provide antidotes for hostility if they model and promote the qualities outlined under the preceding heading "Healthful Behaviors," i.e., attending, sharing, and facilitating. Inevitably these alleviate or at least ameliorate the unpleasantness generated by hostility.

Finally, it is not naive and it should be pointed out that patience is an indispensable prerequisite in counselors who deal with hostile alcoholics. They need to remember that the hostility alcoholics vent toward them and their peer members is never personal but is an emotional trait sown in them early by neglect, indifference, and cruelty. This trait took more than a while to grow and develop in them and the reality is that it is a part of their personalities. Quite apparently, the therapist and the group members can not surgically remove this undesirable trait but both can contribute an emotional climate conducive to developing insight into the why of it. This insight combined with the acquisition of healthful behaviors mentioned can help alcoholics better control their hostility.

Nonparticipating. Defenses interpretation does not effectively explain the why of nonparticipation in group by some alcoholics because the defenses associated with nonparticipation are many and varied. The reasons for it in a group include these reasons for silence detailed and explained in Chapter 8 under Practical Techniques. A rereading at this point might prove helpful. Now, while these reasons for silence may explain the whys for individual nonparticipation and silence in an 'ndividual and even in a group, they do not explain why a whole group may become silent.

The three following reasons are fairly common ones. Other reasons may indeed exist but these are most common. The author's experience is that group nonparticipation often occurs because

1. The group does not want to deal with an anxious or embarrassing issue,

2. the group and the leader are not communicating, and/or

3. the group feels affronted and wants to get back at the leader.

What group leaders know is that silence in a group precipitates a lot more tension than it ever does in individual counseling. Happily and not uncommonly, alcoholic counseling groups include a member who has very little tolerance for such tension. A tense silence broken by an anxious alcoholic, however, does not explain the why of the silence. If the reason is that the group is reluctant to deal with an anxiety provoking issue, confrontation through questioning by the therapist is in order. The one to question first would be the one who broke the silence as that member is probably the one interested in abating the tension.

When the reason has to do with communication the author has discovered that confrontation by questioning is again the best way to resolve the issue. Questioning each member in turn or selecting articulate members has been effective for this author. The answer(s) which come out of a group have been both startling and amusing. For example, early in the author's career, when he was employed in a V.A. psychiatric hospital, he was leading a new group. In its several early encounters, the group was beset with protracted silences regularly. Frustrated, bewildered, and not a little threatened, I questioned the group. The answer which came back readily was simple and not a little pointed. What I learned was that my questions, probing, and interpretations had been couched in language more appropriate for a graduate school setting than one where the average length of education for members was seventh grade. Mike, the little man who sat directly opposite to me looked me right in the eye and summed it up simply and succinctly, *"Big words, doc. Too many big words!"*

The third reason for group nonparticipation is usually due to hostility. If an entire group is angry or resentful, the therapist is probably in some measure responsible. Several approaches for resolution can be considered.

1. Careful and intense self-examination by the therapist focusing especially on his/her perception of the group.

2. Discussion with a colleague, again focusing on perception of the group and consideration of new strategies.

3. If the therapist can honestly admit to inadequacies, then an apologetic, deferential discussion about these inadequacies with the group is very much in order. Quite apparently, no group has ever been offended by an honest admission of fault. After all, it is the essence of very effective self-disclosure previously described.

Absenteeism. The prime defense for absenteeism is denial. Absentee members are so because for whatever reason they need to hold on to the illusion that they are not alcoholic. Absence from group concretizes that illusion.

Reasons for an absence may be legitimate but they are few and dire—death, a contagious illness, and/or a crippling accident. No other excuse can and should be tolerated by the therapist or the group. The point, ***attendance at every single session is mandatory.*** It is an indispensable requisite. The therapist should make this point and with conviction when the alcoholic attends his/her first meeting. Many groups have rules about absences, i.e., one, two, or more absences for reasons other than those indicated and a member is expelled. Such rules should not be imposed by the therapist imperiously as they might engender hostility unnecessarily. Rather they should be issued as policy from the group so that it can have more meaning, more force, and can be more easily identified with.

Unjustified absences hurt not only the absentee but the group as well. Every group has a palpably unique personality just as do individuals. When a member is absent from the group without explanation, then the group's personality is different. The difference is rarely a healthier one, for the absence—always painfully obvious—engenders talk which is rarely complementary to the absentee and even more rarely to the members who discuss him/her.

The author's position is that absence without justification needs to be discussed. Why? Because unjustified absence invariably engenders much, much hostility. Like it or not, justified or not, it is perceived as rejection of the group by most if not all members. The reason for this is simple. Rejection is in the background of virtually all alcoholics. Indeed, for many it was precisely rejection which contributed, often precipitated the alcoholism.

Even though some steam needs to be let out by the group an effective leader will not let discussion about an absentee deteriorate into just a complaining, belittling session about the absentee. Such a leader will help the group develop a constructive plan to help the absentee. Each plan will necessarily be different as its design will be determined by both the needs of the group and absent member. Even so every plan should include ideas about communicating to absentees that they are needed, that they are important to the group personality and that they were missed. An important point is for the plan to provide time for the group to discuss with the absentee his/her motivation, commitment, and readiness for the group.

Buffoonery. From time to time the group might include a person who is genuinely funny, whose jokes are only ironic and not directed personally. Such a person is perceived as a clown. He/she is loved by all the members not only because the humor is devoid of hostility but because the jokes and buffoonery entertain and relieve group tensions.

Alcoholics especially in the treatment center are generally not perceived as sources of entertainment. But this is exactly what a clown is—an entertainer. When the clown is in especially good humor, he/she can precipitate honest belly laughs.

Clowning like most human behavior serves a purpose. In group therapy it hides the denial defense and more often than not it does so exceedingly well. Effective clowns make people laugh, and ironically, every laugh feeds denial. Effective clowns make members forget that clowns are in a group for the same reason as the rest of the members—namely to achieve and maintain sobriety.

The alcoholic clown is an anomaly. Alcoholism and clowning are really like oil and water, they don't mix. Why? Because alcoholics ordinarily are preoccupied with their own selves, are inclined to emotional isolation or at least structure their lives to keep people at a distance. Clowns on the other hand, are emotionally attuned to others and enjoy being with others (how else can they get laughs?). The clown who is an alcoholic, then, is as conflicted as any alcoholic and probably more than most.

The actual buffoonery of the clown can be understood as nothing more than a sophisticated veneer to belie the harsh reality of the alcoholism. Thus clowns who are effective are able to mask their problems. Good and constant *buffoonery in the alcoholic group can be understood as nothing more than a unique form of classical resistance to dealing with the problem of alcoholism.*

After having provided the usual moments of entertainment the clown can sit back comfortably and let others take over to interact therapeutically. If the therapist is not vigilant, the clown can stay quite uninvolved in the actual attending, sharing, and facilitating. The sensitive and conscientious therapist will not let this happen. The problem is not especially difficult to remedy. All the counselor needs to do is to direct an occasional simple question or remark at the clown in his/her role as a member of the alcoholic group. In this way, the therapist is able to remind both the clown and the rest of the group why he/she is there.

Psychologizing. Today, more people than ever have sophisticated vocabularies in psychology and psychotherapy. Words like defenses, rapport, transference, and countertransference are, if not part of every day usage, then at least readily understood. This is probably due to the popularization of psychology, of counseling and group process through literature and television, and the substantial increase in the number of people with some college education during the past generation. Whatever the reason, today we meet people who love to interpret the whys and wherefores of human behavior in general and in particular of the people they know. We call these people psychologizers.

Psychologizers are to be found everywhere and too often in the counseling group. Like the clown, psychologizers deny their alcoholism and engage in idiosyncratic behavior to divert attention from themselves. An important difference exists between the two however: clowns usually are lovable and psychologizers usually are not.

Psychologizers effectively support their denial defense with intellectualization. Thus they engage in analyzing, interpreting, and explaining the motives and behaviors of other group members both when appropriate and when not. Given free rein they can do so ad nauseam.

At the same time it should be noted that their long intellectualized defining of peer behavior can be, often is, smooth and cogent. Usually a response to their fantasies regarding being powerful, these monologues are controlling because of the amount of time they demand of listeners.

Many of the psychologizers one encounters in the alcoholic group learned to be so in past groups and in individual counseling. Even though they may need more treatment, they display a remarkable knowledge of both the language and the techniques of counseling.

How much of a problem psychologizers pose is determined by just how hostile they are. An especially angry one can indeed be an unfortunate burden for the group, i.e., while one might give feedback timidly another might give it brutally. Even worse, those psychologizers, who are especially adept, can and do impress the newer, more naive members with their cognitive expertise. The psychologizers win them over and ally with them against another member or members, thereby creating a sub-group within the group. In short, some psychologizers, especially the hostile ones make themselves out to be rivals for the group leader. Understandably the inexperienced therapist can be threatened by such a person. More unfortunately still these hostile psychologizers are very much aware of the threat felt by such a therapist and consciously or unconsciously thoroughly enjoy the prospects of vying for group leadership and control.

The best way that the therapist can obviate the possibility of such an embarrassing prospect or eventuality is to meet with the psychologizer alone. At the meeting the therapist should point out in the clearest fashion what the respective roles and responsibilities of each of them are and that rivalry for the leadership role is not one of them.

The behavior of psychologizers can strain the patience threshold of the best therapist. The constant temptation is to confront. This may or may not be a good idea. It is if the psychologizing has been going on for some time and the therapist sees that the group collectively or particular members are being silenced or alienated. It is not a good idea to confront the psychologizer or any member for that matter if the therapist is not emotionally and cognitively convinced that he/she understands the member's dynamics.

Assaulting. The assaultive streak, while not common among alcoholics, does indeed exist. It is especially rare among females. Alcoholics who periodically lash out physically have a defense structure which also is not common for those with the disease. Denial is secondary to displacement and projection, with projection usually the more dominant force between the two.

Among assaultive types the constantly seething nag is that people are out to do them in by hook or by crook which leads them to lash out, displace upon others. Admittedly, many, if not most, alcoholics are inclined to some displacement. What is important to note here is that displacement by most alcoholics is done *verbally* not *physically*. For the assaultive types the physical approach to ventilation is just as common as the verbal. Even worse, the assaultive alcoholic is more likely to engage in physical attacks which are not displacements. (The definition of displacement is to vent hostility upon a person other than the one who engendered the hostile feeling.) In other words, the alcoholic may indeed physically vent the anger engendered not only upon the innocent and unknowing but upon those perceived as responsible. When the behavior is such the assaultive individual is especially able to justify his/her behavior.

What may be true of course is that some alcoholics live with hostility so intense that they are quite unable to control it and/or they simply have not learned how to do so. For them, a group might not be the place to learn controls as the process might involve too much hurt to too many people. Quite apparently, no member ever joined a counseling group to become a whipping boy for a hostile alcoholic!

Most alcoholic groups include one or more members who come from homes where physical violence occurred if not regularly then at least sporadically. When such members see violence in the group, it can indeed precipitate many traumatic feelings. To reiterate, members of an alcoholic group do not become members to become traumatized. This author's conviction is that alcoholics with a history for assault and **who commit a physical in the group** must be expelled. In such circumstances, referral to individual counseling is in order.

The astute therapist recognizes the alcoholic who is or might be assaultive. When he/she thinks that one or more of the members is of this type then he/she is obligated to tell the entire group what the policy is regarding physical assault during a session. Fairness dictates that potential assaultees be told the policy in private also.

Housekeeping. Occasionally the counseling group includes a very active individual, one who is constantly busy doing for the group. This person will set up chairs and make coffee before the meeting on a regular basis and on occasion will provide snacks. While the group is in session this busy bee will buzz around the group pouring the coffee and serving the snacks. Such an individual is called a housekeeper.

Housekeepers keep busy for the same reasons that buffoons buffoon and psychologizers psychologize—namely, to divert attention from their alcoholism. Like others previously described, housekeepers are in denial. Also, they cultivate a rich fantasy life. In their fantasy world they are nurturant, servant-like, and enhancing. Thus the image they project fits pretty much with the image they hold of themselves.

Basically, housekeepers are "nice guys and gals." Like the clown, to not like them is hard for the simple reason they seem (and do) find much pleasure in doing for and giving to others.

The personality of the giving, active, serving individual that they display in the group counseling is consistent with the one they display prior to entry and pretty much the one they display after they terminate.

Although exceedingly private in disposition, housekeepers are usually people beset with strong submissive and acceptance needs. By doing, doing, doing for group members they are able to meet both needs. Their busy frenetic ways can and often serve as a camouflage for the alcoholism and obviate their involvement during the more intensely dramatic moments of a session.

If their dynamics are understood and appreciated, housekeepers are usually excellent candidates for group counseling and invariably profit much from it. Guided by the counselor, the members should be encouraged to praise and reward the housekeeper's physical efforts for the group. What the author has discovered is that questioning after being verbally rewarded by the group makes the housekeeper receptive to self-disclosure and a rapid movement toward emotional growth.

Some housekeepers, however, are more complex in nature. These are the ones whose fantasies go beyond nurturance and service to others and include parental-like role. These housekeepers on some level see themselves as protector types and they try to expand the housekeeper role to fit that self-image.

Their own submissive streak notwithstanding, and/or perhaps because of it, they are able to detect those members who have dependency needs. Finely attuned to such needs in the group session they anticipate and act ahead of the therapist or peer who is about to protect a member from the verbal abuse of another or of a clique. The dependent prone members are usually grateful to the housekeeper and quickly come to perceive him/her as a kind of emotional crutch.

Housekeepers who continually try to function as protectors can be likened to over-protective parents and like the overprotective parent the protector-housekeeper seeks not to nurture but to control. Unrestrained in the group, housekeepers could become destructive.

If just plain told this, housekeeper would be astonished. They would not understand. Such astonishment would be a good thing because it would mean that they are oblivious of the demeaning nature of their protector need and that their penchant for it is unpremeditated.

A most effective technique for the author with this kind of housekeeper is to lead the group in a discussion of the traits of the controlling alcoholic enabler. Most of the members know the enabler type only too well. This topic invariably precipitates a discussion which gives off a lot of heat but light too. Not only the housekeeper, but all the members who incorporate even remotely comparable qualities find they can suddenly become the objects of more than a few acerbic comments. More often than not the session seems to have a healthful sobering effect (no pun intended!) on the enthusiastic housekeeper.

Manipulating. In a therapy group composed of alcoholics the participant most likely to accuse the housekeeper or anyone else about being controlling is the person guilty of the same. This person is termed the manipulator.

If one understands the defense structure underlying it, one can better understand the why of manipulator behavior. The structure is comparable to that of the hostile member. Denial is foremost. Manipulators continue to adhere to the notion that they are not alcoholic. Projection is a strong prop for denial. Manipulators feel they are themselves constantly being manipulated and not uncommonly view the group leader as one out to brainwash them.

A common streak in the manipulator personalities, blatant or latent, is **blaming.** Manipulators tend to look out, not in, for the reasons for their problems. They justify their feelings and behavior upon attitudes, talk, and actions of others. In their own view, their misfortunes especially their alcoholism, is a function of the dark motives and manners of other people. Simply put, they hold a victim's view of life.

Shastrom (1967) has developed a comprehensive description of manipulator types. Two types may be considered, those who operate from a position of strength and those who operate from a position of weakness. The list is provided in Figure 9.1.

From a position of weakness	
weakling	sensitive to hurt
clinging vine	dependent
nice guy	warm

From a position of strength	
the judge	critical
the bully	aggressive
the calculator	controlling
the dictator	strong
the protector	supportive

Figure 9.1. Manipulator behavior from two positions: Weakness and strength.

The most effective way to deal with manipulators is to address their perception of themselves and others. Openness, candor, and authenticity may confound the manipulator but ultimately and inevitably lead them to a realistic self-view of their lives.

Seducing. The seducer is that person who uses words, emotional charms, and body to obtain sexual favors. The successful seducer is the manipulator par excellence. He/she operates from a position of strength or if the position demands, from a position of weakness. Seducers can be, to put it delicately, emotionally flexible if not ambidextrous. To them from where they are coming does not matter. What matters to them is where they're going and most importantly, what they expect to get.

The description here is of seducers and the seductive process in general. Add alcohol and the whole manipulative process becomes exacerbated. Now, though inveterate manipulators, the dynamics of the alcoholic seducers are very different from those of the alcoholic manipulator not interested in seduction. Alcoholic seducers are not necessarily blamers, nor do they usually hold an especially victimized view of themselves or of life. In fact, effective seducers who are alcoholics, especial when in their sober states operate with a fairly adequate self-esteem.

The defense which helps to explain them best is not denial or projection but *fantasy.* Male seducers fantasize most about being in control of others, especially of women. Females fantasize about being the focal point of attention, having their proverbial simple wishes treated as commands and dispensing favors sexual and otherwise with discrimination.

The addiction to alcohol for a disproportionate number of both these males and females is related in no little way to their inability to make a long term emotional commitment to the opposite sex. Their heterosexual stance rather is promiscuous.

Despite their apparent sophistication and sometimes "smooth" interpersonal ways, heterosexual alcoholic seducers are a confused and terribly vulnerable lot. The following story illustrates not only how confused and vulnerable they can be but even more just how destructive mutual seduction in a group can be.

Jack had been in the group for almost a month when Connie entered it. Quiet and essentially still nonparticipating he had attended every session (six of them) faithfully. The group was one I led for a local branch of a major industrial concern which at the time had a little over fifteen hundred employees. The group including Connie, consisted of nine alcoholics, seven men and two women.

This was Jack's second time in group with me, both times self-referred. The first time he had been forced to withdraw after two months (eight sessions) because he had been sent by the company to a new plant in a nearby state to set up payroll procedures. Such was the respect in which he was held by central headquarters. Of average height, balding, and more than a little overweight, Jack had been twice married— the first time for three years and the second time for three months. In the middle-manager classification he earned seventy-five thousand dollars a year and paid no alimony.

*During his membership in the first counseling group, Jack had displayed a quiet but affable, easy-going disposition. His questions and general responses to group members and his self-disclosures toward the end of his first counseling group, while few, had been thoughtful. These had shown not only that he listened well but that he was interested, wanted to help others, and wanted to learn about himself. Even though a waiting list existed, I had been pleased to skip over it to admit him, rationalizing that his was a **readmission.** My conviction was that he was serious about achieving and maintaining sobriety.*

Connie had been on two waiting lists besides mine when she was admitted to the group. Twenty-eight years old, divorced, and with three children, Connie worked as an assembler and earned a little over sixteen thousand dollars per year. Blond and average of both face and figure she came in wearing a shy, wistful look.

Connie started in the group and Jack's demeanor changed. The quiet, nonparticipating member the group had known suddenly become very involved if not assertive, even displaying apt if not skillful counseling skills. At her very first session, he questioned several members with thoughtful questions, made a couple of astute observations, and an interpretation I totally concurred with at the end of a long monologue. He even cracked a joke!

Reflecting on the first Connie session afterwards, I had to conclude that Jack had participated very appropriately and had accomplished something else. He'd made himself noticed. That realization led me to watch the interplay between the two. One didn't have to be especially keen to discern that Connie was attracted to Jack. Her eyes never left him. Jack's tell-tale signs were even more transparent. Even though he continued to be active, if not dynamic, he addressed no comments or questions to Connie. He didn't have to. His way of looking at her had begun to become embarrassing.

Up to the time Connie started in the group, members had been openly warm, encouraging, and active. Within three sessions of her arrival, the talk became strained. At the end of the following session the only person talking besides me was Jack. Connie meanwhile, despite several questions by me and a couple by other members, had smiled with apparent uninterest.

Then I got an unsurprising bit of news. As a consultant counselor on a part-time basis (four to six hours per week) I've neither access nor interest in gossip about plant personnel. Access and interest notwithstanding, I learned from an anonymous message on my telephone machine that Jack and Connie were dating.

As I saw it, the problem was not just mine or Jack's or Connie's or Jack's and Connie's together. It was the group's problem. At the next session I confronted the group with comments and questions such as these. **"I used to look forward to coming to this group. I find myself dreading it now. What has happened to alter my feelings? What changes have taken place in this group during the past couple of weeks?"** *This last question precipitated a veritable storm of comments, all very pointed, very bitter and all directed at Jack and Connie. The substance and emotional sum were that the members were resentful. The only other woman stated it succinctly:* **"I don't mind what you do with each other before and after but I really wish you'd both stop making goo-goo eyes here!"** *More than a few told Connie that they thought and felt she was not ready for the group.*

The session was Connie's last. After her second absence the group voted to drop her. Jack stayed. With her departure he returned to the more quiet listener type he'd shown himself to be prior to her joining. He progressed healthfully and terminated from the group four months later.

P.S. A month after his termination he and Connie were married and he adopted her children. Within a year she left him. He now pays alimony.

FUNCTIONS OF THE
GROUP ALCOHOLISM COUNSELOR

In a prior work (Perez, 1986) the author outlined the functions of the group therapist. These functions are of two categories:

1. administrative and

2. therapeutic.

The author's experience since describing those functions has only reinforced his belief in their validity. These functions together with their specifics are summarized in the following paragraphs.

Administrative Functions

The first decision the therapist needs to make is to *decide what the size the group will be.* As so much else about counseling work and particularly group work, the ideal depends upon the therapist's personality. A group with a minimum of six members and a maximum of nine seems to work best for this therapist.

A second administrative duty *is to screen candidates.* This can be done by interviewing members individually or in couples. The author's experience has been that the more he knew about a potential member's past the better he was able to facilitate interaction between and among members. He has found it especially valuable to know about a member's past counseling experience, if any, and especially if the member has or has not been in trouble with the law. The author's experience is that potential members who are court mandated referrals because they were arrested for D.U.I. (driving under the influence) are not the best candidates. This is precisely because they are ordered into counseling. They are usually resentful and hostile. As participants, they go through the motion, complete their "sentences," and in most cases return at a later date. The best potential candidates are the self-referred. These individuals are usually motivated to achieve sobriety.

A third administrative function has to do with *hosting and launching the group.* This duty involves arranging and coordinating the session times. This is an enterprise which the author has found at best tedious and more often frustrating. Another function is to explain to each member, either during screening or at the first session, the therapist's basic rules regarding interaction among members, i.e., to talk *to* and not *about* each other, policy regarding assaultive behavior, and policy about absence from a meeting. Many rules members make themselves. These usually have to do with eating during the group, smoking, and walking around. All of these behaviors, the author permits. A group should not be launched unless members hear what their roles and obligations are in the group especially regarding attending, sharing, and facilitating.

Therapeutic Functions

The four therapeutic functions are defending, supporting, observing, and intervening.

How much *defending* the therapist does is determined by the emotional climate, context, and vitriol and the counselor's personality and disposition.

Supporting involves rewarding and encouraging the shy, inhibited, and fearful member—the one who has more than the usual difficulty involved in the counseling group.

Observing is what the therapist does all the time. It has to do with being exquisitely sensitive to any and all member dynamics. It is perhaps the most draining of all the therapeutic functions as it is constant.

Intervening means sharing. When the therapist intervenes, he/she is essentially modeling counseling skills, i.e., questioning, listening, clarifying, reflecting, etc., the skills outlined in Chapter 8.

Finally, some personal thoughts on you, the therapist. How you do therapy is a function of your personality. How you perceive the group, how you interact with it, and the meanings you derive from each and every session are critical aspects of your personality. They are the determinants for how effective you will be as a group counselor.

Effective group therapists need to be healthy enough to trust their feelings. These are an excellent if not the best criteria for judging your effectiveness, for whether a session was productive or not. Good feelings at the end of a session usually means that the session went well. Queasy feelings tell you either that it did not go well or at least that you were not at your best. If you are beset periodically by queasy feelings of dissatisfaction about your counseling experiences in a group, it's O.K. It may even be desirable because such feelings reflect a person of conscience and only a person of conscience worries about his/her performance. Queasy feelings about how you are doing mean that you seek to travel on the road to excellence. For you, the person of conscience, it is the only road because finally you have only two alternatives—to travel, move forward toward excellence, or to regress. You can not stand still. You can not stay the same. Time does not permit it.

STAGES AND TECHNIQUES

Prefatory Notes

Counseling groups are of two kinds—the open group or on-going group and the closed group. The **on-going group** is one where members come and go. They enter, go through the stage in the treatment process to termination and discharge.

The **closed group** begins with all new members. It may be run in one of two different ways. Thus the group members stay together until all members terminate. This is rare. More commonly, members terminate in terms of their own particular motivation, speed, and needs but no new members are introduced into the group until all the starting members have terminated. The type the author had in mind in the descriptions which follow was the open group.

Group therapists understand that a member passes through stages in the treatment process. Only with a clear knowledgeable frame of reference will they be able to understand what is happening and why it's happening and be in a more effective position to help the member. Each of the stages will be described in terms of dynamics, defenses, and the techniques which seem to be most effective to facilitate treatment.

The stages as listed and defined here do not usually occur in nice, sequential order. The stage concept was adopted here so that the therapist can know all that can and usually does take place. The dynamics and defenses described are all exhibited in a group and usually occur in the respective stage described. At the fourth session, a member may seem to exhibit the dynamics of one at the third stage. Then at the next session, the member may have regressed back to the first stage and stay there for the next half dozen sessions! Thus, in the same way that alcoholics do not adhere to a neat stage process of progression into and recovery from alcoholism, neither do they proceed neatly and logically through group process. Quite apparently, neatness and logic are not indigenous to human dynamics.

With the exception of the first one, stages do not begin with any clear indicator. They never end clearly either. Rather they meld and merge. For this reason to tell on what stage a member is in the treatment process is difficult. Only when he/she is close or at the termination stage can one know. Even then, the knowing (both by the counselor and the member) is fraught with more than a few doubts. Finally, we are discussing alcoholism recovery!

The length of time necessary to pass from the first to fifth stage is a function of much: the energy and motivation of the member, how well the members get along with each other, how articulate the member is, not a little the skill of the therapist, and finally the reality of the administrative circumstances in which the group work is performed, i.e., if a city, country, or state locale, what length of treatment time is prescribed, etc.

The five stages are

1. adaptation,

2. rapport,

3. conflict,

4. progression, and

5. termination.

Adaptation

At this first stage the only thing alcoholics know is that they are embarking on a new experience and with strangers! Even for normal people a new experience can be perceived with embarrassment, shyness, and not a little bit of fear. Add strangers to it and all these feelings become stronger.

To alcoholics beset as they are with a perception which leads them to effect distance rather than closeness with others, thereby rendering them interpersonally inept, normal feelings become exacerbated. The fear, for example, for some becomes a kind of latent terror.

The defenses most new members use to defend against this terror is **denial.** At this stage the most common supports for it are **projection, fantasy,** and **rationalization.** The best way to deal with these defenses at this early point is simply not to. Even gentle and kindly couched questions might be perceived as challenges and conceivably could result in a stranger-like sense of estrangement and even dropping out.

Members' interaction at this stage is best understood in terms of their emotional immaturity and their acutely fearful perception. Acutely uncomfortable then, they relate with silence often, with hostility sometimes, and not uncommonly, with awkwardness.

An important point to note is that whenever a new member is introduced the personality of the new member will change the personality of the group. A critically important point, then, is for the therapist personally to do anything and everything to help the new person to feel welcome and comfortable. Truly as the new member feels and goes so will the group. Members usually know this and are usually exceedingly helpful.

At this first stage when new members come to talk they do so about externals, little or nothing meaningful about themselves but rather about the weather, sports, current political events, etc. Not uncommonly, they make many contradictory statements about their opinions and feelings even about these externals. Such contradictions can be understood as a function of their emotional discomfort and their fear.

The techniques explained and described in Chapter 8 and most effective at this stage include the following:

1. listening,

2. questioning,

3. reiterating,

4. recapitulating, and

5. reflecting.

These techniques can be utilized by both counselor and members.

Rapport

At this second stage, members begin to perceive themselves and the group more kindly and more realistically. This is due to a new found feeling of acceptance by them and of them. Blended with this feeling is one newer still—trust.

In this emotionally but still alien climate new members want and begin to explore themselves through group interaction. These first fumbling attempts are precisely that—fumbling, awkward. The reason for this is simple. While members might be feeling more accepted and accepting and more trusted and trusting, they still have not learned how to self-disclose, even though they've been exposed to the self-disclosure of others.

By listening to these others, the new members begin to accept, trust, and realize that their problems are not external but internal, that they are the cause of their own problems. Before the end of this stage, for many members the longest of the five, the members begin to make little comments about the pain they have felt and are feeling.

This second stage, rapport, is a learning one. At this stage, members begin to learn who they are. This they **learn by listening** and **becoming emotionally attuned** to the self-disclosure of the other members. The mutuality, the warmth, and the sense of relationship and membership in the group help them to **clarify their sense of self.** This clarification comes from the first time realizations of where they are coming from emotionally and where they are. At this stage, members **learn to stop drifting emotionally.** They learn to do what they have never done; **to make goals and resolutions** for their interpersonal lives. Remember, however, much of this learning is in an embryonic phase. New members are still far more familiar with alcoholic than with nonalcoholic ways of perceiving and interacting. In most people old perceptions and behaviors die hard. This is true for alcoholics, especially scared alcoholics as are these new members.

Denial and **projection** especially are still operating, albeit more weakly. **Regressions** and **minor relapses** occur at this stage. **Group warmth and identification** with that warmth, however, help the majority of the new members to continue their rehabilitation.

All the techniques used in stage one continue to be of value. At this stage, the focus of the leader and peer members (by leader direction) should be to **reward** all fumbling behavior and movement toward growth and to ignore and **overlook any behaviors which are inappropriate** especially if they are self-destructive or destructive to the group.

Especially valuable as a technique at this stage, besides those alluded to, is **reflection of feeling** because it is so nonthreatening and more than any other technique seems to facilitate self disclosure.

Conflict

At this stage, members accelerate their search to discover whom they are. The honest **ventilation of emotion** is common. The ventilation is both in response to others and is part of their own **self-disclosures.** This ventilation includes the spectrum of emotion from hostility to empathy. Now while ventilation of hostility is fairly common among alcoholics, *expression and communication of empathy are not.* Since it is learned in the group, this behavior is a brand new one for most members. It is one with which they quickly come to identify and learn to incorporate into their personalities.

This *ventilation of feeling* by the members is of course what characterizes this stage as the conflict stage. Ventilation facilitates periods of *countertransference* and the *empathy of transference.* Both of these are expressions of the members needs and movement toward trying to build and *develop relationships*—another brand new experience.

During the first two stages, when and if members expressed and shared they did so in terms of *past* experiences. The feelings they expressed also were described as past feelings, i.e., how they felt long ago when they were children or early adolescents. At this stage, feelings are expressed as *now* feelings. *The feelings are owned now.* In other words, the members are admitting to whom they feel they are presently. These kinds of self-disclosures are the ones which communicate the ultimate in authenticity and which bring people close, again something alcoholics have not been able to do with these kinds of self-disclosures.

The self-perception of victim begins to erode rapidly. Concomitant with this erosion comes another brand new experience for members—namely they begin to *take responsibility* for their own behavior.

Sessions where the members have shared and felt in these authentic ways are the ones which they leave feeling like they are just now experiencing life.

The denial defense diminishes at this stage. Interestingly, the projection defense continues to hold on. This is seen in the fact that most alcoholics continue to show that they are very angry people. Indeed, those who previously were not displacers of their anger become so. Continued or sudden displacement is not usually long lived. Both ultimately stop doing it. It's a marker indicating the end of the stage for most alcoholics. Sudden displacement is not usually long lived. Both ultimately stop doing it. It's a marker indicating the end of the stage for most alcoholics. Sudden displacement by non-displacers should be read as an encouraging sign, as much as an unfortunate one, as it reflects a comfortableness felt with peers that they had not felt before. Also, it is a period of emotional transition in their movement toward sublimation (channeling other energy into enhancing behavior.)

At this stage the two techniques most effective are **confrontation** and **questioning.** Both can be effectively employed now because members at this stage have a surer sense of themselves and are solidly identified with the group.

Progression

At this stage, members perceive confidently and optimistically. Their interactions reflect an honest geniality and **interest in others.** Among other things what this indicates is a dramatic diminution in the narcissistic preoccupation with self so typical of the alcoholic. It is precisely because they are not preoccupied with their own selves that they have the emotional wherewithal not only to **enhance others** but to *want* to do so.

At this stage, when they give feedback they feel free to express any and all feelings. They are still awkward with enhancing feelings, but ones which might hurt they do with gentleness and tact. At this stage they admit easily and freely both to past and present contradictions in their behavior.

Perhaps the most important change in the members' behavior is indicated by a **questioning of their own self-perception** which they harbored prior to and on the way to becoming alcoholic. Among the most examined has to be their sense of victimization. At this point when the sense of victimization is pretty much erased, most alcoholics seem to be determined to find out why they had such a self-perception. They want badly to understand it so that they will not redevelop it. As they explore it with their peers, they begin to **discard old values and attitude,** to begin to **investigate new ones.**

This is a stage when the phases of transference and countertransference are resolved. Such resolutions inevitably precipitate healthful changes because they provide previously unshown **insights into the self.**

The **movement toward sublimation** begun in the preceding stage is accelerated. At the same time the **projection defense particularly declines** precipitously.

Termination

When members reach this final stage they look as they feel— healthy. Their perception and expectations of others while optimistic is far from naive. (Their experience with alcohol and the group experience obviate any possibility of naivete.)

A perception, devoid of threat, facilitates and promotes interactions which are generally rewarding. So it is with members who reach this stage. Their system of **communication is congruent,** words, emotions and behavior all gibe. Put simply, the person at this stage gives and gets messages easily.

Terminating members realize full well that continued good health is contingent on the maintenance of sobriety. They know maintenance is premised upon constant, **persevering self-examination.** Why? Because they are in a process of **recovering,** non-ending, ever-continuing.

These members have learned to **accept themselves** and in their **ability to improve and grow.** It is this self-perception which leads them to **accept and tolerate the differences and idiosyncrasies of others.**

Finally, the learning of trust begun at the second stage and strengthened throughout the group process leads them to achieve the confidence that they can **risk.** They can risk trusting and loving; risk the trauma of rejection; the joy of acceptance.

SUMMARY

The goal of group counseling is **to help the alcoholic achieve and maintain sobriety.**

The benefits of this kind of counseling for members include learning to help, learning to accept help, learning about self, learning interpersonal skills, learning tolerance of others and of their own selves.

Two kinds of member behaviors in a group can be considered— the healthful and the unhealthful. The healthful ones include attending, sharing, and facilitating. The unhealthful ones are hostility, non-participating, absenteeism, buffoonery, psychologizing assaulting, housekeeping, manipulating, and seducing.

The functions of the group counselor can be categorized into two—the administrative and the therapeutic. Administrative functions include determining size of the group, screening candidates, and hosting and launching the group. The therapeutic functions include defining, supporting, observing, and intervening. It was noted that counselors can either move forward toward excellence or regress. They can not stand still.

The kind of counseling considered here was the open group. The five stages considered were adaptation, rapport, conflict, progression, and termination.

TOPICS FOR
DISCUSSION AND REFLECTION

1. After studying the group approach to alcoholism counseling, do you think you would prefer to work with groups or with individuals? Why? Why not?

2. Among the benefits listed for group counseling, which one do you think has the most value?

3. Among the healthful behaviors listed, can any of them be learned more effectively in individual counseling than in a group?

4. Are there any unhealthful behaviors listed in group counseling which are also apparent in individual counseling? If so, what are they?

5. Which one(s) of the counselor's therapeutic functions would be the most difficult to learn? Why? Which one the least? Why?

6. Are you a counselor who will continue to move forward toward excellence? If yes, what evidence can you point to that supports your "yes"?

7. Which technique(s) among the stages considered will be the easiest to master? Which the most difficult? Why?

8. Whenever a new member is introduced into the group, the personality of the group is changed. Explain the why of this.

9. What personal qualities do you possess which will promote rapport in group?

10. Will you go out of your way to contact individuals who have gone through formal termination process from group?

BIBLIOGRAPHY

Alexander, A. (1991, February). Alcohol abuse in adolescents. *American Family Physician, 43* (2).

Argeriou, M., & Manohar, V. (1978). Relative effectiveness of nonalcoholics and recovered alcoholics as counselors. *Journal of Studies on Alcohol, 39*(5), 793-799.

Athenelli, R.M., & Schuckit, M.A. (1991). Genetic studies of alcoholism. *International Journal of the Addictions, 91* '90 25 (1A).

Axelson, J.A. (1967). The relationship of counselor candidates empathic perception and rapport in small group interaction. *Counselor Education and Supervision, 6* (4), 287-292.

Barnes, G.E. (1980). Characteristics of the clinical alcoholic personality. *Journal of Studies on Alcohol, 41*, 894-909.

Barnes, B.M., & Welte, J.W. (1990, November). Production of adults' drinking patterns from the drinking of their parents. *Journal of Studies on Alcohol, 51* (6).

Beckman, L.J. (1978). The self-esteem of alcoholic women. *Journal of Studies on Alcohol, 39*, 491-498.

Beckman, L.J., Day, T., Bardsley, P., & Seeman, A.Z. (1980). The personality characteristics and family backgrounds of women alcoholics. *International Journal of the Addictions, 15* (1), 47-54.

Begleiter, H., Porjesz, B., Binari, B., & Kissin, B. (1984, September 28). Event-related brain potentials in boys at risk for alcoholism. *Science, 225*, 1493-1496.

Begleiter, H., Porjesz, B., Rawlings, H., & Eckardt, M. (1987, July/August). Auditory recovery function and P3 in boys at high risk for alcoholism. *Alcohol, 4*, 315-321.

Berk, R.S., Montgomery, I.N., Hazlett, L.D., & Abel, E.L. (1989, December). Paternal alcohol consumption: Effects on ocular response and serum antibody response to Pseudonomas aeruginoso infection in offspring. *Alcohol Clinical and Experimental Review, 13* (6).

Brammer, L.M., & Springer, H.C. (1971). A radical change in counselor education and certification. *Personnel and Guidance Journal, 49* (6), 806.

Brown, R.A., & Cutter, H.S.G. (1977). Alcohol, customary drinking behavior and pain. *Journal of Abnormal Psychology, 86,* 179-181.

Bucheimer, A. (1961, March 28). Empathy in counseling. Paper delivered at APGA convention.

Buchsbaum, M.S., & Ludwig, A.M. (1981). Effects of sensory input and alcohol administration on visual evoked potentials in normal subjects and alcoholics. In H. Begleiter (Ed.), *Alcohol intoxication and withdrawal.* New York: Plenaum

Cattell, R.B., Eber, H.W., & Tatsuoka, M.M. (1970). *Handbook for the sixteen personality factor questionnaire (16PF).* Champaign, IL: Institute for Personality and Ability Testing.

Chaikin, A.L., Derlega, V.J., & Miller, S.J. (1976). Effects of room environment on self-disclosure in counseling analogue. *Journal of Counseling Psychology, 23* (5), 479-481.

Cheng, A., & Hsin, H. (1973). Rapport in initial counseling interview and its impact in effectiveness. *Acta Psychologica Taiwanica 15,* 31-40.

Chess, S.B., Neuringer, C., & Goldstein, G. (1971). Arousal and field dependency in alcoholics. *Journal of General Psychology, 85,* 93-102.

Cisin, I.H., & Cahalan, D. (1968). Comparison of abstainers and heavy drinkers in a national survey. *Psychiatric Research Reports, 24,* 10-21.

Connor, R.B. (1962). The self-concepts of alcoholics. In D.J. Pittman & C.R. Shyder (Eds.), *Society, culture, and drinking patterns.* New York: Wiley.

Cook, W.L., & Goethe, J.W. (1990, March). The effects of being reared with an alcoholic half-sibling; a classic study reanalyzed. *Pam Process, 29* (1).

Cooney, N.L., Kadden, R.M., & Litt, M.D. (1990, January). A comparison of methods for assessing sociopathy in male and female alcoholics. *Journal of Studies on Alcohol, 51* (1).

Craddick, R.A., & Leipold, W.D. (1968). Note on the height of draw-a-person figures by male alcoholics. *Journal of Project Techniques, 32,* 486.

Curlee, J. (1970). A comparison of male and female patients in an alcoholic treatment center. *Journal of Psychology, 74,* 239-247.

Cutter, H.S.G., Maloof, B., Kurtz, N.R., & Jones, W.C. (1976). Feeling no pain, differential responses to pain by alcoholics and nonalcoholics before and after drinking. *Journal of Studies on Alcohol, 37,* 273-277.

Davis, V.E., & Walsh, M.J. (1970). Alcohol, amines, and alkaloids: A possible biochemical basis for alcohol addiction. *Science*, Vol. 167.

DePalma, N., & Clayton, H.D. (1958). Scores of alcoholics on the sixteen personality factor questionnaire. *Journal of Clinical Psychology, 14*, 390-392.

DeRivera, J. (1977). A structural theory of the emotions. *Psychological Issues, 10* (4), 34.

Eastman, C., & Norris, H. (1982). Alcohol dependence, relapse, and self-identify. *Journal of Studies on Alcohol, 43* (11) 1214-1231.

Ekman, P., & Friesen, W.V. (1969). Non-verbal leakage and clues to deception. *Psychiatry, 32*, 88-105.

Freud, S. (1959). The dynamics of the transference. In S. Freud, *The Collected Papers, Vol. II.* New York: Basic Books.

Fromme, K., & Samson, H.H. (1983). A survey analysis of first intoxication experiences. *Journal of Studies on Alcohol, 44* (5).

Fuller, G.B., Lunney, G.H., & Naylor, W.M. (1966) Role of perception in differentiating subtypes of alcoholism. *Perceptual and Motor Skills, 23*, 735-743.

Galanter, M., Talbot, D., & Ballegos, K. (1990, january). Combined Alcoholics Anonymous and professional care for addicted and physicians. *American Journal of Psychiatry, 147* (1).

Geller, B., Faden, R.R., & Levine, D.M. (1990). Tolerance for ambiguity among medical students; implications for their selection training and practice. *Social Science and Medicine, 31* (5).

Glatt, M.M. (1959). A chart of alcohol addiction and recovery. *British Journal of Addictions, 54* (2).

Goldstein, G., & Chotlos, J.W. (1965). Dependency and brain damage in alcoholics. *Perceptual and Motor Skills, 21*, 135-150.

Goodwin, D.W., & Moller, N. (1974). Drinking problems in adopted and non-adopted sons of alcoholics. *Archives of General Psychiatry*, Vol. 31.

Goodwin, D.W., Schulsinger, F., Hermansen, L., Guze, S.B., & Winokur, G. (1973). Alcohol problems in adoptees raised apart from biological parents. *Archives of General Psychiatry*, Vol. 28.

Goodyear, R.K. (1981). Termination as a loss experience for the counselor. *The Personnel and Guidance Journal, 59* (6), 347-350.

Goss, A., & Morosko, T.E. (1969). Alcoholism and clinical symptoms. *Journal of Abnormal Psychology, 74*, 682-684.

Goss, A., & Morosko, T.E. (1970). Alcoholism and clinical symptoms. *Journal of Abnormal Psychology, 74*, 682-684.

Gredd, J.A., & Greengard, P. (1990, December). An analysis of synapsin II, a neuronal phosphoprotein, in post mortem brain tissue from alcoholic and neuropsychiatrically ill adults and medically ill children and young adults. *Archives of General Psychiatry, 47* (12).

Gross, H., & McCaul, M.E. (1990). A comparison of drug use and adjustment in urban adolescent children of substance abusers. *International Journal of Addictions, 25* (4A).

Gross, W.F., & Adler, L.O. (1970). Aspects of alcoholics' selfconcepts as measured by the Tennessee Self Concept Scale. *Psychological Reports, 27,* 431-434.

Gynther, M.D., Presher, C.H., & McDonald, R.L. (1959). Personal and interpersonal factors associated with alcoholism. *Quarterly Journal of Studies on Alcohol, 20*, 321-333.

Haase, R.F. (1970). The relationship of sex and instructional set to the regulation of interpersonal interaction distance in a counseling analogue. *Journal of Counseling Psychology, 17* (5), 233-236.

Haase, R.F., & DiMattia, D.J. (1976). Spatial environments and verbal conditioning in a quasi-counseling interview. *Journal of Counseling Psychology, 23* (5), 414-421.

Haase, R.F., & DiMattia, D.J. (1970). Proxemic behavior: Counselor, administrator, and client preference for seating arrangements in dyadic interaction. *Journal of Counseling Psychology, 17* (7), 319-325.

Hagnell, O., & Tunving, K. (1972). Mental and physical complaints among alcoholics. *Quarterly Journal of Studies on Alcohol, 33*, 77-84.

Haley, J. (1971). *Family therapy: A radical change. Changing Families: A Family Therapy Reader.* New York: Greene and Stratton.

Hannon, R., Day, C.L., Butler, A.M., Larson, A.J., & Casey, M. (1983). Alcohol consumption and cognitive functioning in college students. *Journal of Studies on Alcohol, 44,* (2).

Harada, S. (1989, August/September). Polymorphism of aldehyde dehydrogenase and its application to alcoholism. *Electrophoresis, 10* (8-9).

Harburg, E., Gleiberman, L., Russell, M., & Cooper, M.L. (1991, March-April). Anger-coping styles and blood pressure in black and white males. *Psychosomatic Medicine, 53* (2).

Harford, T., & Spiegler, D. (1982). Environmental influences in adolescent drinking. National Institute on Alcohol Abuse and Alcoholism. Special Population Issues. Alcohol and Health Monograph, No. 4, D.H.H.S. Pub No. (ADM) 82-1193. Washington, DC: Sup. of Doc. U.S. Gov't Printing Office.

Harford, T.C., & Spiegler, D.L. (1983). Developmental trends of adolescent drinking. *Journal of Studies on Alcohol, 44* (1), 181-188.

Hawthorne, W., & Menzel, N. (1983). Youth treatment should be a programming priority. Alcohol Health and Research World. *National institute on Alcohol Abuse and Alcoholism, 7* (4), 46-50.

Hays, R.D., & Revetto, J.P. (1990). Peer cluster theory and adolescent drug use: A reanalysis. *Journal of Drug Education, 20* (3).

Hertzman, M., & Mitnick, L. (1978-79). Ethics, evaluation, and training in alcoholism. *Drug Forum, 7* (2), 145-154.

Highlen, P.S., & Baccus, G.K. (1977). Effect of feeling and probe on client self-referenced affect. *Journal of Counseling Psychology, 24* (5) 440-443.

Hobbs, N. (1962). Sources of gain in psychotherapy. *American Psychology, 17,* 741-747.

Hobson, P. (1989, November). Psychological profile of social drinkers. *British Journal of Addictions, 84* (11).

Hoffman, H. (1970a). Depression and defensiveness in selfdescriptive moods of alcoholics. *Psychological Reports, 26,* 23-26.

Hoffman, H. (1970b). Personality characteristics of alcoholics in relation of age. *Psychological Reports, 27,* 167-171.

Hoffman, H., & Bonyge, E.R. (1977). Personalities of female alcoholics who became counselors. *Psychological Reports, 41* (1), 37-38.

Hubbard, R.L., Cavanaugh, E.R., Rachal, J.V., Schlenger, W.E., & Ginzburg, H.M. (1983). Alcohol use and problems among adolescent clients in drug treatment programs. Alcohol Health & Research World. *National Institute on Alcohol Abuse and Alcoholism, 7* (4), 10-18.

Imber, S.D., Miller, A.E., Faillace, L.A., & Liberman, B. (1971). Temporal processes in alcoholism. *Quarterly Journal of Studies on Alcohol, 32,* 304-309.

Jackson, D. (1957). The question of family homeostasis. *The Psychology Quarterly Supplement, 31* (1), 79-90.

Kahn, M.W., & Stephen, L.B. (1991, December). Counselor training as a treatment method for alcohol and drug abuse. *International Journal of Addictions, 16* (8).

Kanner, L. (1963). The scope and goal of psychotherapy with children. *American Journal of Psychotherapy, 17,* 366-374.

Karp, S.A., Poster, D.D., & Goodman, A. (1963). Differentiation in alcoholic women. *Journal of Personality, 31,* 386-393.

Katsuhiko, S. (1969). An analysis of the change in rapport during counseling. *Japanese Journal of Child Psychiatry, 10* (3), 180-188.

Kaufman, E. (1990). Critical aspects of psychodynamics of substance abuse and the evaluation of their application to a psychotherapeutic approach. *International Journal of Addictions, 25* (2a).

Kaul, T., Kaul, M., & Bednar, R.L. (1973). Counselor confrontation and client depth of self-exploration. *Journal of Counseling Psychology, 20* (2), 3, 132-136.

Keller, M. (1980). Alcohol and youth. In J.E. & W.J. Filstead (Eds.), *Adolescence and alcohol.* Cambridge, MA: Ballener.

Kelly B.J. (1975). Concerned confrontation: The art of counseling. *Social Journal of Educational Research, 9* (3), 110-122.

Kendon, A. (1972). How people interact. In A. Ferber, M. Mendelsohn, & A. Napier (Eds.), *The book of family therapy.* Science House: New York.

Knight, P.H., & Blair, C.K. (1976). Degree of client comfort as a function of dyadic interaction distance. *Journal of Counseling Psychology, 23* (1), 13-16.

Koeppen, A. (1972). Confrontation: A threat and a promise. *Texas Personnel and Guidance Journal, 1* (1), 9, 39-43.

Konovsky, M., & Wilsnack, S.C. (1982). Social drinking and selfesteem in married couples. *Journal of Studies on Alcohol, 43* (3), 319-333.

Kristianson, P.A. (1970). A comparison study of two alcoholic groups and control group. *British Journal of Medical Psychology, 43,* 161-175.

Kubicka, L., Kozeny, J., & Roth, I. (1990, January). Alcohol Abuse and its psychosocial correlates in sons of alcoholics as young men and in the general population of young men in Prague. *Journal of Studies on Alcohol, 51* (1).

Laird, J.T. (1962). A comparison of male normals, psychiatric patients, and alcoholics for sex drawn first. *Journal of Clinical Psychology, 18,* 302.

Lawson, G. (1982). Relation of counselor traits to evaluation of the counseling relationship by alcoholics. *Journal of Studies on Alcohol, 43* (7), 834-839.

Leake, G., & King, A. (1977). Effect of counselor expectations on alcoholic recovery. *Alcohol, Health, and Research World, 1* (3), 16-22.

Lewis, C.E., & Bucholz, K.K. (1991, February). Alcoholism, antisocial behavior and family history. *British Journal of Addictions, 86* (2).

Little, S.C., & McAvoy, M. (1945). Electroencephalographic studies in alcoholism. *Quarterly Journal of Studies in Alcohol,* Vol. 6.

Long, D., Floyd-Walker, D., & Foreman, R. (1989, November-December). Therapeutic counseling skills of nurses working in an alcohol treatment program. *Rehabilitation Nursing, 14* (8).

Loper, R.G., & Kammeier, M.L., & Hoffman, H. (1973). MMPI characteristics of college freshman males who later became alcoholics. *Journal of Abnormal Psychology, 82,* 159-162.

MacLeod, L.D. (1950). Biochemistry and alcoholism. *British Journal of Addictions,* Vol 47.

Machover, S., Puzzo, F.S., Machover, K., & Plumeau, F. (1959). Clinical and objective studies of personality variables in alcoholism. *Quarterly Journal of Studies on Alcohol, 20,* 528-542.

Manohar, V. (1973). Training volunteers as alcoholism treatment counselors. *Quarterly Journal of Studies on Alcohol, 34* (3), 869-877.

Maslow, A.H., & Mintz, N. (1956). Effects of aesthetic surroundings: Initial short-term effects of three aesthetic conditions upon perceiving "energy" and well being in faces. *Journal of Counseling Psychology, 41,* 247-254.

McClelland, D., & Davis, W.N. (1972). The influence of unrestrained power concerns on drinking in working class man. In D.C. McClelland, W.N. Davis, R. Kalin, & E. Wanner, *The drinking man.* New York: The Free Press.

McClelland, D.C., Wanner, E., & Vanneman, R. (1972). Drinking in the wilder context of restrained and unrestrained assertive thoughts and acts. In D.C. McClelland, W.N. Davis, R. Kalin, & E. Wanner, *The drinking man.* New York: The Free Press.

McCord, J. (1972). Etiologica factors in alcoholism; family and personal characteristics. *Quarterly Journal of Studies on Alcohol, 33,* 1020-1027.

McDermott, D., Tricker, R., & Farna, N. (1991). The effects of specialized training in alcoholic information for counseling students. *Journal of Drug Education, 21* (1).

McKenna, T., & Pickens, R. (1981). Alcoholic children of alcoholics. *Journal of Studies on Alcohol, 42* (11), 1021-1029.

McKenna, T., & Pickens, R. (1983). Personality characteristics of alcoholic children of alcoholics. *Journal of Studies on Alcohol, 44* (4).

McKirnan, D.J., & Peterson, P.L. (1989). Psychosocial and cultural factors in alcohol and drug abuse: An analysis of a homosexual community. *Addictive Behaviors, 14* (5) 555-563.

Menne, J.M. (1975). A comprehensive set of counselor competencies. *Journal of Counseling Psychology, 22* (6), 547-553.

Milliger, C., & Young, M. (1990, August). Perceived acceptance and social isolation among recovering homosexual alcoholics. *International Journal of Addictions, 25* (8).

Mills, D.H., Chestnut, W.H., & Hartzell, J.P. (1966). The needs of counselors: A component analysis. *Journal of Counseling Psychology, 1341,* 82-84.

Mills, D.J., & Abeles, N. (1965). Counselor needs for affiliation and nurturance as related to liking for clients and counseling process. *Journal of Counseling Psychology, 12,* 353-358.

Milman, D.H., Bennett, A.A., & Hanson, M. (1983). Psychological effects of alcohol in children and adolescents. Alcohol Health and Research World. *World National Institute on Alcohol Abuse and Alcoholism, 7* (4).

Mintz, W.L. (1956). Effects of aesthetic surroundings: Prolonged and repeated experience in a "beautiful" and ugly room. *Journal of Psychology, 41,* 459-466.

Moss, H.B. (1989). Psychopathy, aggression and family history in male substance abuse patients: A factor analytic study. *Addictive Behaviors, 14* (5).

Moustakas, C.E. (1966). *The authentic teacher.* Cambridge, MA: Howard A. Doyle Publishing.

Mukasa, H., Nakamura, J., Yamada, S., Inove, M., & Nakazawa, Y. (1991, November). Platelet monoamine oxidase activity and personality traits in alcoholics and methamonetamise dependents. *Drug and Alcohol Dependence (Ireland), 26* (3).

Mungas, D. (1988, February). Psychometric correlates of episodic violent behavior. A multidimensional neuropsychological approach. *British Journal of Psychiatry,* 152.

Munroe, R. (1955). *Schools of psychoanalytic thought.* New York: Henry Holt.

Munson, J. (1961). Patterns of client resistiveness and counselor response. *Dissertation Abstracts, 21,* 2368-2369.

Nespor, K. (1990). Treatment needs of alcohol-dependent women. *International Journal of Psychosomatics, 37* (1-4).

Newlin, D.B., & Pretonius, M.B. (1990, October). Sons of alcoholics report greater hangover symptoms than sons of nonalcoholics: A pilot study. *Alcohol Clinical and Experimental Research, 12* (5).

Newlin, D.B., & Thompson, J.B. (1990, November). Alcohol challenge with sons of alcoholics: A critical review and analysis. *Psychological Bulletin, 108* (3).

Parker, F.B. (1959). A comparison of the sex temperament of alcoholics and moderate drinkers. *American Sociological Review, 24,* 366-374.

Parker, F.B. (1969). Self-role strain and drinking disposition at a pre-alcoholic age level. *Journal of Social Psychology, 78,* 55-61.

Patterson, C.H. (1959). *Counseling and psychotherapy: Theory and practice.* New York: Harper and Row.

Patterson, C.H. (1963). Control, conditioning, and counseling. *The Personnel and Guidance Journal, 41,* 680-686.

Penick, E.C., Nickel, E.J., Powell, B.J., Bingham, S.F., & Liskow, B.I. (1990, September). A comparison of familial and nonfamilial male alcoholic patients without a co-existing psychiatric disorder. *Journal of Studies on Alcohol, 51* (5).

Perez, J.F. (1979). *Family counseling: Theory and practice.* New York: D. Van Nostrand.

Perez, J.F. (1985). *Counseling the alcoholic.* Muncie, IN: Accelerated Development.

Perez, J.F. (1986). *Counseling the alcoholic group.* New York: Gardner Press.

Petrie, A. (1967). *Individuality in pain and suffering.* Chicago, IL: University of Chicago Press.

Pinl, R.D., Peterson, J., & Finn,P. (1990, August), Inherited predisposition of alcoholism: Characteristics of sons of male alcoholics. *Journal of Abnormal Psychology, 99* (3).

Rachal, J.V., Guess, L.L., Hubbard, R.L., Maisto, S.A., Cavanaugh, E.R., Waddell, R., & Benrud, C.H. (1983). The extent and nature of adolescent drug use. The 1974 and 1978 national sample studies. Adolescent Drinking Behavior, 1. Rockville, MD: National Institute on Alcohol Abuse and Alcoholism. *Alcohol Health and Research World, National Institute on Alcohol Abuse and Alcoholism, 7* (4).

Rakos, R.F., & Schroeder, H.E. (1976). Fear reduction in help givers as a function of helping. *Journal of Counseling Psychology, 23* (5) 428-435.

Robins, L.N., Bates, W.M., & O'Neal, P. (1982). Adult drinking patterns of former problem children. In D.J. Pittman & C.R. Snyder (Eds.), *Society, culture, and drinking patterns.* New York: Wiley.

Rogers, C.R. (1961). The place of the person in the new world of the behavioral sciences. *The Personnel and Guidance Journal, 39* (6), 442-451.

Roos, P., & Albers, R. (1965). Performance of alcoholics and normals on a measure of temporal orientation. *Journal of Clinical Psychology, 21,* 34-36.

Roy, A., DeJong, J., Lamparski, D., Adinoff, B., George, T., Moore, V., Barnett, D., Kerich, M., & Linnoila, M. (1991, May). Mental disorders among alcoholics. Relationship to age of onset and cerebrospinal fluid and neuropeptides. *Archives of General Psychiatry, 48* (5).

Rutter, D.R., & Hagart, J. (1990). Alcohol training in south-east England: A survey and evaluation. *Alcohol Alcohol, 25* (16).

Sargent, M.J. (1966). Frata House, an Australian alcoholic Unit. *Medical Journal of Australia, 2,* 753-757.

Sattler, J.M., & Pflugrath, J.F. (1970). Future-time perspective in alcoholic and normals. *Quarterly Journal of Studies on Alcohol, 31,* 839-850.

Schuckit, M.A. (1985). Genetics and the role for alcoholism. *Journal of the American Medical Association,* Vol. 245, No. 18.

Segal, B., Huba, G.J., & Singer, J.L. (1980). Reasons for drug and alcohol use by college students. *International Journal of the Addictions, 15* (4), 489-498.

Shastrom, E.L. (1967). *Man the manipulator: The inner journey from manipulation to actualization.* New York: Abingdon Press.

Shore, E.R., Rivers, P.C., & Berman, J.J. (1983). Resistance by college students to peer pressure to drink. *Journal of Studies on Alcohol, 44* (2).

Skinner, B.F. (1956). Critique of psychoanalytic concepts and theories. In H. Feigl & M. Scrivin (Eds.), *Minnesota studies in the philosophy of science* (p. 85). Minneapolis, MN: University of Minnesota Press.

Skuja, A. (1981, August). Treatment attitudes of recovered alcoholic counselors and nonalcoholic counselors. *Journal of Drug Dependence, 8* (1).

Skuja, A.T., Schneidmuhl, A.M., & Mandell, W. (1975). Alcoholism counselor trainees: Some changes in job related functioning following training. *Journal of Drug Education, 5* (2), 151-157.

Smart, R.G. (1968). Future time perspectives in alcoholics and social drinkers. *Journal of Abnormal Psychology, 73,* 81-83.

Smith, S.S., & Newman, J.P. (1990, November). Alcohol and drug abuse-dependence disorders in psychopathic and nonpsychopathic criminal offenders. *Journal Abnormal Psychology, 99* (4).

Spiegel, D., Hadley, P.A., & Hadley, R.G. (1970). Personality test patterns of rehabilitation center alcoholics, psychiatric inpatients and normals. *Journal of Clinical Psychology, 26,* 366-371.

Stone, G., & Morden, C. (1976). Effect of distance on verbal productivity. *Journal of Counseling Psychology, 23* (5), 486-488.

Strupp, H.H. (1957). A multi-dimensional comparison of therapist activity in analytical and client centered therapy. *Journal of Counseling Psychology, 21,* 293-312.

Sussman, S., Charleen, V.L., Marks, B., Freeland, J., Harris, J.K., Vernan, S., & Alfrod, B. (1990, August). Physical features, physical attractiveness and psychological adjustment among alcohol abuse inpatients. *International Journal of Addictions, 19* (8).

Szasz, T.S. (1961). *The myth of mental illness.* New York: Harper and Row.

Tahka, V. (1966). *The alcoholic personality: A clinical study. 13.* Helsinki: Finnish Foundation for Alcohol Studies.

Talbot, J., & Gillen, C. (1978). Differences between nonprofessional recovering alcoholic counselors treating bowery alcoholics: A study of therapist variables. *Psychiatric Quarterly, 50* (4), 333-342.

Thorne, F.C. (1950). Principles of personality counseling: An eclectic viewpoint. *Journal of Clinical Psychology, 233.*

Tweed, S.M., & Ryff, C.D. (1991, March). Adult children of alcoholics: Profiles of wellness amidst distress. *Journal of Studies on Alcohol, 52* (2).

Vaillant, G. (1983). *The national history of alcoholism: Causes, patterns and paths to recovery.* Harvard University Press.

Valle, S.K. (1981). Interpersonal functioning of alcoholism counselors and treatment outcome. *Journal of Studies on Alcohol, 42* (9), 783-790.

Waller, J.A., & Casey, R. (1990, November). Teaching about substance abuse in medical school. *British Journal of Addictions, 85* (1).

Walter, D., Nagoshi, C., Muntaner, C., & Haerzen, C.A. (1990, October). The prediction of drug dependence from expectancy for hostility while intoxicated. *International Journal of Addictions, 25* (10).

Wehler, R., & Hoffman, H. (1978). Personal orientation inventory scores on female alcoholism counselors before and after training. *Psychological Reports, 43* (2), 500-502.

Westcott, R. (1966). Introducing coenetics. *American Scholar, 35,* 342-356.

Widgery, R., & Stackpole, C. (1972). Desk position, interviewer anxiety, and interviewer credibility: An example of cognitive balance in dyad. *Journal of Counseling Psychology, 19* (5), 173-177.

Williams, A.F. (1965). Self-concepts of college problem drinkers. A comparison with alcoholics. *Quarterly Journal of Studies on Alcohol, 26,* 586-594.

Wilson, W.M. (1968). Hospitalized alcoholic patients: Training personnel to work with alcoholic patients. *Hospital and Community Psychiatry, 19* (7), 211-215.

Windle, M. (1990, April). The HK/MBD Questionnaire: Factor structure and discriminant validity with an adolescent sample. *Alcohol Clinical and Experimental Research, 14* (2).

Winokur, G., & Corgell, W. (1991, February). Familial alcoholism in primary unipolar major depressive disorder. *American Journal of Psychiatry, 148* (2).

Wisotsky, M. (1958). A note on the order of figure drawing among incarcerated alcoholics. *Journal of Clinical Psychology, 15,* 65.

Wisotsky, M., & Birner, L. (1960). Preference for human or animal drawings among normal and addicted. *Perceptual and Motor Skills, 10,* 43-45.

Witkin, H.A., Dyk, R.B., Faterson, H.F., Goodenough, D.R., & Karp, S.A. (1962). *Psychological differentiation.* New York: Wiley.

Wolberg, L.R. (1954). *The technique of psychotherapy.* New York: Greene and Stratton.

Wrenn, R.L. (1960). Counselor orientation: Theoretical or situational. *Journal of Counseling Psychology, 7,* 40-45.

Yori, C.D. (1989, September). Homosexuality and illegal residency status in relation to substance abuse and personality traits among Mexican nationals. *Journal of Clinical Psychology, 45* (5).

Zucker, R.A. (1968). Sex-role identity patterns and drinking behavior of adolescents. *Quarterly Journal of Studies on alcohol, 29,* 868-884.

OTHER READINGS OF INTEREST

Barnes, B.M., & Welte, J.W. (1990, November). Prediction of adults' drinking patterns from the drinking of their parents. *Journal of Studies on Alcohol, 51* (6).

Berg, N.L. (1971). Effects of alcohol intoxication on self-concept: Studies of alcoholics and controls in laboratory conditions. *Journal of Studies on Alcohol, 32,* 442-543.

Boy, A.V., & Pine, G.J. (1976). Equalizing the counseling relationship: Psychotherapy. *Theory, Research, and Practice 13* (1), 20-25.

Chodorkoff, B. (1964). Alcoholism and ego function. *Quarterly Journal of Studies on Alcohol, 25,* 292-299.

Cowan, L., Auld, F., & Begin, P.E. (1974). Evidence for distinctive personality traits in alcoholics. *British Journal of Addictions, 69,* 199-206.

Cutter, H.S.G., & Fisher, J.C. (1980). Family experience and the motives for drinking. *International Journal of the Addictions, 15* (3), 339-358.

Donovan, J.E., Jessor, R., & Jessor, L. (1983). Problem drinking in adolescence and young adulthood. *Journal of Studies on Alcohol, 44.*

Fitzgerald, K.W. (1988). *Alcoholism: The genetic inheritance.* New York: Doubleday.

Freud, S. (1949). *A general introduction of psychoanalysis.* New York: Perma Giants.

Frey, D., & Carlock, C.J. (1989). *Enhancing self esteem, 2nd ed.* Muncie, IN: Accelerated Development.

Galanter, M., Talbot, D., Ballegos, K., & Rubenstone, E. (1990, January). Combined Alcoholic Anonymous and professional care for addicted physicians. *American Journal Psychiatry, 147* (1).

Goss, A., & Morosko, T.E. (1970). Relation between a dimension of internal/external control and the MMPI with an alcoholic population. *Journal of Consulting and Clinical Psychology, 34,* 189-192.

Harford, T.C., & Grant, B.F. (1990, October). Alcohol abuse among grandsons of alcoholics: Some preliminary findings. *Alcohol Clinical and Experimental Research, 14* (3).

Jones, M.C. (1968). Personality correlates and antecedents of drinking patterns in adult males. *Journal of Consulting and Clinical Psychology, 32,* 2-12.

McKirnan, D.J., & Peterson, P.L. (1989). Alcohol and drug use among homosexual men and women: Epidemiology and population characteristics. *Addictive Behaviors, 14* (5) 545-553.

Meer, B., & Amon, A.H. (1963). Age-sex preference patterns of alcoholics and normals. *Quarterly Journal of Studies on Alcohol, 24,* 417-431.

Milliger, C., & Young, M. (1990, August). Perceived acceptance and social isolation among recovering homosexual alcoholics. *The International Journal of Addictions, 25* (8).

Needle, R., McCubbin, H., Lorence, J., & Hochlauser, M. (1983). Reliability and validity of adolescent self-reported drug use in a family-based study: A methodological report. *The International Journal of Addictions, 18* (7), 901-902.

Pepinsky, H.B., & Karst, T.O. (1964). Convergence: A phenomenon in counseling and psychotherapy. *American Psychologist, 19,* 333-338.

Rudikoff, L.C., & Kirk, B.A. (1961). Goals of counseling: Mobilizing the counselee. *Journal of Counseling Psychology, 8,* 243-249.

Rudio-Stipec, M., Bird, M., Canino, B., Bravo, M., & Alegria, M. (1991, January). Children of alcoholic parents in the community. *Journal of Studies on Alcohol, 92* (1).

Satir, V. (1975). You as a change agent in helping families to change. In V. Satir, J. Stachowiak, & H. Taskman (Eds.), *Helping families to change* (p. 41). New York: Jason Bronson.

Transeau, G., & Eliot, J. (1990, August). Individuation and adult children of alcoholics. *Psychological Reports, 67* (1).

Williamson, E.G. (1966). Value options and the counseling relationship. *The Personnel and Guidance Journal, 44,* 617-623.

INDEX

A

Abel, E.L. 5, 267
Abeles, N. 117, 274
Ability to persevere 48
Absenteeism 241-2
Acceptance 259
  others 230-1, 263
  self 229, 263
Acclimation 9
Acetaldehyde 6, 7, 10
Acetaldehyde dehydrogenase
  (ALDH) 8
Activities, learning 191-223
  art of role-playing 212-3
  confrontation technique 222-3
  technique of recapitulation
    215-6
  to reflect feeling 210-1
Adaptation 7-9
  stage in group counseling
    258-9
  techniques for 259
Addiction 10-1
  cycle of, *Figure* 77
Adinoff, B. 276
Adler, L.O. 270
Adolescents, alcoholic 43-5
  number of 43
  starting age 44
  view of drinking 44
Adult Children of Alcoholics (ACOA)
  45-58, 59
  ability to persevere 48
  attraction to pain 50-1
  emotionally distant from others
    51-2
  frantic way of life 54

inability to trust 48-9
need for approval 47-8
relationships based on pity
  52-3
tendency to lie 50
terror of being evaluated 53-4
unreliability 49
vacillation 51
Albers, R. 20, 276
Alcohol dehydrogenase (ADH) 8
Alcoholic
  adolescents 43-5
  approaches to counseling
    145-50
  family 37-60
  group members behavior
    231-53
  meaning of 77-112
  perception 29, 34
  treatable 141-3
  untreatable 141-3
Alcoholics Anonymous 130, 177-82,
  228, *Figure* 132-3
  Membership Survey,
    Figure 132-3
Alcoholism
  genetic predisposition 4, 5
  inherited 3-7
  learned 3-7
  predisposition 12-3
  progression 63-7, *Figure* 64
  recovery process 68-9,
    Figure 65
  relapse 70-4
Alegria, M. 280
Alexander, A. 43, 267
Alfrod, B. 277
Amon, A.H. 280

F

Facilitating 235-6
Faden, R.R. 116, 269
Faillace, L.A. 271
Family, alcoholic
    research 37
Fantasy 18, 185, 236, 250, 258
Farna, N. 129, 131, 273
Faterson, H.F. 29, 278
Fear 190
Feedback 236
Feeling 193, 260
    owned 261
    ventilation 261
Feelings, reflection 205-11
    See reflection of feelings
Feigl, H. 276
Ferber, A. 272
Fifth step 181
Figure-drawing test 21
Finn, P. 275
First step 178-9
Fisher, J.C. 279
Fitzgerald, K.W. 279
Floyd-Walker, D. 1116, 273
Foreman, R. 116, 273
Frame of of reference 177-82, 223
Freeland, J. 277
Freud, S. 161, 269, 279
Frey, D. 279
Friesen, W.V. 163, 269
Fromme, K. 44, 269
Fuller, G.B. 22, 269
Functions
    administrative 254-5, 264
    group alcoholism counselor
      253-6
    therapeutic 255-6, 264
Functions, administrative 254-5, 264
    group size 254
    hosting the group 254-5
    launching the group 254-5
    screening candidates 254
Functions, therapeutic 255-6, 264
    defending 255
    intervening 255
    observing 255
    supporting 255

G

Galanter, M. 177, 269, 279
Gamma-aminobutyric acid (GABA)
    10, 11
Gay community
    alcoholism 32-3, 34
Geller, B. 116, 269
Genetic view 3-13
George, T. 276
Gillen, C. 116, 277
Ginzburg, H.M. 43, 44, 271
Glatt, M.M. 63, 64, 74
Gleiberman, L. 20, 270
Goal setting 145-150
Goals in counseling 143-150
    primary 143
    secondary 143-4
Goethe, J.W. 37, 268
Goldstein, G. 29, 268
Goodenough, D.R. 29, 278
Goodman, A. 29, 272
Goodwin, D.W. 3, 4, 269
Goodyear, R.k. 173, 269
Goss, A. 22, 270, 279
Grant, T.C. 280
Gredd, J.A. 7, 270
Greengard, P. 270
Gross, H. 270
Gross, W.F. 22, 270
Group
    approach to alcoholism
      counseling 227-78
    closed 256
    on-going 256
    open 256
Group counseling 227-78
    See stages in group counseling
    benefits 227-31
    hosting 254-5
    introduction of new members
      258
    launching 254-5
    number of members 254
    screening candidates 254
Group counselor
    functions 253-6, 264
Group members
    behaviors 231-53
    screening 254
Group warmth 260

Guess, L.L. 275
Guidelines
    developing a personal philosophy
        of counseling 136-7
Guze, S. B. 269
Gynther, M.D. 26, 270

H

Haase, R.F. 156, 157, 270
Hadley, P.A. 22, 277
Hadley, R.G. 22, 277
Haerzen, C.A. 277
Hagart, J. 131, 276
Hagnell, O. 270
Haley, J. 130, 270
Hannon, R. 44, 270
Hanson, M. 274
Harada, S. 7, 270
Harburg, E. 20, 270
Harford, T.C. 39, 45, 271, 280
Harris, J.K. 277
Hartzell, J.P. 117, 274
Hays, R.D. 45, 271
Hazlett, L.D 5, 267
Help
    learning to accept 228-9
Helper
    learning to become 228
Henry, case of 103-6
Hermansen, L. 269
Hertzman, M. 117, 271
Highlen, P.S. 271
Hobbs, N. 172, 271
Hobson, P. 23, 271
Hochlauser, M. 280
Hoffman, H. 23, 25, 31, 131, 271,
    273, 277
Hostility 189, 237-9, 240, 246
Housekeeper 246-8
    destructive 248
    fantasies 247
    protector types 247-8
Housekeeping 246-8
Hsin, H. 150, 268
Huba, G.J. 28, 276
Hubbard, R.L. 43, 44, 271, 275
Humor 237-8

I

Identification 260
Imber, S.D. 20-271
Indifference 111
Indifference in communication
    159-60
    avoiding behaviors 159, 160
    quasi-indifference 159, 160
    silence 159-60
Inebriation 111
Inove, M. 23, 274
Insecurity 110
Insensitivity 111
Insight 172-3
    definition 172-3
    importance 173
Integration 190
Intellectualization 164-6
Intervening 255

J

Jack, case of 251-3
*Jackson Personality Research Form
    (PRF)* 23-4, 25
Jackson, D. 37, 271
Jellinek, E.M. 63, 74
Jessor, L. 279
Jessor, R. 279
Jones, M.C. 280
Jones, W.C. 30, 268
Judson, case of 106-10
Julia, case of 94-8
Justification 191

K

Kadden, R.M. 22, 268
Kahn, M.W. 128, 271
Kalin, R. 273
Kammeier, M.L. 31, 273
Kanner, L. 143, 272
Karp, S.A. 29, 272, 278
Karst, T.O. 280
Katsuhiko, S. 150, 272
Kaufman, E. 177, 272
Kaul, M. 272

Montgomery, I.N. 5, 267
Moore, V. 276
Morden, C. 163, 277
Morosko, T.E. 22, 270, 279
Moss, H.B. 29, 274
Moustakas, C.E. 192, 274
Mungas, D. 22, 274
Munroe, R. 172, 274
Munson, J. 117, 274
Muntaneer, C. 277

N

Nagoshi, C. 20, 277
Nakamura, J. 23, 274
Nakazawa, Y. 23, 274
Napier, A. 272
National Institute on Alcohol Use 43
National Institute on Alcohol Abuse 8
Naylor, W.M. 22, 269
Need for approval 47-8
Needle, R. 280
Nespor, K. 38, 275
Neuringer, C. 29, 268
Newlin, D.B. 5, 275
Newman, J.P. 22, 277
Nickel, E.J. 37, 275
Nondirectivist 145, 148-50, 153-4
   counselor 166, 203-4, 218-20
Nonparticipation 239-41
Norepinephrine 9
Norris, H. 28, 269

O

O'Neal, P. 31, 273
Observing 255

P

Pain 111
   attraction to 50-1
Pain tolerance 30
Parker, F.B. 21, 275
Patience 239
Patterson, C.H. 143, 193, 275

Penick, E.C. 37, 275
Pepinsky, H.B. 280
Perception
   alcoholic 29, 34
   analysis-therapist 126
   therapist 116-7
Perception 15-6
Perez, J.F. 117, 157, 253, 275
Personality
   clash 155-6
   elements 15-9
   prealcoholic 30-2, 34
   research findings 20
Personality dynamics
   elements 15-9
Personality tests
   See tests, personality
Peterson, J. 275
Peterson, P.L. 32, 274, 280
Petrie, A. 30, 275
Pflugrath, J.F. 20, 276
Phasis 193
Photo-preference test 21
Pickens, R. 45, 273
Pine, G.J. 279
Pinl, R.D. 5, 275
Pittman, D.J. 268, 276
Pity
   relationships resulting 52-3
Plumeau, F. 21, 273
Porjesz, B. 267
Poster, D.D. 29, 272
Posture 232
Powell, B.J. 37, 275
Prealcoholic personality 30-2, 34
Predisposition
   alcoholism 12-3
   genetic 12-3
Presher, C.H. 26, 270
Pretonius, M.B. 5, 275
Progression in group counseling 262-3
   discard old values and attitudes 262
   enhance others 262
   interest in others 262
   investigate new values and attitudes 262
   questioning of self-perception 262

ABOUT THE AUTHOR

Prior to publication of the original version of this book, *Counseling the Alcoholic,* no books were devoted exclusively to alcoholism counseling. Since its publication in 1985, more than one-half dozen other books have appeared on the market. In reviewing them, the author found that none addressed the causes of alcoholism (particularly genetic predisposition) nor do any of them treat the problems associated with both individual and group counseling. This book does all of that.

A licencsed psychologist in Massachusetts, Joseph F. Perez is Professor and Chairman of the Department of Psychology at Westfield State College. He took his bachelor's degree Magna Cume Laude at the University of Connecticut in 1954 and five years later he obtained a Ph.D. from the same University. In recognition of his scholarly achievements, the University in 1987 inducted him into Phi Beta Kappa as an alumnus.

Dr. Perez's initial exposure to alcoholism counseling began in 1961 when he was a staff psychologist at the V.A. Hospital in Northampton, Massachusetts. Although he continued his counseling work for the following two decades, he did not focus his attention upon alcoholism until the early 80s. Since then his abiding professional interest has been the theory and practice of alcoholism counseling as a teacher, a practitioner, and a researcher.

As a teacher, he teachers courses and conducts seminars both at the graduate and undergraduate levels. As a practitioner, he facilitates groups and conducts workshops in private industry for recovering alcoholics. As a researacher, he has been something more than involved and occupied. *Alcoholism: Causes, Effects, and Treatment* is the fifth book he's had published on alcoholism counseling since 1985.

On the lighter and personal side, Joe Perez has reached that point in his life, because of age and looks, where he's asked periodically when he's going to retire. His response delivered with increasing impatience remains the same, "I don't want to!" He doesn't because he loves all his work. Teaching permits him to fulfill his need to be a ham. Writing, particularly his efforts in the pure trade market lets him translate his fantasies into reality. His counseling work gives special meaning to his life. His other loves include tennis, scrabble, the New York Yankees, and cooking (soups, squid, and trip).

He lives with Gerri, his wife of 38 years, and Mimi, his youngest of four children in Northamptom, Massachusetts.